Closed for Democracy

Every year, over 1,000 public schools are permanently closed across the United States. And yet, little is known about their impacts on American democracy. *Closed for Democracy* is the first book to systematically study the political causes and democratic consequences of mass public school closures in the United States. The book investigates the declining presence of public schools in large cities and their impacts on the Americans most directly affected – poor Black citizens. It documents how these mass school closure policies target minority communities, making them feel excluded from the public goods afforded to equal citizens. In response, targeted communities become superlative participators to make their voices heard. Nevertheless, the high costs and low responsiveness associated with the policy process undermines their faith in the power of political participation. Ultimately, the book reveals that when schools shut down, so too does Black citizens' access to, and belief in, American democracy.

Sally A. Nuamah is an assistant professor at Northwestern University. She is the author of the multi-award-winning book, *How Girls Achieve* (2019), and the recipient of over thirty additional honors including *Forbes Magazine* "30 under 30 in Education," the Marilyn J. Gittell Activist-Scholar Award, and the Andrew Carnegie Fellowship.

T0371085

Closed for Democracy

How Mass School Closure Undermines the Citizenship of Black Americans

Sally A. Nuamah
Northwestern University

CAMBRIDGE UNIVERSITY PRESS

CAMBRIDGE
UNIVERSITY PRESS

Shaftesbury Road, Cambridge CB2 8EA, United Kingdom

One Liberty Plaza, 20th Floor, New York, NY 10006, USA

477 Williamstown Road, Port Melbourne, VIC 3207, Australia

314–321, 3rd Floor, Plot 3, Splendor Forum, Jasola District Centre,
New Delhi – 110025, India

103 Penang Road, #05–06/07, Visioncrest Commercial, Singapore 238467

Cambridge University Press is part of Cambridge University Press & Assessment,
a department of the University of Cambridge.

We share the University's mission to contribute to society through the pursuit of
education, learning and research at the highest international levels of excellence.

www.cambridge.org
Information on this title: www.cambridge.org/9781009247450

DOI: 10.1017/9781009247436

First published 2023

A catalogue record for this publication is available from the British Library.

Library of Congress Cataloging-in-Publication Data
Names: Nuamah, Sally A., 1989– author.
TITLE: Closed for democracy : how mass school closure undermines the citizenship
  of Black Americans / Sally A. Nuamah, Northwestern University, Illinois.
DESCRIPTION: First Edition. | New York : Cambridge University Press, [2022] |
  Includes bibliographical references and index.
IDENTIFIERS: LCCN 2022016934 (print) | LCCN 2022016935 (ebook) |
  ISBN 9781009247450 (Hardback) | ISBN 9781009247443 (Paperback) | ISBN
  9781009247436 (ePub)
SUBJECTS: LCSH: School closings–United States. | Education, Urban–Political aspects–
  United States. | Education, Urban–Social aspects–United States. | African Americans–
  Education–Social aspects. | Education and state–United States. | Racism in education–
  United States. | Community and school–United States.
CLASSIFICATION: LCC LB2823.2 .N83 2022 (print) | LCC LB2823.2 (ebook) |
  DDC 379.1/535–dc23
LC record available at https://lccn.loc.gov/2022016934
LC ebook record available at https://lccn.loc.gov/2022016935

ISBN 978-1-009-24745-0 Hardback
ISBN 978-1-009-24744-3 Paperback

They closin' all the schools and all the prisons gettin' open.
Philadelphia native Meek Mill, "Championships" (2018)

CONTENTS

FIGURES

TABLES

ACKNOWLEDGMENTS

This book has been in progress for about ten years. It started from a personal place; schools were closing in my neighborhood in Chicago, and my community was fighting to save them. I was attending these events before I realized they would become the subject of my research. So first, I want to thank the near north community, all of whom welcomed me back home in the middle of historic battles to save schools and keep what was left of an area that was changing fast due to gentrification. I also want to give a special thanks to organizations such as Journey for Justice (J4J) and the Legal Assistance Foundation (LAF), in addition to the people who were not formally a part of any organization but were just as involved in the work of advocating for public education.

Second, I want to thank my academic advisors and now friends, Reuel Rogers and Traci Burch, at Northwestern University. They supported this project very early on, even when others asked me whether this was "real political science" because of its focus on schools. When I got the idea to compare Chicago to Philadelphia, they encouraged me to apply for a visiting role at the University of Pennsylvania, and I was fortunate to be awarded their Office of Vice Provost Excellence in Diversity Fellowship. As a result of this experience, I had the privilege of being mentored by another set of amazing scholars, particularly in political science and education, at the University of Pennsylvania (Penn). In political science, I would especially like to thank Rogers Smith, Marc Meredith, and Dan Gillion, who gave me support as if I were one of their students, throughout my years in Philadelphia; and in education, I'd like to thank Sigal Ben-Porath, Rand Quinn, and Krystal Warner, who did the same. I was also lucky to have support from other faculty and administrators from across Penn including Anita Allen, Lorene Cary, Wendell Pritchett, and Annette Lareau. Further, I met a community of peers across the east coast interested in similar topics. Together, we organized a school closures conference, academic panels, and op-eds. This collaboration especially benefited from the support of the Urban Studies Program, and its director Elaine Simon, as well as Ariel Bieurbaum and Ryan Good. The city of Philadelphia more generally was good to me: From the incredible youth groups, such as the Philadelphia Student Union and Youth Action, to the long-serving adult organizations, such as Parents United and Action United, everyone was very generous in welcoming me into their lives and sharing their stories about education and politics in the city. I felt at home.

Third, at Princeton University, I must acknowledge the University Center for Human Values, especially Melissa Lane and Anna Stilz; the Center for the Study of Democratic Politics; and the School of Public and International Affairs, and its incredible dean at the time, Cecil Rouse. For two years, they provided me with funding, office space, mentorship, and other research support as I worked to transition this project from a dissertation into a book.

I must also acknowledge my colleagues and friends Kevin Levay, Jonathan Collins, Domingo Morel, Patricia Posey, Paul Frymer, Thomas Ogorzalek, Quinn Mulroy, David Figlio, Alvin Tillery, Dara Strolovitch, Jessica Trounstine, Jane Mansbridge, Steve Balla, Jeff Colman, Nancy Loeb, William McHenry, and Lily Morkli; my colleagues at Duke University; my longtime editor, Amy Reeve; all my writing groups; and many more people than I can recount here. With their help, and that of my mentors, I was able to publish several versions of this work in academic journals including the *Journal of Urban Affairs, Politics, Groups, and Identities* and *the American Political Science Review*, in addition to public media including the *Washington Post's* "The Monkey Cage" and *Education Week*. The following have been reprinted with permission: Nuamah, S. A. 2021. "Close to Home: Place-Based Mobilization in Racialized Contexts." *American Political Science Review* (with Thomas Ogorzalek); Nuamah, S. A. 2020. "The Cost of Participating While Poor and Black: Toward a Theory of Collective Participatory Debt." *Perspectives on Politics;* Nuamah, S. A. 2017. "The Paradox of Educational Attitudes: Racial Differences in Public Opinion on School Closure." *Journal of Urban Affairs.*

Last, but certainly not least, I want to thank my mom, Afua Serwaah; my brother, Robert Nuamah; my life partner, Ezekiel Richardson; my nephew, Jayden Tyler Nuamah; and my late father, Francis Antwi-Nuamah. None of them understood what I was getting into when I started this project, but they willingly and generously supported me through it all. They attended community meetings with me, gave me food and transportation, listened to my talks, celebrated my achievements, and consoled me during my rejections. They helped me to overcome the tremendous obstacle of being a first-generation Ph.D. working to write about communities similar to where I grew up and having it "accepted" in academia. I am grateful for their presence and their constant reminders that this work is important.

Ultimately, I have interfaced with *hundreds* of people during this project, so it's impossible to thank them all, but if nothing else, I hope that this work is a recognition of the harm that has been done to them and provides insights on a path toward reparation.

INTRODUCTION: CLOSED FOR SCHOOL, OPEN FOR BUSINESS
When Citizens Become Targets in the Era of Mass School Closure

When I met Leanne Woods[1] in 2013, she was the proud mother of four kids, all of whom had attended or were attending Steel Elementary, a public school in North Philadelphia. She was an involved parent: She regularly attended parent meetings available to her, got to know her kids' teachers, and stayed abreast of what was happening at the school. As a working parent, she did not have time to do much else.

One year later, in 2014, Leanne found herself unemployed and decided to spend her excess time involving herself in city, state, and regional parent groups. Through participation in one of these groups, she discovered something shocking: Steel Elementary was marked for closure and conversion into a charter school. She thought: "My school is slated to be a charter and I didn't know ... How did I, an involved parent, not know?"

The fact that Leanne considered herself an involved parent and yet was unaware of the district's decision was suspicious to her, so she decided to dig deeper. "I got my hands on a copy [of their plan] ... well, actually someone leaked it to me ... and it said that Mastery Charter was looking to build a network. Steel falls between two Mastery high schools ... so they were trying to fit this into their charter expansion ... so I am like, okay, this is somebody's *business* plan."

---

[1] All names of persons interviewed are pseudonyms. School names are not.

After Leanne realized that the closure of Steel Elementary was connected to a larger "business plan," she reached out to other parents and shared what she knew, and the community began organizing a response. In particular, she recalls, "We are known in this community, we live in this community, we know our neighbors. So, we went door to door talking to parents and telling them the truth. Little did I know Mastery [Charter Schools] had been doing this for a year ... they told the parents that it was already going to happen."

At this point, I would like to make it clear that Leanne's story is not novel: Public institutions have been threatened for closure in cities like Boston, Philadelphia, and Chicago for decades (US National Commission on Excellence in Education, 1983; Orr & Rogers, 2011; Common Core of Data – National Center for Education Statistics, 1993–2013). Across the nation, these closures are disproportionately affecting public schools like Steel Elementary with large low–income Black and Brown populations.

The large scale and racialized nature of closures raise serious concerns about the fairness by which the government distributes public goods and the impacts on the political beliefs and actions of those most affected. Despite the common nature of Leanne's story, and the concerns it raises, there are no major authoritative texts on the interplay between mass public school closures and democratic participation. The field of political science is largely silent on this topic, and the field of education offers little commentary on the effects of school closures on political behavior.

Closed for Democracy is about the mass closing of public institutions and the consequences for Black Americans' relationship with democracy. It is an investigation of the impacts of shuttering schools – one of America's last remaining public institutions – on the political beliefs and civic participation of those most affected. It interrogates the response and political engagement of parents like Leanne who demand these institutions remain open. It illustrates how members of affected communities take the initiative to become informed about the closure policies and, in turn, protest them, even when the government claims the closures are in their interest. Further, this book highlights how affected communities go on to engage in the political process more than any other group, despite lacking the resources traditionally associated with high levels of participation. Yet, the book ultimately reveals, they feel a sense of loss even when they successfully save their school because many participants realize that theirs is a Pyrrhic victory: They have won but at a great and unsustainable cost.

The Cost of Empty Victories: The Collective Participatory Debt of Black Americans

Closed for Democracy exposes the costs of "winning" while poor and Black in American democracy. It describes the feeling of empty victories that hard-fought battles tend to leave behind but that remain under-discussed as the efforts of Black citizens continue to be described through a static and binary lens of total wins *or* losses. For instance, it is perhaps unsurprising that those who lost their schools felt a sense of loss, but what about those who were able to keep their schools open, or lost and then regained their schools? Were they any more relieved? Did *they* win?

Leanne and the Steel Elementary community, for example, do win the battle to stop Mastery's larger "business plan" and keep Steel open, but they lose faith in the democratic establishment altogether. While Leanne could have viewed the victory as an indication of external efficacy and/or her value as a citizen, she and other affected citizens conclude the opposite: that their wins felt more like losses.

These feelings of loss, even when those targeted appear to "win" can be described as indicative of their *collective participatory debt* (CPD),[2] defined as a type of mobilization fatigue that transpires when citizens' repeated participation is met with a lack of democratic responsiveness. Citizens affected by CPD question the utility of political participation even when they achieve policy gains as they recognize those gains are inconsistent with, or represent an insignificant fraction of, their broader demands.

These feelings of CPD, or loss even when supposedly "winning," are not new. Decades after the civil rights movement, scholar Manning Marable (2007) wrote in his classic text *Race, Reform and Rebellion* that the "movement was flushed with victory, yet in retrospect, it was a victory in defeat" (p. 144). Following the murder of Michael Brown by the Ferguson police in 2014, political theorist Melvin Rogers described Blacks as "perpetually losers in American

---

[2] Described in more detail later and in Chapter 4.

democracy." Relatedly, more than ten years ago, Zoltan Hajnal (2009) found that Black voters tend to lose "more regularly than other voters" in American democracy (p. 50). He concluded that this persistent loss "could, if not addressed, lead to disillusionment with the democratic process" (p. 55).

Drawing on the concept of CPD, the book demonstrates how the experience of being targeted for school closure leads to prolonged disillusionment and disengagement with government and politics. And through their disillusioned responses, we learn that affected citizens were never simply seeking to save their schools. Rather, their fight to save public school was and is indicative of their larger fight for racial justice and liberation. The impending chapters explain how.

But first, some necessary context.

The Era of Mass School Closures

Each year, nearly 1,000 public schools close, affecting nearly 200,000 students (Tilsley, 2017). One fundamental reason for the mass closure of public schools in recent years is the passage of federal policies such as No Child Left Behind in 2001 and Race to the Top in 2009.[3] Both policies emphasize high-stakes standardized testing and implement punishments for failure to meet preset standards.[4] The punishment for failing to meet these standards includes, but is not limited to, takeover by charter operators and/or the state, reduced federal funding, and closure (Manna, 2006; McGuinn, 2006; Morel, 2018).

In 2009, for example, the US Department of Education proposed a "turn-around"[5] of the nation's 5,000 lowest performing public schools within five years. In 2013, nearly 2,000 public schools were closed, in part due to this turnaround effort. The number of schools closed that year represented nearly double the number of schools closed across the United States only a decade earlier in 2003 (US Department

---

[3] For details related to No Child Left Behind, see www2.ed.gov/nclb/landing.jhtml. For details related to Race to the Top, see www2.ed.gov/programs/racetothetop-district/index.html?

[4] For example, No Child Left Behind requires that states "restructure" any school that fails to make "adequate yearly progress" (McGuinn, 2006).

[5] "Turnaround" refers to a set of actions funded by school improvement grants, including: (1) students stay in the same school, and staff are replaced with new public school staff; (2) students stay, and staff are replaced with a charter operator; (3) new standards and strategies are developed to better tailor to the needs of students; or (4) the school is permanently shut down. For more details, see www2.ed.gov/news/speeches/2009/06/06222009.pdf.

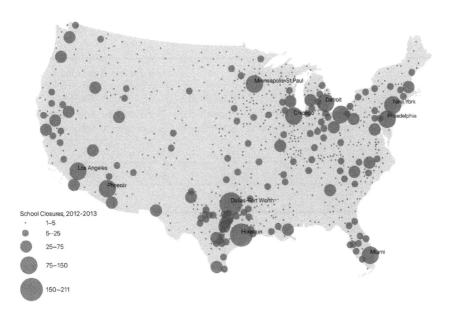

Figure I.1 Map of school closures across the United States (1993–2013)

of Education, National Center for Education Statistics, 2018). In other words, they were indicative of a new *era of mass school closure* across the United States.

An increasing number of these closures occurred in large cities, such as Chicago and Philadelphia (see Figure I.1). Of the 2,000 schools closed in 2013, for example, 49 were from the Chicago Public Schools (CPS) district, the highest number of schools closed in a single year in US history (Ahmed-Ullah, Chase & Secter, 2013). That same year Philadelphia, New York, Washington, DC, and Newark, New Jersey, also experienced enrollment declines followed by subsequent closures in their respective districts (Cohen, 2016). In each city, a disproportionate number of the students affected were low-income and Black; see Table I.1.

Mass School Closures in Context

While I frame school closures as a modern issue, they can be documented at least as far back as the 1920s. These early closures were generally thought of as rural issues and typically occurred through the merger of multiple districts of one-room schoolhouses. For example, in 1929, Arkansas legislators advocated for the passage of Act 149,

Table I.1. Percentage of public school population in top three cities affected by closures, by race and income in 2013

City	Number of Schools Closed	Black Population		Low-Income Population	
		% Affected in School System	Total % of Population in School System	% Affected in School System	Total % of Population in School System
Chicago	49	87	42	94	76
Philadelphia	23	85	55	93	81
New York	22	55	30	81	73

Source: Local school data for Chicago, Philadelphia, and New York

which facilitated the consolidation of smaller school districts into a single district. Its proponents argued that because migration to larger cities had resulted in lower enrollments and fewer resources, the consolidation of school districts would improve education for all students by distributing more resources to fewer schools. Following its passage, more than 1,500 public school districts closed.[6]

Act 149 is illustrative of the type of education policies (and rationales) made across rural areas struggling with similar issues of industry and population decline in the early years of closure (Ledbetter, 2006). Yet, by the 1960s, the population across the United States was estimated to be shrinking by 1 percent each year and up to 3 percent in the largest school districts. Soon, public school closures began to affect urban areas as well, albeit in the form of closed school buildings rather than districts.[7] This shift was partly due to the desegregation of schools as a result of Brown v. Board of Education in 1954 and subsequent "White flight" to the suburbs from the more racially mixed cities in the 1960s (Faust, 1976; McPherrin, 1979).

To a significant degree, once public education was "uniformly" available (at least legally) through Brown v. Board of Education, school

---

[6] Act 149 was followed by a similar, but unsuccessful, effort called Act 1, which sought to reduce the number of school districts from 1,900 to 500 in both 1946 and 1948.

[7] It is important to distinguish between school district consolidation and school closure. The former refers to the collapsing of multiple smaller school districts into a single district, which is common in rural areas. The latter refers to the shuttering of a single school building and/or school program, which is common in urban areas. While consolidation can lead to the shuttering of a physical school and/or program, this is not necessarily the case. This book is specifically interested in school closure, not consolidation.

closure became primarily a racial issue. The complete history of racial segregation is complex and out of the scope of this text, but it is well known that Blacks were historically blocked from education in the United States, as many states made it illegal for them to learn and attend school (e.g., Todd-Breland, 2018). Even once they were allowed to attend school, through Jim Crow laws, Black Americans were segregated into colored-only schools that were unequally funded and of inferior quality compared to White-only schools. Recognizing this clear racial disparity in schooling, leaders of the civil rights movement made the issue of school integration central to their efforts because they understood that the attainment of equal education would be critical for accessing full citizenship and, thus, all that democracy promised.

The fight for equal education culminated in the passage of *Brown v. Board of Education* in 1954, barring school segregation that had come under *Plessy v. Ferguson*'s separate but equal precedent (Todd-Breland, 2018). While states were forced to desegregate, school districts in places such as Arkansas decided to close all their high schools for an entire year rather than integrate. The limited research on this topic, referred to as the "lost year," finds that 3,665 students were left out of their public schools once they reopened and suggests that 50 percent of the Black students impacted did not attend school for over a year (Gordy, 2009).[8]

By the end of the 1970s, more than approximately 7,000 public schools had been closed across 80 percent of the nation's school districts. But this time, the lion's share of these closures occurred in the twenty-five largest districts, in places such as Chicago, New York City, St. Louis in Missouri, and Cleveland and Columbus in Ohio. Still, the publicly stated reasons for these closures in the 1960s and 1970s are like those of today. Proponents cited enrollment decline and expected cost savings from consolidated resources. More specifically, school districts expected to gain savings from either the lease or sale of high-maintenance buildings. Nonetheless, these cost savings were rarely realized because most of the budget was typically expended on personnel costs, an issue unresolved through the closure of schools (Colton & Frelich, 1979; Valencia,

---

[8] I should note that, in the case of Arkansas, I am referring to the fact that there was an emphasis on the closure of schools rather than school districts *and* the specific racialized reasons, in this case, integration, as justification for closure (as opposed to industry decline, cited in the earlier example).

1984b). In some cases, the difficulty of selling a building and the cost of maintaining a closed building resulted in almost no cost savings at all. Instead, new costs were created as school districts struggled to pay realtors and leasing agents to intervene under public pressure to document the utility of the closure. As scholar Richard Valencia (1984b) deduced, "one can infer from the literature that closing schools reduce [s] per-pupil costs very little, if at all. Thus, it appears that the strategy of closing schools to save money is largely symbolic" (p. 10).

Similar to today, those affected by school closures raised questions about the legitimacy of the process, specifically the policy's seemingly racially targeted nature (Cuban, 1979). In fact, national data going back to 1975 demonstrate how public school closures were unequally stratified along the lines of race and income (Valencia, 1980, 1984b; Dean, 1981). For example, a study conducted on school closures in St. Louis between 1968 and 1977 found that of the seven schools shut down before 1975, all of them had majority Black enrollments because White enrollment had been declining in those neighborhoods (Colton & Frelich, 1979). In particular, the study found that "closed main site schools ... tended to be ... located in neighborhoods serving clients who were poor and African American. Schools in these neighborhoods were also relatively close together" (pp. 17–18). Another report conducted by Valencia (1980) further confirmed these findings and discovered that "investigations of school closings in five major cities indicate that schools with primarily low socioeconomic status and minority students have suffered the brunt, if not the exclusive burden, of closings" (p. 6). These historical findings make evident that when schools close in the United States, there are clear winners (the White and affluent) and losers (the minority and low income).

The Racially Targeted Nature of Closings Today

Today, racial disparities in school closings persist. In urban areas, specifically, school closures affect Black people more than any other group, including Whites, across class.[9] In fact, some studies have

---

[9] For urban closure see, https://apps.urban.org/features/school-closures/child_map.html. The literature is much less clear regarding the racial and economic impacts of rural closure. More specifically, there exists competing literature on this topic, with a slight majority suggesting that its racial and economic impacts are uneven. Since this is not the focus of my

demonstrated that closure can be predicted by determining the percentage of Black students in a school (Burdick-Will, Keels, & Schuble, 2013; Weber et al., 2018). Further, schools that have high concentrations of students on free or reduced lunch are more likely to be threatened with closure (Han et al., 2017). Since economic segregation and racial segregation are closely linked in the United States, the burden of school closures is often borne by communities at the intersection of socioeconomic deprivation and anti-Black racism. It is unsurprising, then, that when a school closes, the most devastating effects are concentrated in communities that can least afford them.

Increasingly, cities with declining economies and high rates of poverty are the central sites of uneven school closure by race (Tieken & Auldridge-Reveles, 2019). For example, in Chicago and Philadelphia, which have two of the largest public school districts in the nation, nearly 90 percent of the students attending schools targeted for closure in 2012 were Black or Latinx (US Department of Education, National Center for Education Statistics, 2018). In Chicago, Black students made up about 47 percent of the total public school population in 2013; yet 88 percent of these students, many of whom were also eligible for free or reduced lunch, were affected by closure. In Philadelphia, Black students made up 48 percent of the public school population; yet they represented nearly 81 percent of those targeted for closure (Good, 2017).[10] Across the nation, the racialized patterns of closures are the same: Black students are overrepresented as targets for closure relative to their proportion in the public school system. The large number of closures in cities such as Chicago and Philadelphia – and their disproportionate racial impacts – should raise serious questions about how the closures of public institutions shape the political beliefs and actions of the Americans most directly affected.

---

investigation, I hesitate to uphold or deny this claim, but see Tieken and Auldridge-Reveles (2019) for more information.

[10] See Chicago Public Schools website, CPS Schools Data – Race and Ethnic Report, 2012–2013, http://cps.edu/SchoolData/Pages/SchoolData.aspx. See School District of Philadelphia, School Information, https://dashboards.philasd.org/extensions/philadelphia/index.html.

How Engagement with Educational Policies Forms Black Political Behavior

Citizens learn about politics through their engagement with the local institutions they encounter in their everyday lives. The education system is an institution that directly affects most people's lives daily, first as students and then as parents, with most Americans directly acquiring civic skills through public schools (Hochschild & Scovronick, 2003). For example, schools may be the first place where students take a formal civics course or parents engage in politics, usually via school board elections. In either case, Americans likely use their experiences with education as a microcosm for understanding not only related policies that affect them but also politics and government at large.

Political and social scientists have long acknowledged the importance of examining the political consequences of public policies, including education policy, on citizens' political attitudes (e.g., Soss, 1999; Mettler & Soss, 2004; Mettler, 2011; Jacobs & Weaver, 2015; Cramer & Toff, 2017; Lerman & McCabe, 2017; Bruch & Soss, 2018). Yet, while some scholars of policy feedback have touched on education policy and political behavior specifically (e.g., Bruch & Soss, 2018; Rose, 2018), the field has tended not to focus on it. Instead, the focus is typically on nationalized issues such as the GI Bill, Social Security, Medicare, and Medicaid.

Suzanne Mettler (2005), for instance, finds that veterans' experiences with the benefits of the GI Bill (Servicemen's Readjustment Act of 1994) increased their civic engagement. More recent scholarship demonstrates the potential demobilizing effects of Medicaid policy on those who rely on it (e.g., Michener, 2018a), although these same experiences can "lead to meaningful opinion formation or attitude change," particularly among voters (Lerman & McCabe, 2017, p. 624). Together, these studies of policy feedback demonstrate the significant role of personal experience in a range of political dispositions (e.g., attitudes, behavior, self-conceptions) that one would expect could be easily applied to educational issues.

The relative lack of focus on educational issues by policy feedback scholars, then, may be due to the decentralized complexity of education governance, especially at the K-12 level. But this oversight is unfortunate because K-12 education is an area of government from which students, their families, and members of the broader community receive a variety of essential resources, from free meals to flu shots. The ability of schools to provide these resources in addition to academic learning should make them central sites of investigation for feedback scholars, especially when one considers their essential role during the global COVID-19 pandemic.

Amid the global COVID-19 pandemic, over 50 million children across the United States experienced the temporary closing of their schools, thus removing access to the crucial assistance that public schools provide. And while the effects of temporary school closures differ in many important ways from permanent closures, one would expect similar consequences – beyond the much–discussed loss of learning – to ripple across the many dimensions that tie local communities to their schools.

In response to protests and rebellions to bring attention to Black people killed by the police in May 2020, for example, Chicago Public Schools decided to temporarily suspend its meal program for twenty-four hours due to safety concerns. Yet, this decision left thousands of students without access to free food. In a city where an average of more than 200,000 meals had been handed out daily to families in need since March 2020, the decision was an illustration of how easily the issues of racism, the shuttering of public institutions, and COVID-19 can converge in detrimental ways, reemphasizing the significant role of schools in this moment. Despite this, the effects of school closure, whether temporary or permanent, on the behaviors conventionally measured by political scientists – government trust, efficacy, citizenship – remain unclear.

Even fewer studies have examined school closures in relationship to race and political behavior.[11] Measures of Black political behavior such as group consciousness – expressions of how much people view their life chances as connected to other members of their same constructed category – may provide a useful approach (e.g., see Miller et al., 1981; Dawson, 1994; Chong & Rogers, 2005). For instance, it could be the case that group consciousness explains the ensuing actions of community members affected by closure, meaning that their behaviors are rooted in historical experiences with race.

Nonetheless, as Paula McClain and colleagues (2009) have observed, it is also "important for scholars to understand better the

---

[11] The recent scholarship that focuses on K-12 education is perhaps best exhibited in Domingo Morel's book *Take Over*, in which the author illustrates the varying patterns of mobilization among Black and Latinx citizens following the decision by the state to take control over the local school district.

contexts that activate and those that might limit or stymie the development of group consciousness" (p. 471). Further, as Chryl Laird (2019) argues in an analysis of racial group identification, "political context ... shapes the way group members see their own interests as connected with those of the group" (p. 3). Accordingly, while historical connectedness to a racial group may in some cases shape how policies are understood, contemporary policies can also play a critical role in constructing race and thus the extent of connectedness to a racial group.[12]

In this book, I conceive of group consciousness as a racial attitude modified by citizens' policy experiences. In particular, I view low-income minority groups as making political decisions not only based on historical experiences with race but also through their engagement with specific contemporary policies happening in their community. By examining community members' experiences with school closings, I demonstrate how they provide an opportunity for racial consciousness to be activated and community mobilization to ensue, particularly once policies identify certain groups as targets.

How Citizens Become Targets

Policies often construct citizens as targets before they go on to engage with them. According to Anne Schneider and Helen Ingram (1993), "by specifying eligibility criteria, policy creates the boundaries of target populations" (p. 335), for example, income requirements for Temporary Assistance for Needy Families (referred to as "welfare") or age qualifications for Social Security. Schneider and Ingram show that, through the process of defining criteria, social policies send messages to citizens about who is worthy of receiving public services and goods – and who is not. These messages are based on stereotypes, cultural characterizations, or popular images about the targeted group that policy makers utilize and citizens internalize. As Schneider and Ingram further explain, "there are strong pressures for public officials to provide beneficial policy to powerful, positively constructed target populations and to devise punitive, punishment-oriented policy for negatively

---

[12] To be sure, group norms and racialized social pressure play an important role in forcing connectedness (White & Laird, 2020), but an independent policy event can still shape how that pressure operates and its overall effectiveness.

constructed groups" (p. 334). In sum, the various ways in which a group is socially constructed shape how policies are developed and, consequently, how citizens view themselves in relationship to others affected by the policy (Schneider & Ingram, 2005).

Despite the important findings from Schneider and Ingram's work, related studies typically struggle to connect social construction frameworks with political outcomes and behavior, especially those related to race. A close example is an investigation by Joe Soss (1999), in which he demonstrates how recipients of Social Security Disability Insurance are essentially constructed as "deserving" and respond positively to their experiences with this federal government program, whereas recipients of Aid to Families with Dependent Children are constructed as "undeserving" and thus view their experiences with government bureaucracy negatively. These constructions align with race and gender stereotypes and contribute to recipient experiences with a program and its administrators. Recipients then generalize their experiences to the nature and goals of the political system more broadly.

These findings, like much of the literature, have serious implications for race, but race remains decentered in the analysis. By *decentered*, I mean that race may be discussed as an outcome of the research but not as a central framework for conceiving the project, theoretically or empirically. Recognizing this gap, Jamila Michener (2019a) develops what she describes as a *racialized feedback framework*. The framework suggests specific conditions when race should be especially salient in research on policy feedback: (1) the policies under consideration are heavily disproportionate, in their allocation of benefits to or burdens on particular racial groups; and/or (2) the policies are decentralized. Using this framework, if a policy is both highly disproportionate and decentralized, then race should be centered in the analysis.

In this case, the closure policy disproportionately targets low-income Blacks for the removal of resources in the form of schools. Consequently, they are also disproportionately burdened with the labor involved in opposing the policy (e.g., meetings, protests, voting). Further, these actions are occurring at the neighborhood and community level, away from state and district authority. Together, the negative impacts of the school closure policy are racialized, decentralized, and unevenly distributed, which has serious consequences for the political behavior of those targeted for closure.

Becoming a Shared Target of School Closures

It is important to note, however, that the political behavior of those targeted is based not on their experiences with distantly formulated policy or policy messages but rather their contextual experiences as members of the community in which the policy occurs. By *contextual*, I mean that while citizens may not have direct or personal exposure to the policy, they may still identify as a policy target through their shared geographic location, racial identity, and/or resources with those who are personally and directly affected. This makes them *shared policy targets*.

My shared policy target conceptualization is similar to recent scholarship that describes the effects of policies on individuals who may not be direct targets of a policy but share proximity to those who are. Traci Burch (2014), for example, finds that the racially targeted policies associated with mass incarceration decrease the political participation of those directly affected as well as fellow members of their neighborhood. Similarly, Hannah Walker (2014, 2020) finds that those who have proximal – not just direct – experiences with the criminal justice system engage in increased protest actions. Jamila Michener (2018a) examines the impacts of concentrated disadvantage on political participation and finds that as the percentage of persons on Medicaid increases in a county, ties to civic engagement associations and aggregate voting declines. While these works are specific to the justice and healthcare system, they illustrate how feedback effects are often not limited to direct beneficiaries but also entire communities.

Nonetheless, a shared policy target conceptualization differs from these established works in that it recognizes that mobilization toward a policy is incited (or depressed) not only because of the ways the recipients are constructed by government or even their geographic proximity to the policy's impacts, but also because of the counter-constructions of the policy that are *actively* developed and shared between members of the target community. Regarding the policy issue of school closure, the book highlights how target communities collect and disseminate information contrary to government rationale for closure. In fact, they frame school closure as a *race and neighborhood* concern, which means that the target category is not only inclusive of those who have children that attend schools threatened for closure but also poor Black communities where those schools are located more generally. Understood this way, the construction of who is included as a target of school closure is not just an empirical issue (where direct and indirect targets of policy happen to behave similarly in the data because they live in the same community), it is a substantive political tool and strategy, likely used by communities to facilitate collective investment and mobilization against the government. In other words, *citizens may come to see themselves as directly impacted by a policy as a community*, even if they are only indirectly affected at the individual level and live outside of the directly impacted community. This intentional inclusion of oneself as a shared member of an affected community facilitates opportunities for both informal and formal political participation (read more about *place-based mobilization* in Nuamah & Ogorzalek, 2020).

I examine participation around public schools, specifically, because these institutions have been a central channel for minority populations to access socioeconomic mobility, community empower- ment, and, most important for this analysis, democracy (Lipman, 2009; Caref et al., 2012; Todd-Breland, 2018). Public schools represent some of the first institutions in which Blacks held leadership roles, such as principal and superintendent, before taking on formal political roles like mayor; for example, W. W. Herenton became the first Black superin- tendent of Memphis Public Schools in 1979 and then the first Black mayor of Memphis in 1991. Public schools have also acted as central sites for organizing around social and political issues for Blacks; for example, the Freedom Schools throughout the 1960s were used to provide students with the educational tools needed to attain political equity (e.g., Perlstein, 1990; Todd-Breland, 2018). In addition, Black schools have acted as centers of employment through the hiring of teachers, staff, and administrators as well as mechanisms to sustain Black businesses, which have benefited from contracts such as those to serve lunch and/or provide janitorial services. In a context where most programs of social welfare have been disinvested, schools have become, and continue to be, engines of social, economic, and political mobility. In the words of one parent, "schools are the last remaining public institutions" (interview, Philadelphia, 2017). Therefore, the closures of public schools act as a threat to Black futures and are deserving of attention.

In examining this topic, I highlight the importance of research on how racialized political events or policies affects the collective polit- ical behavior of entire communities. I extend the theory on social construction of target populations, policy feedback, race, and urban politics using evidence that policies, particularly those related to public school closures, can and do shape Blacks' relationship to government and democracy. Together, the combination of becoming a target of closure by living in an affected community, the creation and promotion of counternarratives, and the acute threat of losing shared public resources, creates a local and unique body politic that facilitates formal and informal participation against school closures.

Case Studies: Chicago Public Schools and the School District of Philadelphia

Perhaps no two places are better candidates for an investigation of public school closure and political behavior than Chicago and Philadelphia. Both cities have large racial and ethnic minority populations (roughly 32% of Chicagoans and 43% of Philadelphians identify as Black). In addition, both cities are very racially segregated: In Chicago, most Blacks reside in areas located on the South and West Sides of the city, while in Philadelphia, Blacks are mostly located on the North, Southwest and West sides of the city (US Census Bureau, 2019).

However, the key shared characteristic of both cities is that they experienced the largest number of school closures in their respective histories in 2013. That year, Chicago closed a total of forty-nine public schools, and Philadelphia closed twenty-three.[13] As noted earlier, although Blacks make up approximately 50 percent of the total public school population in these cities, nearly 80–90 percent of students attending the closed schools were Black.

Due to their similar closure rates and racial dynamics, Chicago and Philadelphia are useful case studies, but there are other factors that facilitate valuable comparisons for understanding the effects of school closures on the political attitudes of racial and ethnic minorities more broadly. To see this connection, it is helpful to look briefly at the historical details and context surrounding public school closures in each city.

---

[13] Chicago Public Schools action guidelines are available at www.cps.edu/about/school-transitions/school-actions, and the consideration guidelines for Philadelphia are available at http://media.phillyvoice.com/media/documents/District_Closure_Considerations.pdf.

Chicago Public Schools

Before his untimely death in 1987, Chicago's first Black mayor, Harold Washington, laid the groundwork for one of Chicago's first contemporary education reforms, the Chicago School Reform Act of 1988.[14] The act was in response to a citywide summit on creating a community-based approach to school-level decision-making. These efforts led to the establishment of more than 6,000 local school councils by 1989 as well as a commission (elected by the local school councils) that nominated school board members (Hess & Easton, 1991).[15]

But all that changed when, following Washington's death and two interim mayors, Richard M. Daley was elected mayor of Chicago in 1989. In 1995, he orchestrated a takeover of Chicago Public Schools, giving the mayoral office unprecedented power. In turn, the school board was filled via appointment rather than elected process, creating direct mayoral control. The collective bargaining power of the Chicago Teachers Union also came under fire (Lipman, 2011). Further, services previously under contract with CPS were outsourced to private companies or organizations. Perhaps most critically, Mayor Daley appointed Paul Vallas as chief executive officer (CEO) of CPS. In a marked shift from the previous community-based approach to school leadership and learning, under Vallas's leadership, CPS promoted a privatized "high-stakes" approach, focusing heavily on teacher and school accountability through test scores of students (Russo, 2004).

This shift can be best described as the *neoliberal turn*, the gradual embrace of the general idea that society works best when it follows the principles of the market (Spence, 2015). In a neoliberal conception of education, specifically, schools are conceived of as commodities that produce successful individuals (measured by academic performance) as opposed to public goods that produce good citizens. The goal then is to generate competition by bringing more options to the market, commodifying them, and then distributing rewards or punishment based on traditional measures of performance (e.g., Lipman, 2011; Spence, 2015).

---

[14] The Chicago School Reform Act of 1988 rewrote Article 34 of the Illinois School Code, the portion of state law that deals only with Chicago's public schools.
[15] The final commission members were approved by the mayor.

Undergirding this neoliberal perspective are the long-standing constitutive systems of racism and capitalism,[16] which contribute to the promotion of individual-level solutions to systemic issues. Yet these individual-level solutions do not fundamentally alter the racial and labor order. In other words, neoliberal efforts do not address the fact that the systematic inequality produced through institutional racism, and its intrinsic connection to capitalism,[17] cannot be dismantled through market competition and individual success (e.g., Robinson, 1983; Leong, 2013). Instead, the neoliberal turn in education replaces potentially democratic efforts with those relevant to the free market, thereby elevating individual-level solutions while ignoring structural problems.

The case of Chicago is particularly illustrative of this: Along with Gery Chico, president of the CPS school board from 1995 to 2001, Vallas proposed that Chicago create at least fifteen smaller schools and charters outside of the traditional district. By 1997, thirty-eight organizations applied to open such schools; in all, ten were approved and six ultimately opened (Ayers & Klonsky, 2006; Bulkley, Henig, & Levin, 2010). The transformation of public education in Chicago, under the auspices of accountability, had commenced.

Citing increasing differences between himself, Daley, and local education groups, Vallas resigned as CEO of CPS in 2001, and Arne Duncan, his chief of staff, was appointed as the new CEO. From 2001 to 2002, Duncan oversaw the official closing of three CPS schools. The justification provided for the closure policy was under-enrollment and/or that the schools performed persistently poorly (Duncan, 2006). (Vallas left Chicago in 2002 to become CEO of the School District of Philadelphia, which is discussed next.) In Chicago, the Office of New Schools was created, and the charter cap was raised from 15 to 30 in 2003 (Vergari, 2007).

In 2004, the Renaissance 2010 initiative was passed in Chicago. The purpose of the initiative was to take a "portfolio management approach" to improve schools by developing shared metrics for

---

[16] *Racism* is typically defined as oppression and subordination of people based on the social construction of race. *Capitalism* is typically defined as an economic system in which the central means of production are privately owned and operated for the purposes of profit.

[17] This is often referred to as *racial capitalism*, a term coined by Cedric Robinson to describe "the process of deriving social and economic value from the racial identity of another person" (Leong, 2013). The use of the term *capitalism* in this book implies racial capitalism.

evaluating schools, making determinations about which schools to close, and making space for the creation of new schools.[18] With the birth of this initiative, the school closing policy became official. Mayor Daley and Superintendent Duncan intended to close as many as 60 schools, based on low performance, to make room for 100 new schools, mostly charter, by 2010 (Bulkley, Henig, & Levin, 2010).

In 2008, Duncan left CPS to become secretary of education under President Barack Obama. A succession of CEOs was appointed for CPS in the years that followed, and in 2012, newly elected Chicago Mayor Rahm Emanuel replaced all the appointed school board members with new members, at the same time creating an independent commission tasked with providing recommendations to the board. In 2012, Barbara Byrd-Bennett[19] was appointed as CEO of CPS. Under her leadership, the city underwent the largest number of school closures in a single year in history. As was the case with earlier closings, under-utilization was the main justification given, along with potential cost savings in the millions. Between 2001 and 2013, Chicago saw more than 120 schools close.

School District of Philadelphia

Over the years, Philadelphia has been home to multiple educa-tion reforms, perhaps the most significant ones being the Children Achieving initiative in 1994 and the Pennsylvania Charter School Law, passed in 1997 (similar legislation was passed the same year in Illinois). The Children Achieving initiative, developed by then–Superintendent of the School District of Philadelphia David Hornbeck, emphasized high-stakes accountability through testing and embraced alternative schools and public–private partnerships. The Pennsylvania Charter School Law was introduced and passed under Governor Tom Ridge, allowing independent organizations to operate public schools with less regulation. Thereafter, Philadelphia went on to embrace one of

---

[18] To learn more about the Renaissance 2010 initiative, visit www.cps.edu/PROGRAMS/ DISTRICTINITIATIVES/Pages/Renaissance2010.aspx or https://www.austinweeklynews .com/2007/10/31/cps-approves-18-new-renaissance-2010-schools.

[19] Barbara Byrd Bennet was accused and eventually convicted for engaging in education-related corruption and bribery in 2015. She was sentenced to 4.5 years in federal prison.

the most liberal charter school laws in the nation (Bulkley, 2007).[20] Nonetheless, while this law was implemented and expanded over the years, Philadelphia and its public school district faced ongoing economic decline. In response, Act 46 was passed in 1998 by the Pennsylvania General Assembly to authorize a state takeover of any district in financial or academic distress.[21] By 2001, the School District of Philadelphia had succumbed to the policy and was subjected to the supervision of the state. As a consequence of the state takeover, multiple outside partners were recruited to provide recommendations and management services for low-performing Philadelphia public schools. The most important partner, in this case, was Edison Schools Inc., an organization given management responsibility for nearly twenty Philadelphia public schools, representing the largest share of schools allocated to any single provider (Peterson & Chingos, 2009; Cucchiara, 2013).

Hornbeck resigned in 2001, and Vallas, the former CEO of CPS, was appointed superintendent in 2002. While in office, Vallas removed Edison from operations, established and mandated a district-wide curriculum, increased the number of small schools, and promoted select charter operators that he thought were strong. In short, he replicated many of the reforms he had put in place in Chicago (Bulkley, 2007; Useem, 2009). Yet, under Vallas's leadership, enrollment continued to shrink, and financial constraints increased. In addition, he was accused of a lack of transparency and public engagement. Consequently, Vallas resigned in 2007 and was officially replaced by Arlene Ackerman in 2009.

Ackerman continued many of Vallas's policies under her own initiative, Imagine 2014.[22] Through Imagine 2014, which began in 2009, Ackerman identified low-performing public schools and labeled them "Renaissance schools" (reminiscent of Chicago's Renaissance 2010 initiative). These identified schools could be subjected to the following actions by 2014: (1) closure or conversion to charter status;

[20] As of 2016, there were nearly 60,000 students in about eighty charter schools in Philadelphia (see Philadelphia School District 2016 data at www.philasd.org/performance/programsservices/open-data/school-information/#district_enrollment).

[21] The Education Empowerment Act, which identifies "districts with a history of low-test performance," was also passed under Governor Ridge in 2000.

[22] Ackerman also promoted public engagement as a cornerstone of her work through the development of local organizations, most notably Parents United and Parent Power (Peterson & Chingos, 2009). Details related to Imagine 2014 are available at https://wayback.archive-it.org/1950/20110330123833/http://www.phila.k12.pa.us/announcements/Imagine_2014_041509.pdf.

(2) management by outsiders; or (3) district management through a turnaround or management by people selected by the superintendent or central office. As a result, much like Chicago, schools began to close but not yet in large numbers or systematically. After her involvement in a cheating scandal in 2011 as well as major protests and campaigns by youth groups such as the Philadelphia Student Union, Ackerman was forced to resign (Conner & Rosen, 2013; Caskey & Kuperberg, 2014).

In 2012, William Hite, previous superintendent of Prince George's County School District in Baltimore, was appointed superintendent of the School District of Philadelphia. Upon his arrival, Hite faced one of the biggest economic crises to hit the school district in the recent past because of a discontinuation of federal funding and a significant drop in state funding under then–Governor Thomas Corbett. Furthermore, charter school growth continued to increase, at this point accounting for more than 30 percent of the public school system (Jack & Sludden, 2013). In an effort to save money and under the pretext of academic underperformance, Hite proposed sixty schools for potential closure, potentially affecting nearly 10,000 low-income students, 81 percent of whom were Black. Since 2012, more than thirty schools have been closed in Philadelphia (Jack & Sludden, 2013).

Comparing School Closings in Chicago and Philadelphia

The decision to close schools was met with resistance by those affected in both Chicago and Philadelphia. Thousands of people attended protests about potential closures (DeJarnatt, 2013), and legal cases in opposition to these decisions were filed.[23] State reform laws were passed in both Illinois and Pennsylvania to mandate public announcements on school closure decisions as well as public input and a ninety-day window between announcement and closure.[24] In

---

[23] For details about court cases in Philadelphia, see www.washingtonpost.com/news/answer-sheet/wp/2013/11/23/in-philadelphia-schools-is-the-right-to-know-the-new-pay-for-play/?noredirect=on&utm_term=.1c3be9191cd7. For more information about court cases in Chicago, see https://www.americanbar.org/groups/litigation/committees/childrens-rights/articles/2019/spring2019-school-closing-victory-the-fight-to-save-national-teachers-academy/.

[24] See, for example, details regarding implementation of the Illinois law (IL P.A. 097-0474) at www.ilga.gov/legislation/publicacts/fulltext.asp?name=097-0474; for the Pennsylvania law, see www.education.pa.gov/Documents/K-12/Safe%20Schools/Chapter%2010%2042%20PaB%204574.pdf.

addition, both cities successfully passed moratoria that limited each state's ability to close schools in upcoming years.[25] Finally, Get Out the Vote campaigns targeting elected officials associated with the closures were launched in both cities.

Despite the similar actions that the closures generated in Chicago and Philadelphia, there are notable differences in the history of school closures in these cities. First, Philadelphia has a much shorter history of school closures. Official announcements to close schools were first made in 2010, and nearly two years passed before eight schools were closed in 2012, followed by twenty-three more in 2013. In contrast, Chicago officials closed the first three schools in 2001 and consistently closed more schools every year until a peak of forty-nine in 2013.

Second, the capacities of the teacher unions in these cities were considerably different. Compared to the Philadelphia Federation of Teachers, the Chicago Teachers Union is larger and stronger, in part due to the Chicago School Reform Act of 1988, which decentralized power to the schools. In fact, the Chicago Teachers Union has often been cited as providing a model for many efforts of the Philadelphia Federation of Teachers as well as other teachers' unions. For example, the Caucus of Working Educators, the Teacher Action Group–Philadelphia, and Philadelphia Coalition Advocating for Public Schools were often described as the products of an initiative to strengthen the position of the Philadelphia Federation of Teachers. In so doing, these organizations could advocate for district teachers and students in ways similar to the Chicago Teachers Union's Caucus of Rank and File Educators, or CORE, group. Finally, the reasons for closure were framed differently across both cities. While CPS framed the 2013 iteration of closings as primarily an underutilization issue because of more seats than students in a classroom, in Philadelphia the criteria for closure was bundled into concerns related primarily to academic performance as well as the quality of the school buildings.[26]

---

[25] See www.dnainfo.com/chicago/20121126/chicago/schools-chief-announces-five-year-moratorium-on-school-closures and http://thenotebook.org/articles/2013/01/24/city-council-passes-resolution-to-support-moratorium-on-school-closings for details related to the school closing moratoria in Chicago and Philadelphia, respectively.

[26] The proposal to close schools was handled by Philadelphia's facilities department. Deviations in policy framing in these cities allow for a more nuanced investigation of how the framing of a closure policy might influence citizens' receptivity to it. Altogether, comparing across cities facilitates a discussion on the broader applicability of the findings and contributes to a more nuanced understanding of these phenomena.

Larger structural similarities such as city size and racial composition, shared district leadership (e.g., Paul Vallas), district initiatives (e.g., Renaissance 2010, Renaissance schools), similarities in the scale of closures, the closure processes, and outcomes ensure that the cases of Chicago and Philadelphia are analogous enough to be examined together. Yet, the variable factors between the cases (e.g., the difference in length of experience with closure, union capability, framing) facilitate valuable comparisons between each city. Perhaps most important, comparing the school closure experiences of Chicago and Philadelphia produces findings that can be applied to similar cities facing mass closure across the nation.

Beyond Chicago and Philadelphia: The Closure of Black Communities

Beyond Chicago and Philadelphia, decades of gentrification (e.g., replacement of affordable public housing with private condos) and neoliberal reform (e.g., replacement of public schools with private charter schools) have contributed to the significant displacement of populations in what were once Black- and Brown-led areas. Mara Tieken and Trevor Auldridge-Reveles (2019), for example, describe how threats to close schools "may serve as a signal ... that a place is in 'transition' or 'decline,' that its current community is not worthy of investment, that its spaces are open for the use and exploitation of others" (p. 939). Understood this way, school closures threaten to deal several communities across the nation their final blow.

While this investigation focuses on urban areas, closures often send similar messages in rural communities and are thus similarly disfavored by those who experience them (Bastress, 2003; Alsbury & Shaw, 2005). However, those affected in rural areas often exhibit less resistance to these efforts, compared with urban areas. This is likely due to a lower concentration of organizations that citizens can rely on to build political power and, in some cases, the decision by White parents to opt out of the public school system or be reassigned to another public school of their choice (Berger, 1983; Desimone, 1993; Bastress, 2003; England & Hamann, 2013). In the face of relatively low levels of resistance, however, more schools are likely to be closed in rural areas in the coming years, highlighting the need for research on school closures' distinctive impacts from urban areas.

Ultimately, I use the examples of Chicago and Philadelphia to dive deeply into the political consequences of school closures on the lives of those affected the most. But, as illustrated thus far, this study is not just about Chicago and Philadelphia; it is about how urban areas across the United States with similar histories of displacement and reform are subjected to the contemporary closure of their schools. And by virtue of where those schools are, it is about how school closures are interpreted by those affected as indicative of the slow but deliberate diminution of Black communities, more generally.

Research Approach

To study the political consequences of public school closures in urban areas, I used multiple data types and methodologies. I constructed a national-level data set containing the location of nearly every public school in the United States known to be closed between 1994 and 2014. Using this data, I created novel survey measures of exposure to school closures. I then merged data on these measures with data from multiple individual-level surveys of citizens living in Chicago and Philadelphia, focused specifically on education and politics. I selected and analyzed responses to items from surveys of Chicagoans conducted by the Cooperative Congressional Election Study (CCES), the Joyce Foundation, and the National Opinion Research Center (NORC) at the University of Chicago as well as surveys of Philadelphians conducted by Pew Charitable Trusts.[27]

In addition to the quantitative data, I also relied on original qualitative data, including interviews, ethnographic observations, and public transcripts. I conducted interviews and attended community meetings about school closings for forty-two months between 2012 and 2017 in both Chicago and Philadelphia. Overall, I collected 100 interviews with parents and elites as well as participant responses from community meeting[28] observations or transcripts of these meetings.

---

[27] The surveys vary widely in what they offer, but each provide data on numerous key variables, such as perceptions of school closures, approval and blame toward various political actors involved with the school closure, and measures of political trust, political efficacy, and political participation.

[28] These are meetings set up by the district that those affected by pending closures were encouraged to attend.

I used ethnographic observations of meetings and meeting transcripts to determine how the community forums related to school
closures act as spaces to learn about politics (or political learning).
I then used in-depth interviews with parents and community residents
to illustrate how participants describe their experiences and the lessons
they learned from these experiences. In particular, I focused on aspects
of the meetings that play an important role in teaching citizens about
accountability and the responsibility of school officials and other political leaders (e.g., meeting size, format, follow-up), and that influence
beliefs about government and democracy.

Although the data on citizens from each city differ and possess
respective limits, as a whole, the information allows me to effectively
hone in on the precise relationship between race, living in a neighborhood with high concentrations of public school closures, and political
attitudes/engagement. Additionally, while I focus on public school
closures, I expect that this work may provide a blueprint for analyses
of other important policy decisions that often have racially and geographically concentrated effects that are felt most powerfully by poor
Black and Brown communities across the United States, in areas such as
policing, environmental justice, and immigration. The Appendix will
detail the methods of data collection for each chapter in much greater
detail than is valuable to address in this introduction or the chapters.
Yet, together they enable an investigation that highlights the temporal
dynamics of democratic loss for Black citizens beyond bureaucratic
interactions with federal programs such as Supplemental Security
Income and Aid to Families with Dependent Children, and/or the ballot
box; focuses on other forms of non-electoral participation, particularly
those considered more accessible to, and representative of, commonly
marginalized groups, such as community meetings (Collins 2021); and
centers "community" as a site of co-identification and political action
for marginalized groups.

Looking Ahead

The chapters ahead take us on a journey through what it was
like for these communities to learn that their school was closing, to form
an opinion about it, to determine who to blame, to go after them, and
then to experience the result of their actions. All of this work is centered
on low-income Black Americans and traditional public schools. This

work is especially focused on the experiences of low-income African American women, who were and are primarily affected by the threat of traditional public school closure in their local communities. Accordingly, while there are references to several racial groups, in pursuit of comprehensiveness, this book will offer less examination of their experiences. It will focus on the specific relationship that Blacks have with public institutions, particularly schools, and illustrate how the threat of their closure disrupts not only their relationship to public institutions but also democracy broadly.

As alluded to earlier, the central unit of analysis is the community rather than the individual.[29] Although I fully recognize that students and parents are especially affected by school closure, the community focus of the investigation makes it such that their views are understood as one part of a shared grievance around the collective social and political impacts of closure, as opposed to a disruption to a student's or parent's individual-level achievement. Relatedly, while I describe the value of community organizations and unions for mobilizing people to participate, they are not the focus of this work. This decision is not an indication of the insignificance of community organizations in the fight to save schools – an entire book could be written on their powerful influence – but rather an empirical move to center the voices of low-income Black people who do not ordinarily participate in politics and are not ordinarily discussed in relevant research. In doing so, I take seriously the idea that ordinary citizens can use their policy experiences to develop their own ideas about government and democracy, even if they work with community organizations or leaders in the process.

Focusing on low-income Blacks, I investigate the attitudes of citizens toward school closure; how policy attitudes toward school closure shape broader political attitudes, in particular, political blame; and the effects of school closure on citizens' political engagement, efficacy, and belief in American democracy. More specifically, in Chapter 1, I investigate what citizens' perceptions of the school closure policy are and how these attitudes vary by race. Further, I examine how divisions across racial attitudes likely shape government response to the

---

[29] While in practice, the investigation relies on various measures that range from individual-level to aggregate data (depending on availability), all of it is interpreted through a collective lens. Thus, there is also very little discussion of individual students or children.

largely Black population affected by closure. Chapter 2 looks at how and to whom targeted citizens' attribute blame and responsibility for school closure actions. In so doing, it brings forth issues of race and representation, demonstrating the ability of those affected by closure to assign blame based on who holds the most power over closure decisions. In Chapter 3, I expand on the previous chapters by demonstrating how citizens' negative attitudes toward school closure policies, and their attributions of blame, have broader consequences for their political engagement. From their actions, I show that some communities are successful at evading school closure and shaping other political outcomes, but I raise the question of whether their efforts are enough to produce lasting policy change. Chapter 4 demonstrates the real limits of citizen participation in producing the type of changes that targets of school closures desire: transparency about the process, saving and strengthening all their schools, and true racial justice. Using the concept of *collective participatory debt*, this chapter illustrates the disillusionment that those affected by the closure have with future participation, even when they win their battles to save some schools.

Together, this work brings the agency of marginalized and disaffected communities to the fore and demonstrates how these groups navigate complex political relationships to form opinions on, and take action toward, important political issues. It provides clear support for the notion that low-income racial minorities can, and do, make informed decisions about politics, even if they appear inconsistent with what policy makers deem as beneficial to them. Further, they can, and do, go on to participate more than any other group to make their voices heard, even as they lack the resources traditionally associated with high levels of participation. Yet, they also can, and do, hold negative attitudes toward government and future participation, even when they secure policy wins – as those wins fail to materialize in the ways expected.

To be sure, Carole Pateman's (1970) classic work on participatory democracy makes clear that "the major function of participation in … participatory democracy is … an educative one, educative in the very widest sense" (p. 41). And indeed, citizens affected by closure learn productive lessons about democracy and their position in it, regardless of the outcome. Yet, as stated by Francesca Polletta (2012), if "democracy comes to mean simply public participation, then spectacles of participation may be made to stand in for mechanisms of democratic accountability" (p. 41). Similarly, in the words of the late Charles

Hamilton (Carmichael and Hamilton, 1992), this type of participation may be "quick, intense, theatrical … but it is not very likely to be deep and sustaining" (p. 211). In sum, while there is use in participation for the sake of education, the goal should be that citizens receive a lasting democratic response from the government.

The Cost of Participation: Closed for School, Closed for Democracy

Democratic responsiveness cannot exist without participation, but for some Americans – particularly low-income Black citizens – participation may not guarantee democratic responsiveness. Even if they are heard, they may find that the costs they endured during their participation were so dire it was not worth it.

Ultimately then, the school closure case provides insight for questions that have always been central to the study of Black politics more broadly: (1) How much should Black citizens persist in the fight for equity in a capitalist democracy?; (2) and, what, if any, are the right pathways for doing so? As stated by Michael Dawson (2018) in his recent work on race and capitalism: "Not only do Blacks and their allies continually resist White supremacy, victories that not only reshape but fundamentally undermine it are won at an inevitably high cost of blood and sacrifice." Juliet Hooker (2016) asks, "whether the display of exemplary citizenship by Blacks in the face of such unequal bargaining constitutes an unjust form of democratic suffering?" (p. 449). Cornell West goes a step further, questioning whether "*Black suffering* is required" for American democracy to function.[30]

This book is about those who have experienced the high costs and suffering associated with participating while poor and Black. It chronicles and details their experiences with becoming highly informed, superlative political participators to save their schools and, by proxy, their neighborhoods. It then follows their realization that they must pay uneven costs repeatedly because the battle is unending. It demonstrates how these citizens are everything a liberal democracy demands. And yet, democracy is closed to them.

---

[30] Referenced by Manning Marable (2007).

1

WHAT TARGETED CITIZENS THINK
Racial Differences in Public Opinion on School Closures

Sharon is an Black woman who has a daughter in the fourth grade at a public school in the city of Chicago. The school is in her neighborhood, and so every morning she walks her daughter to school before she heads to work.

One morning in December 2012, on the walk to school, Sharon runs into her friend Leslie, who is also an Black woman and whose daughter attends school in a nearby neighborhood. To Sharon's surprise, Leslie mentions that she just read in the paper that Sharon's daughter's school is under threat of closure. Sharon is in disbelief, so when she gets to the school that morning, she asks one of the teachers, who confirms the story. He hands her a flyer providing the details of two meetings coming up over the next few weeks. He tells her that attending the meetings is the *only* way to save the school. If the school is not saved, next year Sharon's daughter will be reassigned to another school.

Sharon attends both meetings, and Leslie joins her because, as she tells Sharon, she is vehemently against the school closing. At these meetings, Sharon and Leslie are told by the district that the closures of some schools will facilitate the allocation of more resources to the remaining schools. Yet, they remain opposed to the closures.[1]

---

[1] Details for all meetings, including URLs for meeting transcripts, can be found in the Appendix.

Everyone who attended the meetings waits to hear if they have had any impact on the district's decision. In March 2013 it is announced that the school will be closed, disappointing Sharon, Leslie, and many others.

Sharon, like Leanne in the Introduction, represents one of thousands of parents across large cities, including Chicago, New York, Philadelphia, and Boston, who have been faced with the threat of school closure and have had to participate in the formal meetings available to them to defend against the closure. Leslie represents one of thousands of community members who are not direct targets of school closure policy (i.e., do not have a child in the school scheduled to be closed or work there) but who has also participated in the process to stop schools from closing. While school districts often frame school closures as a contributing to the allocation of more resources, how do those directly affected, like Sharon; those indirectly affected, like Leslie; and the general American population feel about these policies? And why?

Parents such as Sharon and Leanne, as well as teachers and staff have a negative reaction when their school is closed or even only threatened to be closed. Perhaps more surprisingly, Leslie and others who are not directly affected have an adverse reaction as well. This chapter will focus on which citizens are targeted by school closure policies, directly or indirectly. Further, it will demonstrate how and why targeted citizens develop negative feelings about these policies, even when these policies are framed as being beneficial for them. Finally, and perhaps most important, this chapter will illustrate the significant role of race in structuring the attitudes of different populations toward the policy. It will show how Black and Latinx attitudes toward the school closure policy look very different than that of Whites.

The Process of Closing a School

When discussing the impacts of school closure policies and how citizens view them, it is important to begin with a basic understanding of how the decision to close a school is made (Figure 1.1). Typically, school districts generate a closure list based on a set of criteria. These criteria can change based on the priorities of a school district as well as from year to year or even within a year. Common criteria include low performance (typically measured by standardized test scores that fall

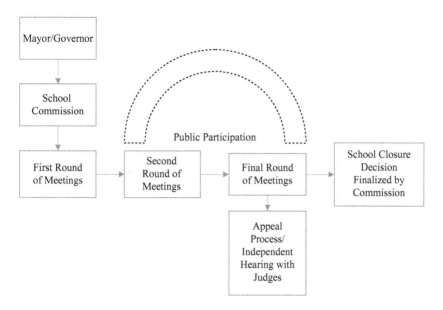

Figure 1.1 How school closure decisions are made

below a specified benchmark) and under-enrollment (calculated based on a school district's estimate of each school's student enrollment capacity relative to the actual student population).

In the case of Chicago, which will be the focus of this chapter, the Chicago Public School (CPS) system began officially closing schools in 2001 under then–CEO Arne Duncan. The justification provided for the policy was to address schools that performed persistently poorly (Duncan, 2006). School closings continued through 2012 under the next CEO, Barbara Byrd-Bennett, at which time the policy was justified as the result of population loss in particular areas of the city. CPS officials provided the public with the following statement as a rationale for the use of the policy at that time:

> Chicago has experienced a significant population decline; it has 145,000 fewer school-age children today than it did in 2000, centered primarily on the south and west sides. This population decline has been the primary driver of underutilized schools in our District; CPS has space for 511,000 students but only 403,000 are enrolled. (CPS presentation, network meeting, Austin-North Lawndale, Chicago, January 31, 2013, p. 1)

According to CPS, the decline in student population created an under-utilization crisis, in which there are more seats than students in a given classroom.

Once established, all schools that fit the closure criteria, in this case underutilization, were placed on a closure list. This list is distributed to the public and to the governing body, mostly typically a board, which makes final decisions about closures. In Chicago, the mayor-appointed school board made school closure decisions (technically, an independent commission in Chicago has the final say on school closures, although its decisions are nonbinding), while in Philadelphia, they were made by a school reform commission, to which the governor appoints three members, and the mayor appoints two.

Generally, after a closure list is generated but before a board or commission takes a final vote, the district announces scheduled meetings for public comment and feedback on the proposed school closings. At these meetings, participants may offer arguments about why their schools should not be closed and provide testimonial about issues the district may have overlooked. Alternative proposals may also be introduced in hopes of saving a school from being closed. Ideally, the public comments and feedback should contribute to the board or commission's final decision.

Typically, there are at least two rounds of meetings, potentially consisting of dozens of individual meetings, after the release of an initial school closure list. After the first set of meetings, a shortened school closure list may be constructed by the board or commission based on participant feedback. After that, a second round of public meetings is held for those schools that remain on the list. Once the second set of meetings are complete, the board or commission votes on which schools should remain on the final closure list for that school year. In Chicago, once the final list is generated, the public can attend a hearing with retired judges, appointed by the school district, to make a final appeal. The judges can recommend saving a school from closure, but only the board can officially decide to remove the school from the list. Once the public meetings are complete and vote is final, the schools that remain on the list will eventually be closed. The entire process takes at least four months, with the announcement of which schools are on the potential closure list made in late November/early December and final decisions typically released in March.

Targeting Chicago Public Schools for Closure

In November 2012, CPS compiled a list of 330 schools that could potentially be closed. By June 2013, 49 of those 330 schools were closed, which is the highest number of school closings in a single year in US history (School Reform Commission Report, 2013). Through closing those schools in 2013, CPS claimed it would be able to not only resolve the underutilization issue but also "redirect those dollars to ALL schools, then ... make investments that support student growth through new technology, AC, libraries, art/music, more counselors and nurses, and others" (network meeting, Austin-North Lawndale, Chicago, January 2013).

On the surface, the policy makes sense. It seeks to resolve a clear problem – population decline – while also ensuring that the resolution produces more resources to support all students. If the policy is read this way, one could expect a majority of citizens to support school closures.

Regardless of the stated intent to help all students, in practice the policy directly affected a select few: Out of the seventy-seven community areas that make up the city, only seven neighborhoods (across nine zip codes) absorbed close to 60 percent of the school closures (Table 1.1; Chicago Public Schools, 2013). Furthermore, while Blacks made up 48 percent of the public school population, 88 percent of them were affected by the school closure policy (in comparison, less than 10 percent of Latinx and even fewer Whites were affected). Clearly, then, the use of the school closure policy in Chicago resulted in uneven consequences for Blacks. Despite the policy's racially disparate impacts, CPS officials classified it as a nominally nonracial policy (Figure 1.2). The policy's racially disparate impacts shaped citizens' attitudes toward not only school closure policies but also politics, more broadly.

Public Attitudes toward Education and School Closings

To understand the impacts of the school closing process on attitudes toward politics, we need to better understand public opinion toward education. As noted by Jennifer Hochschild and Nathan Scovronick (2003), "most parents have experienced public schools themselves and hold stronger, more fully developed views about education than about most other policy arenas" (p. 80). In addition, they state that "public education uses more resources and involves more people than any other government program for social welfare. It is the main activity of local

Table 1.1. Zip codes with highest number of school closures, by income and percentage of Blacks in 2013

Zip Code	Number of Schools Closed	% Closed	Income ($)	% Black
60628	10	4.00	48,381	6.57
60622	11	4.00	69,889	5.13
60621	11	4.00	27,727	97.81
60653	15	6.00	56,151	31.77
60617	16	6.00	38,487	10.94
60623	17	6.00	35,283	6.75
60612	22	8.00	40,164	17.97
60624	24	9.00	68,324	4.12
60609	27	10.00	36,334	95.54
Total No. of Schools Closed	153 (262)	57.00		
Total No. of Zip Codes	9 (36)			

Note: (262) represents the total number of schools closed overall. (36) represents the total number of zip codes with school closures. Income represents median income per zip code.
Source: Chicago Public Schools, 2013

governments and the largest single expenditure of almost all state governments" (p. 8). The persistent exposure to education and the sheer size of the educational system relative to other forms of social welfare typically studied (e.g., Temporary Assistance for Needy Families, Medicare/Medicaid, Social Security) reemphasize the importance of examining attitudes toward education and its potential consequences on democracy.

Yet, while many surveys have been used over the years to determine attitudes toward education (Hochschild & Scott, 1998; Bushaw & Lopez, 2010, 2013), they have generated very few *investigations* of those educational attitudes. In most investigations, education is included as an independent variable (i.e., measured as the impact of educational attainment on an outcome). Thus, we still know very little about attitudes toward education as a dependent variable (e.g., the impact of income on preferences for a specific educational policy).

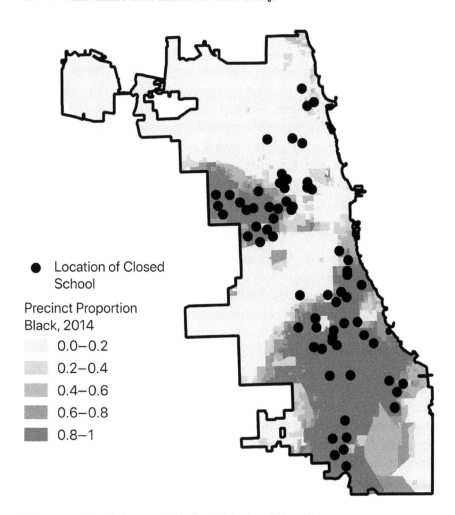

Figure 1.2 School closures in Black neighborhoods in Chicago

It is unsurprising then that we know even less about attitudes toward school closing policies specifically. The few studies that have collected information on attitudes toward school closures report generally negative feelings toward these policy decisions among parents of children affected, even when provided with evidence of budget and performance crises facing the school. In a survey conducted by Phi Delta Kappa in 2010, for example, when parents were asked, "What should be done about low performing schools?," more than half (54 percent) said the best solution was to "keep the school open with existing teachers and principals and provide comprehensive outside support" (Bushaw & Lopez, 2010, p. 10). Only 11 percent of those surveyed supported "closing schools and sending the students to other higher performing schools nearby" (p. 11). These same questions were asked again in a 2013 survey; that year, 47 percent of White parents supported public school closings compared to 33 percent of non-White parents (Bushaw & Lopez, 2013, p. 21). Even though a majority of parents (53 percent) surveyed expressed opposition to closure, the findings from the 2013 survey raised questions about exactly who opposed closures and for what reasons. This chapter answers these questions by demonstrating the powerful role of race.

The Role of Race in Opinion on School Closures

Indeed, many Americans express a strong commitment to public schools and oppose policy proposals that they perceive as undermining them, such as the establishment of vouchers and charter schools (Henig, 1995; Moe, 2001; Howell & Peterson, 2006; Loveless, 2007; Howell & West, 2009; Jacobsen & Saultz, 2012). Yet, what seems to be similar attitudes toward education policies begin to fall apart when Americans are asked about *race-based* education policies.[2] For example, classic studies find that White support for affirmative action declines significantly when the words "preferences" or "quotas" are used or when references to the equality of outcome or opportunity are introduced in survey questions (e.g., Bobo, 1998). Similarly, studies on integration find that, while White support for integration has nearly reversed since the 1990s from majority nonsupport to majority support, very few White Americans support policies such as busing that would make integrated schools work (see, e.g., Gillespie, 1999; Hochschild, 2006).

Although closing public schools is not an explicitly race–based policy, it disproportionately affects Blacks. This can be detrimental in cities such as Chicago, where public schools are one of the central sources of economic stability and viability for Blacks and other racial minorities (De la Torre & Gwynne, 2009; Lipman, 2009; Caref et al., 2012). What this chapter investigates is whether racial minorities generally view school closures differently than Whites, as indicated in the

---

[2] For more on racial attitudes toward nominally race–blind policies in the realms of welfare and criminal justice, see Kinder & Sears, 1981; Bobo, 1983; Kluegel & Smith, 1983; Gilens, 1995; and Kuklinski, Cobb, & Gilens, 1997.

Phi Delta Kappa surveys (Bushaw & Lopez, 2010, 2013), and, if so, whether these attitudes extend beyond those directly affected (e.g., Sharon in the earlier example) to those living in the neighborhood at large (e.g., Leslie in the earlier example).

Shared Policy Targets

I argue in this chapter that Black and, to some extent, Latinx residents, oppose school closing policies at significantly higher rates than Whites, even when accounting for other factors such as income. This is, in part, due to the common experience of Blacks and Latinx with racially targeted policies, and the development of cross-cultural counternarratives, which contributes to perceptions of themselves as shared policy targets of school closure.

As described in the Introduction, policy, by design, often targets particular groups (e.g., Social Security targets the elderly and the GI Bill targets veterans). By targeting particular groups, policies send messages about who is eligible for them and who is not. This determination of eligibility is based on certain social constructions (e.g., deserving or undeserving) about targeted groups. Members of these targeted groups may internalize these social constructions, thereby shaping their perceptions of their value and status in society. These perceptions can then influence attitudes toward government, bureaucracy, and democracy at large (Pierson, 1993; Smith & Ingram, 1993; Ingram & Schneider, 1995; Bruch & Soss, 2018; Rose, 2018).

Because of the racially targeted nature of the school closure policy, I expect citizens' experiences with the process of school closures to influence their attitudes in similar ways. Yet, I believe it is necessary to account for the behavior of citizens who are not direct targets of a policy but still perceive themselves as such due, in part, to the counterconstructions they cocreate against the state.

To be sure, there are various ways that one can be directly or indirectly affected by a policy.[3] But in the context of school closures, I define direct, or what I call *actual* targets, as inclusive of teachers and staff at schools threatened for closure as well as parents of students who

---

[3] Research makes clear that indirect targets can range in their level of exposure to the policy (Watkins-Hayes, 2009; Burch, 2013; Walker, 2014; Michener, 2017). They may act as persons who work for institutions affected by a policy, for example bureaucrats at a welfare

attend them; these individuals are directly subjected to the policy's processes and consequences. A *perceived* target refers to an individual who experiences indirect exposure to the policy, such as resident near a targeted school or a person who shares similar demographic character-istics to the *actual* targets but are in no way subjected to the closure process directly. Since a majority of school closures take place in minor-ity neighborhoods, the latter category accounts for the possibility that an individual may feel targeted simply by identifying as a Black or Brown resident.

Theoretically, citizens who are direct (actual) targets of the policy should hold the strongest attitudes against closures. Indirect (perceived) targets can be expected to feel not as strongly but still indignant. An individual who is not directly or indirectly affected by the closure process, classified as a nontarget in this analysis, would likely be ambivalent or have a non-attitude (or possibly a sympathetic attitude, especially given that most Americans support public schools).

How Shared Policy Targets Develop Attitudes toward School Closings

The significant number of people of color who may identify as a perceived target of potential school closings has to do with their shared group consciousness. I will focus first on the experiences of Blacks since they are directly affected most often, numerically, by school closures. Established research on group consciousness and linked fate provides a specific approach for understanding *how* attitudes are formed along racial lines for Blacks. Group consciousness refers to one's identification as a member of a respective group (Jackman & Jackman, 1973; Gurin & Markus, 1989; Chong & Rogers, 2005). Linked fate reflects one particular way of operationalizing group consciousness. This concept refers to a cognitive racial cue – specifically, a sense of commonality – used among Blacks to dictate their political interests (Dawson, 1994). Linked fate describes the political decisions of Blacks as rational

office. They may live in a neighborhood where a policy's effects are concentrated, for example the neighbors of those convicted of a felony. Further, they may be a sibling of an individual impacted by a policy, for example a sister of a person who receives Medicare.

calculations. Both concepts are perhaps best defined as Blacks' expression of how much they view their life experiences as connected to other members of their respective racial group. Per these concepts, one would expect Blacks to express strong attitudes toward school closures if they view the policy issue as affecting members of their same racial group.

Additionally, it is well established in the literature that Blacks tend to express distinctly different attitudes from their majority counterparts on several policy issues. Blacks' divergent attitudes are attributed again to their shared experiences with discrimination in the United States. These shared experiences have contributed to shared political ideologies that are then reflected in their attitudes toward certain policies (Pinderhughes, 1987; Barker, 1988; Lieberson & Waters, 1988; Dawson, 1994, 2011). While Michael Dawson and Ernest Wilson (1991) suggested that, as Blacks' economic situations improved, their shared identities would weaken, later works revealed that racial identities only strengthened as economic status improved (Hochschild, 1993, 1995; Dawson, 1994; Tate, 1994; McClain et al., 2009). This incongruity has been explained by the slow economic progress of Blacks overall and their continued experiences with discrimination in majority White spaces in the workplace. In addition, Blacks have continued to live in segregated neighborhoods stratified by race and class (Massey & Denton, 1998; Sampson, 2012). Consequently, despite the removal of traditional forms of overt racism such as Jim Crow laws, and despite upward mobility for Blacks in the post–civil rights era, Blacks maintain strong collective attitudes relative to non-Black American groups.

Certainly, gender, ethnicity, and sexuality contribute to heterogeneity across the political behavior of Blacks (Gay & Tate, 1998; Cohen, 1999; Harris-Lacewell, 2006; Dawson, 2011). Ethnicity further complicates investigation of Black attitudes. As Reuel Rogers (2006) explains in his work on Afro-Caribbean immigrants, while Caribbean/West Indians are politically incorporated in the United States as Black, they maintain ties to their homelands, which has implications for their policy attitudes (see also Greer, 2013).

Despite these findings, Michael Dawson's (2011) investigation of political attitudes revealed that nearly three quarters of Blacks, across class, still believe that what happens to their racial group affects them. In a more recent comprehensive evaluation of linked fate across groups conducted by the 2016 Collaborative Multiracial Post-Election Survey, researchers found that:

> Nearly 60% of all racial and ethnic groups reported a perceived linked fate with their racial or ethnic in-group. Black respondents at 66% reported the highest level of linked fate, ... Among those respondents who perceived an in-group linked fate, on average, one-third of both Blacks and Latinos believed that what happens to their racial or ethnic in-group will affect them a lot (Frasure-Yokley, Masuoka & Barreto, 2019).

In other words, studies continue to confirm the important role of race in the construction of political worldviews and formation of collective identities.

Still, I view group consciousness and linked fate as only providing a partial explanation for attitudes toward closure because these concepts fail to account for how Blacks determine their status as shared policy targets. Understanding this allows for a more complex, nuanced, and fluid examination of the effect of policy on collective political attitudes. Such an examination finds that these citizens use relevant and recent policy experiences to form opinions rather than relying exclusively on historical references to race and belonging. For example, research in urban politics illustrates how Black and Latinx citizens become particularly mobilized by racial threats from the state to take over their schools and/or reduce their budgets (Orr, 1999; Morel, 2018). Scholar of Race, Ethnicity and Politics (REP), add to this work demonstrating the mobilizing effects of controversial policies such as those related to immigration once they become racialized (e.g., Zepeda-Millan, 2016). Further work on policy feedback illustrates the potentially empowering effects of programs on Black parents depending on how they are designed (Barnes, 2020). Together, this work casts dispersion on the notion that a *latent group consciousness* accounts for attitudes among minority communities and calls for an examination of minority communities as a composition of rational political actors that actively use their policy experiences to update their political identities and preferences.[4]

---

[4] Since linked fate does not discuss the ways that political identity is updated, and this book suggests that a single political experience can contribute to shared identities, this suggests that there is a need to reconsider how these identities develop.

Regarding public school closure, the racially disparate impacts of the current policy coupled with the racially discriminatory policies of the past, likely contributes to a shared perception among Blacks that they are *all potential targets* of school closure, even though these closures are only experienced by a small percentage of the Black population directly. I argue that this broader conception of who the policy is targeting, buttressed by counternarratives promoted by organizations that frame closure policy as racially biased, contributes to a shared group consciousness that likely affects Blacks' political preferences. *Accordingly, I expect Blacks, whether they are direct or indirect targets of closure, to express negative attitudes toward school closure policies.*

For other ethnic minorities, their various subgroups may make it difficult to expect the same patterns seen among Blacks (See Sidney 2002). For example, some racial minorities in the United States might not view themselves as part of the subordinate (e.g., Latinx groups who identify as White; Masuoka & Junn, 2013). Claudine Gay (2004) demonstrates how racial minorities who feel fully integrated into the residential context of higher income neighborhoods identify less with their respective racial group, while those who do not feel fully integrated maintain a strong identification with their racial group.

Research also suggests that examinations of racial group identity and its influence on attitudes should account for specific policy context (e.g., Laird, 2020). While ethnic, class, and generational divisions may discourage group identity, recent immigration legislation may reactivate shared group identity among Latinx populations, for example (Cain, Citrin, & Wong, 2000; see also De la Garza, 2004; Marsh & Ramírez, 2019). Further, recent work suggests that Latinx groups may form a relationship with other minority groups through linked fate around a policy issue (Gershon et al., 2019). In the case of Chicago, 86 percent of the public school population is either Black or Latinx. Thus, these are the racial groups that stand to lose the most when schools in their neighborhoods are closed. Latinx communities also have similar historical experiences to Blacks with fighting for public schools in Chicago (e.g., Little Village Hunger Strike). Accordingly, the racially targeted nature of the closure policy, in addition to the educational experiences of Latinx communities, should shape their attitudes in similar ways to Blacks. *Thus, I expect Latinx groups to also express negative attitudes toward public school closure, although at lower levels.*

At this point, these expectations suggest that negative reactions toward school closure policy by Blacks and Latinx may be mostly interest driven (and less about direct policy experience, per se). It is important to note that, in almost all cases, school closure policy is promoted as a way to gain *more* resources for communities through the consolidation of schools. My expectation, however, is that both Black and Latinx groups do not believe this.

I argue that this skepticism is a product of their experiences as targets of previous school closures and/or other similar social policies, in which the results produced did not match the promises made (see Nuamah, 2019b). Even when alternatives to traditional public schools are utilized by Blacks and Latinx, they do not necessarily lead to the same positive educational experiences as they do for their majority counterparts. For example, John Logan and Julia Burdick-Will (2016) find that attending a charter school only slightly offsets the educational disadvantages that Black and Latinx students in high-poverty areas face when compared with White students due, in part, to the segregated nature of their experiences. In fact, using qualitative and quantitative data, Jessica Trounstine finds that segregation allows governments to disinvest in poor and minority communities, and provide higher access to public goods for White communities. Given that such research shows that White students have more positive policy experiences and that fewer White students are directly affected by school closing policies (nontarget status), one might expect Whites to report sympathetic attitudes, more in line with those expressed by Blacks and Latinx who are not directly affected, or indifferent attitudes regarding school closure policies. At the same time, if White citizens benefit from the divestment of Black and Brown communities via closed schools (as Trounstine's investigation suggests), then one might expect them to have less oppositional attitudes toward school closures, or even supportive attitudes toward them.

In sum, attitudes toward school closure policies should vary across groups. In particular, I expect that being a target of a school closure policy should increase negative attitudes toward it. Further, I expect that many who are indirectly targeted will also have similarly negative attitudes and that these attitudes will be influenced by a person's race. Accordingly, Blacks should express the most oppositional attitudes, followed by Latinx, and then Whites.

Studying Racial Differences in Opinion on Closures in Chicago

My study of racial differences in attitudes toward school closings in Chicago began with the development of an original data set of every single school closed in Chicago between 2001 and 2014. These data were then linked by zip code to census data collected from the American Community Survey 2009–2013 estimates (US Census Bureau, 2019). The linked data were then merged by zip code with the 2013 survey on educational attitudes of parents conducted collectively by the Joyce Foundation, the *Chicago Tribune*, and the National Opinion Research Center (NORC) at the University of Chicago. The survey sampled 1,020 individuals, over half (520) of whom are parents in CPS, and featured multiple questions about education reform, two of which ask specifically about public school closure. The survey also oversampled Black respondents, which represented the population most affected by the threat of school closure, and thus enabled a more reliable and robust analysis of Black attitudes. The survey data facilitated an investigation of how support for school closures are shaped by one's race and proximity to a closed school, while also accounting for other factors that could influence the analysis, including being a parent, low income (defined as earning less than $50,000 a year), and experiencing neighborhood poverty.

The majority of the analysis relies on a single dependent variable asking about attitudes toward closure. This question basically outlines the official explanation for school closures in Chicago. That is, the question echoes the dominant narrative, which makes it a conservative test for my hypotheses related to Blacks and Latinx citizens. The specific question asked is:

> Chicago Public Schools recently announced plans to close some schools that are serving less than half the number of students that the school was built to serve in order to help balance its budget and free up resources to support the remaining schools more efficiently. Would you agree or disagree with a policy that would close these under-enrolled schools in order to balance the district's budget? (NORC, 2013, p. 15).

The question gives respondents the option to select one of the following: (1) strongly agree; (2) somewhat agree; (3) somewhat disagree;

(4) strongly disagree; and (5) neither agree or disagree. (The respondents can also opt to say they don't know or refuse to answer.) I code the variable as a dummy (1 for agree). Given the dichotomous dependent variable as well as the multiple individual and aggregate level independent variables, the analysis is primarily based on logistic regression models. Using these data and measures, I test my expectation that being a target – whether direct or indirect – of school closure should result in negative attitudes toward the policy. All details are available in the Appendix.

Support for Closure

The initial results[5] provide support for my expectations. In particular, living in a neighborhood with a school threatened for closure is associated with a .46-point increase in the probability of opposing closure, while earning an income of $50,000 or less is associated with a .69-point in the probability of opposing school closure. In the models that focus specifically on race, the output reveals a significant relationship between race and attitudes toward closure, with being Black and Latinx associated with a 1.2-point and .93-point increase, respectively, in negative attitudes toward closures compared to Whites' (the baseline group) attitudes. Without the inclusion of controls (or other factors that may matter), at the most basic level, I find that there is a potential relationship between race, living in a neighborhood with a school on the closure list, and income, on attitudes toward school closure in the direction expected (Table 1.2).

Once we account for other individual-level factors such as level of education, renting/owning a home, and having an income of $50,000 or less together, being Black or Latinx remains significant and positively related to opposition to school closure, while being a parent and living in an area that has a school on the closure list does not have a significant relationship to closure in either direction (Table 1.3, Model 1).[6]

[5] Based on bivariate logistic regression.
[6] The same relationships, although at lower levels, are found once we accounted for these same factors at the aggregate level (Table 1.3, Model 2).

Table 1.2. Bivariate logit regression predictors of opposition to school closures

Model	(1)	(2)	(3)	(4)	(5)
(Individual)	Parent	Low-income[a]	On closed list	Rank[b]	Race
Parent	0.112 (0.134)				
Income of $50,000 or less		0.687*** (0.140)			
Closed list neighborhood			0.458*** (0.137)		
Number of Schools Closed					
High closure				0.623*** (0.159)	
Medium closure				0.771*** (0.196)	
Low closure				0.733*** (0.263)	
Race					
Black					1.121*** (0.155)
Latinx					0.934*** (0.188)
Constant	−0.310*** (0.096)	−0.547*** (0.092)	−0.436*** (0.087)	−0.615*** (0.100)	−0.851*** (0.108)

Note: [a] Income of $50,000 of less; [b] Level of closure per zip code. Stars denote level of statistical significance (confidence in results from highest to lowest): ***0.001 (highest), **0.05, *0.010 (lowest); the coefficient of the independent variable is the value without parentheses; the standard error is the value within the parentheses.
Data source: NORC, 2013

More specifically, earning an income of $50,000 or less is associated with a .16-point increase in the probability of a person opposing closure, while being Black or Latinx is associated with .20- and .17-point increase, respectively, at the individual level. At the contextual level, when aggregate variables are added, earning an income of $50,000 or less is associated with a .09-point increase in the probability of a person opposing closure, while being Black or Latinx is

Table 1.3. Multiple logit regression predictors of opposition to school closures

Model	(1)	(2)
(Individual)		
Black	0.960***	0.745***
	(0.175)	(0.211)
Latinx	0.806***	0.493**
	(0.199)	(0.220)
Parent	0.110	0.098
	(0.145)	(0.147)
Gender	0.228	0.196
	(0.151)	(0.152)
Affiliation	0.169	0.194
	(0.147)	(0.150)
Income of $50,000 or less	0.427***	0.343**
	(0.155)	(0.159)
Closed list neighborhood	0.079	0.013
	(0.160)	(0.197)
(Aggregate)		
Age under 15		0.0001
		(0.030)
High school education or less		0.011
		(0.017)
Rent		−0.010
		(0.009)
Family poverty		0.032
		(0.022)
Foreign-born		0.005
		(0.009)
Constant	−1.275***	−1.444**
	(0.193)	(0.680)

Note: Stars denote level of statistical significance (confidence in results from highest to lowest): ***0.001 (highest), **0.05, *0.010 (lowest); the coefficient of the independent variable is the value without parentheses; the standard error is the value within the parentheses.
Data source: NORC, 2013

associated with a .16- and .10-point increase, respectively (for inter-actions see Table 1.4).[7]

To better understand the results, the analysis are converted into models that allow an investigation of how one set of variables impact an outcome of interest (or predicted probabilities). Predicted probabilities "show if there are significant differences in the predicted outcomes and whether these differences vary with the level of the independent variables" (Long, 2009, p. 12). In logistic regression, the effect of a variable depends on the level of all variables in the model (Allison, 1999). I focus on the specific relationships most substantively important for the analysis.[8]

I examine the probability of opposing school closures by inves-tigating whether an individual is a parent *and* lives in a neighborhood with a closure (closed zip code) or a nonparent who lives in a neighbor-hood with a closure, while holding all other variables at their means. In addition, I vary if a person is a Black parent that lives in a neighborhood with a closure, a Black parent that does not live in a neighborhood with a closure, and Black nonparent that lives in a neighborhood with a closure, holding all other variables constant. I run the same models varying race – Latinx and white, respectively.[9]

The results displayed in Figure 1.3 suggest that being a parent is associated with a moderate probability of opposing closure (45 per-cent), even for respondents living in a neighborhood that has a closed school. When we account for race, being Black is associated with a more than 55 percent probability of opposing closure regardless of parental status and/or living in an area that experienced closure. Indeed, it is difficult to test the difference between Black residents on the closed list and not on the closed list, because significantly more Black residents are on the list than not (nearly 70 percent). Yet, it is important to note that Black parents who live in a neighborhood that experiences closure do have a high probability of opposing closure (60 percent). Similar to

---

[7] There are no consistently significant relationships between the interactions and the dependent variable or the contextual controls and the dependent variable (Table 1.4).

[8] As stated in Long (2009), predicted probabilities, "require a great deal of planning about which comparisons are most interesting and at which values you want to hold other variables in the model constant ... it is important to limit your explorations to those regions of the data space that are both substantively reasonable and where there are sufficient observations to justify your conclusions" (p. 12).

[9] I measure confidence intervals in order to interpret the certainty of the results (see Appendix). The confidence interval is a measure of the distance between the sample and population mean.

Table 1.4. Multiple logit regression predictors of opposition to school with interactions

Model	(1)	(2)	(3)
(Individual)			
Black	0.735***	0.835***	0.789***
	(0.211)	(0.251)	(0.218)
Latinx	0.525**	0.486**	0.843***
	(0.222)	(0.221)	(0.311)
Parent	0.268	0.173	0.209
	(0.189)	(0.185)	(0.168)
Gender	0.206	0.197	0.168
	(0.153)	(0.153)	(0.156)
Affiliation	0.198	0.195	0.233
	(0.150)	(0.150)	(0.155)
Income of $50,000 or less	0.547**	0.338**	0.382**
	(0.213)	(0.159)	(0.165)
Closed list neighborhood	0.022	0.012	0.020
	(0.197)	(0.196)	(0.201)
(Aggregate)			
High school education or less	0.012	0.011	0.012
	(0.015)	(0.015)	(0.016)
Rent	−0.010	−0.010	−0.009
	(0.006)	(0.006)	(0.007)
Family poverty	0.031	0.032*	0.030
	(0.019)	(0.019)	(0.020)
Foreign-born	0.004	0.005	0.006
	(0.009)	(0.009)	(0.010)
(Interactions)			
Parent			
Income of $50,000 or less	−0.422		
	(0.293)		
Closed list neighborhood	0.019		
	(0.288)		

Table 1.4. cont'd

Model	(1)	(2)	(3)
Black			
Income of $50,000 or less		−0.080 (0.304)	
Parent		−0.194 (0.292)	
Closed list neighborhood		−0.249 (0.330)	
Latinx			
Income of $50,000 or less			−0.314 (0.379)
Parent			−0.598 (0.376)
Closed list neighborhood			0.383 (0.438)
Constant	−1.542*** (0.325)	−1.467*** (0.319)	−1.519*** (0.379)

Note: Stars denote level of statistical of significance (confidence in results from highest to lowest): ***0.001 (highest), **0.05, *0.010 (lowest); the coefficient of the independent variable is the value without parentheses; the standard error is the value within the parentheses.
Data source: NORC, 2013

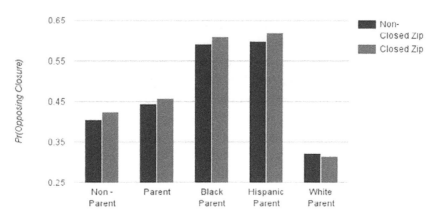

Figure 1.3 Probability of opposing closure by race, parental status, and living in zip codes with closures

Black residents, Latinx residents also have a high probability of opposing closure (57 percent). Although living in a community that experienced a closure does not make a significant difference (as both closed and non-closed groups have relatively high probabilities of opposing closure), it is the case that Latinx parents who live in closed neighborhoods also have the highest probability of opposing closure (61 percent), whereas Whites, overall, have a low probability of opposing closure – only about 28 percent. This probability increases by about 6 percent if they are parents and/or on the closed list.

The results ultimately show that race has the strongest association with opposition toward closure, regardless of whether one is a parent or lives in an area facing the threat of closure. These findings are significant at both the individual and aggregate (contextual) levels. In particular, being Black is associated with the highest probability of opposing school closure policy, at the highest level of significance (.001); this is consistent even at the contextual level. Being Latinx is also associated with high levels of opposition to closure, although the statistical significance lowers when contextual variables are added (.05). Whites, the baseline group, have largely positive attitudes toward school closures when compared with Blacks and Latinx. These findings are significant at both the individual and contextual level (.05). *In sum, while Black and Latinx groups express high levels of opposition to school closure, Whites express high levels of support for school closure.*

However, these results still do not explain *why* these attitudes vary across different racial groups. Nor do the results, by themselves, show that the experience of being an actual or perceived target of closures leads to opposition to the policy. Furthermore, it does not help us understand why living in an area where a school is closed (or threatened for closure) fails to explain negative attitudes toward school closure. Joe Soss and Sanford Schram (2007) point out that the degree to which people perceive that a policy will have a clear, immediate effect on their lives plays an important role in shaping their attitudes toward the policy. Interviews with parents and community members reveal that individuals' beliefs that they were targets of the school closure policy as well as their past experiences with the school district led to negative attitudes toward the policy. These negative attitudes also emerged in individuals that were not directly affected by the policy but were demographically similar to those directly affected by school closure policy. In other words, I find that Black and Latinx communities do not need to live in an area where a school was closed (or threatened for closure) to understand its potential impacts on members of their same race and/or community. As for Whites, their attitudes *and* explanations were different. First, I will describe the experiences of Black and Latinx residents affected by closure before briefly discussing the opposite views of Whites.

Explaining Racial Differences in Attitudes toward School Closures

As mentioned earlier, Blacks are the most impacted by school closures in Chicago and have the most negative views of the process. Relying on data collected across twenty-eight meetings (see Tables A.1A and A.1B in the Appendix) as well as fifty semi-structured interviews (for coding, also see the Appendix), I find that previous experiences with other school policies and perceptions about the fairness of the school closure process make Blacks, in particular, more open to counternarratives about the 2012 policy.

During the 2012–2013 school closure process in Chicago, several groups, including the Chicago Teachers Union, promoted multiple narratives that ran counter to the race neutral one promoted by CPS (i.e., under-enrollment). The primary counternarrative focused on the argument that the school closure policy was racist, as indicated by a Chicago Teachers Union activist in the following statement:

> Malcolm X fought against racism and segregation, and here we are 50 years later fighting to save Black and Brown children. This is not about school utilization … Let's call it what it is, educational apartheid—the definition of an official policy of racial segregation for political, legal, and economic discrimination against non-Whites. In 2011, the CPS Board of Education admitted publicly … and I quote, "If we think there is a chance a building is going to be closed in five years, [we] are not going to invest in that building." The Board of Education has been deliberately starving schools in Black and Latino neighborhoods (network meeting, Pilsen-Little Village, Chicago, March 4, 2013).

This accusation reframes closure decisions as intentionally discriminatory. When Black community members heard statements such as these, they were able to connect with it, in part because of their direct and immediate experiences with other CPS policies. State Representative Mary Flowers elaborated further on this idea at a community meeting:

> You will give an animal air conditioning, and you will make our [Black] children go to school in the cold, in the heat. That's unacceptable. I'm sick and tired of it (network meeting, Englewood-Gresham, Chicago, February 18, 2013).

The comment implies that CPS is treating people from certain communities, Blacks, differently than others and contributes to the counternarrative about the rationale behind the closure. As another Black parent stated at the same community meeting:

> [Representative] Flowers hit the nail on the head when she was talking about Black children. In reading through the history of the schools that you guys want to close, why is it that there's a disproportionate amount of schools ... on the south side and the west side that are closing, and then there are not that many schools, if any, on the north side that are closing? This is hitting the south side and the west side the hardest of anybody ... We notice where the schools are being targeted. It is on the south side. It is on the west side. It is where the students are Black and Brown (network meeting, Englewood-Gresham, Chicago, February 18, 2013).

This statement demonstrates that this community member feels that closure affects a particular group: Black and Brown people who live on the South and West Sides of Chicago. The use of terms such as "hardest hit" and "targeted" are indicative of the negative feelings this Black parent had about the racist nature of the policy.

The parent's inclusion of "Brown" students in her statement reflects the collective racial consciousness of Blacks and Latinx regarding this issue. Even though fewer than 10 percent of schools targeted for closure in 2012 included Latinx families, Latinx community members also endorsed the counternarrative that framed the policy as racist, or unfairly targeting certain groups more than others. One lifetime resident of a majority Latinx neighborhood in Chicago stated:

> When I heard about closing schools in [a nearby neighbor-hood], my heart dropped, so I wanted to show solidarity ... I just don't like how they are treating us at this meeting ... sending us here and there ... But we are going to exercise our freedom of speech ... I've been active for ten years, and I've never quite seen something like this ... It's divisive. But hope-fully this issue brings us together as a neighborhood and shows the powers-that-be that you can't just step on us (network meeting, Fulton, Chicago, February 11, 2013).

Latinx community members also interpreted their experience with the "divisive" nature of the meetings as a microcosm of how local bureau-crats' value and treat them, likely leading them to subscribe to the counternarrative of school closure as racially biased and develop nega-tive attitudes toward the policy. Another Latinx parent stated:

> They are trying to isolate people ... separate them ... So, we are just trying to work together and not step on each other's toes (network meeting, Pilsen-Little Village, Chicago, February 6, 2013).

The fact that Latinx community members feel they are a shared policy target along with Blacks helps them to avoid the inherent aspect of the process that pits schools and communities against each other. Latinx community members instead adopted the counternarrative and "work[ed] together" to develop a unified front with Blacks against the school closure policy.

Latinx residents have negative attitudes toward closure even when they are not direct targets, the same goes for Blacks who are indirect targets. More than 50 percent of those randomly selected for an interview at the closure meetings[10] were not directly affected by the threat of closure. They were past and present community residents, former and current teachers, and cafeteria workers and janitors of unaffected schools who had secondary exposure to the policy through their connections with those who were directly affected. This is demon-strated in the following examples:

---

[10] Details for all interviews can be found in the Appendix.

> One of my neighbors works as a cafeteria lady, and she is afraid she will lose her job. I see her every day, so I see the effects every day (interview, Fulton, Chicago, February 11, 2013)

[* * *]

PARENT: I am a parent, and my son goes to school in the neighborhood.
ME: Is the school slated to be close?
PARENT: Actually, no. I think they are actually a top school in the neighborhood.
ME: So, what brought you here?
PARENT: I want to support public schools, public school education . . . and I want my voice to be heard . . . I just want them to be honest, more honesty on behalf of CPS. What is really their motive for closing down schools? (interview, Pilsen-Little Village, Chicago, February 2, 2013).

The latter dialogue demonstrates how even parents not directly affected by the school closure policy question the intentions of CPS and display negative attitudes about the policy. Further, they attend meeting to intentionally register their support for those groups directly impacted because of their perception of themselves as part of a shared community. The sentiment of standing up for one's community was common, as indicated in these statements:

> My kids go to school somewhere else . . . I mean it doesn't matter; it's the city of Chicago! (interview, North Lawndale, Chicago, January 31, 2013).

[* * *]

> I saw some guys from the environmental groups here today, and why are they here today? It's because of the community . . . they are members of the community (interview, Pilsen-Little Village, Chicago, February 6, 2013).

For Black and Latinx residents, their negative experiences with the threat of school closure is symbolic of its negative impacts on their communities. The counternarrative reflects this and, most importantly, encourages the development of a shared target identity among Blacks and Latinx residents who are both directly and indirectly affected by the school closure policy. It is clear that Blacks interpret school closure as being influenced by racism. Latinx communities share this view, thereby promoting a collective racial consciousness and opposition toward closure policies.[11]

The Opinions of Whites

Most White Chicagoans live in neighborhoods where schools have not been targeted for closure.[12] This is due to the segregated nature of the city. Therefore, they have had no direct stake in the implementation of the school closure policy, and their opinions or actions would in theory not affect the education of their own children. Nonetheless, as discussed by Jessica Trounstine, "segregated places are politically polarized places" making it less likely that Whites and minorities will find a common group on public policy issues (2018, 16). And indeed, the statistical data reveal that – in stark contrast to Black and Latinx citizens – a large percentage of Whites had positive attitudes toward closure. The qualitative data I collected suggest that these attitudes are related largely to many Whites viewing school closures as a fair solution to isolated crises faced by CPS. As one White community member I interviewed stated:

> North and north-west sides of the city are overcrowding. We have to fix the overcrowding. We can't just say we have a budget problem; we need to fix this. We have to rationalize the physical facilities ... We also have to be honest about our teacher quality and variability. We had no way of getting rid of weak teachers; we need to have a process of evaluation. There is now a chance to remove the weakest teachers from the weakest schools (interview, Chicago, January 2013).

White parents, especially those who live on the North Side, do not view school closure through the same lens as minority parents whose children

---

[11] It is important to remember that within-group variation exists. Not all Blacks and Latinx disagree with school closure, and not all Whites agree with the policy (e.g., many teachers or activists in these communities are White and have views that are similar to those of Blacks and Latinx).

[12] This is due to the segregated nature of the city. Closed schools would not have positive or negative effects on Whites (although, in some cases, Whites may view closures as a mechanism for ensuring future gentrification).

are directly affected by closure. The perspective of White parents in unaffected neighborhoods tends to be similar to those of the CPS board members interviewed. As one board member stated:

> Parts of the south and southwest side of the cities ... happen to be majority minority communities, and we had 26 to 30 percent enrollment, which is expensive. Why is that? It is because what we see is that populations have shifted greatly. So, yes, most of the people affected will be minorities (interview, CPS Board of Education member, May 2013).

This statement, which was a response to a question about whether the school closure policy was racially targeting certain groups, demonstrates that school board members view school closures differently than minority groups directly and indirectly affected. In the eyes of White board members and White parents, these policies just *happen* to affect minorities, and particularly Black, the most because they are the ones who leave the city. In contrast, Black and Latinx groups connect school closure policies to a larger effort to tear apart their communities. Whites' supposedly "deracialized" opinion of school closures contributes to their supportive attitudes toward the policy, even though they are not affected by them.

Supporting Public Schools – But Also Their Closure?

Given that most Americans profess support for public schools, and thus oppose policies such as vouchers that can be viewed as undermining traditional public schools, the racial differences in attitudes toward school closure raise important concerns about the nature of this commitment and by whom it is made. The existing public opinion literature would suggest that Whites have indifferent, possibly even sympathetic, attitudes due to their support for public education and their limited experience with school closures. For Whites to support closures and not be perceived as anti–public schools then, one must assume that they believe that closing schools will result in better public schools for all. Yet, there is, in fact, very little evidence of this both historically and to date (Valencia, 1984a; De la Torre & Gwynne, 2009; Good, 2017; Bierbaum, 2018). Further, minorities directly affected by the school closure policy commonly express their disbelief in the dominant narrative that school closures will lead to better public schools.

Thus, it is unclear why Whites would support the closure of public schools if they want what is best for the communities affected.

At the same time, previous research suggests that the loss of access to public goods for minoritized communities are almost always connected to a gain in access to public goods for White people. In some cases, White people are vocal advocates for lower resources for everyone when faced with the option of sharing resources with minority communities (e.g., Oliver, 2010; Trounstine, 2016, 2018). Understood in this context, the supportive opinions of White people might be evidence of more of the same.

Regarding the Latinx population, Latinx attitudes about school closures look strikingly similar to those of Blacks likely due to their similar overall educational experiences. For example, many alternatives to public schools, such as charter schools, do not typically benefit Blacks and Latinx in the same way they do Whites. Their similar educational experiences likely ignite a feeling of being shared policy targets, which then shape public attitudes. They would also help to explain how the Black and Latinx populations in this study shared such similar views, even as their respective populations in the city continue to diverge (Chicago's Black population is declining just as the Latinx population is increasing).[13]

Ultimately, this chapter demonstrates the continued salience of race in shaping education policy preferences. Most importantly, it highlights how nominally nonracial policies that have racially disparate impacts affect the policy attitudes of those targeted. In so doing, it illuminates a mediating factor, experience as a shared policy target, that to varying degrees shapes the link between race and attitudes toward many policies, including school closures.

As Michael Dawson (1994) explains in his classic work *Behind the Mule*, so long as discrimination exists, Blacks will continue to express divergent attitudes when compared to their majority counterparts. In that study, Blacks' political attitudes are looked at through a

---

[13] My initial expectation was that they would hold less negative attitudes than Blacks, given the lack of linked fate typically associated with the Latinx in established research. The question this expectation raised is whether feelings of linked fate or racial identification are more consequential than direct experience with the policy or actual exposure to the threat of school closure. My sense is that experience as a shared policy target and linked-fate feelings interact. Scholars would benefit from understanding how linked fate can be used as a heuristic device for interpreting policy experience. Further research should be done to determine the extent of this cross racial support.

lens of their experiences with discrimination in the country. I find evidence of similar feelings among Latinx. Whites, then, need to be attentive to the ways in which disengagement with the racial consequences of school closure policies might result in the perpetuation of discrimination. In the end, racial differences in attitudes matter not only because they essentially symbolize the role of race and, in some cases, racism in the country, but also because they challenge the ability for groups to work across racial lines and toward political and social progress.

School closures are particularly important to study because public schools continue to act as essential vehicles that provide citizens with the civic skills necessary for upholding democracy as well as the life skills critical for securing better life chances. For Blacks and Latinx especially, public schools are the institutions that represent one of the most central mechanisms for achieving racial equality, ensuring social mobility, translating civic skills, and improving political participation. In many cities, Black communities were able to participate in school politics before they were able to participate in other aspects of city government. In major cities, Blacks earned seats on school boards before being elected to city councils and mayoralties (Henig et al., 2001). In addition, school systems provided jobs and served as an important tool of economic mobility for Blacks (Orr, 1999). Once these schools are removed, these opportunities can be lost to those groups. It is no surprise, then, that Blacks and Latinx express such negative attitudes toward closure, for these attitudes are reflected in their concerns about their contemporary political position relative to other racial groups in the United States.

2 WHO TARGETED CITIZENS BLAME
Blame, Approval, and Black Power

In November 2015, Philadelphians set out to vote for a new mayor less than two years after twenty-three schools had been shuttered, the most in one year in Philadelphia. An exit poll conducted during the primary election the preceding May asked Philadelphian voters, "Of the following Philadelphia issues, which single one is the most important to you personally – that is, the Philadelphia issue that will determine your vote for Mayor and city officials on election day?" While in years past, the answers may have centered around the economy or crime, this election was all about education: In all, 37 percent of the total voters polled answered, "improving education and schools in Philadelphia," easily outnumbering those whose answers revolved around decreasing crime (14 percent), increasing jobs (14 percent), and reducing poverty (8 percent).[1] In other words, after the unprecedented closure of twenty-three schools, there was no other issue more important than education in Philadelphia's 2015 election.

The 2015 election was the first significant opportunity that those affected by the school closures in Philadelphia had to act against the politicians they blamed for the current educational landscape in an electoral context. Studies across policy feedback, public policy, and urban politics have demonstrated that, after negative experiences with policies, citizens construct negative attitudes not only toward the policy

[1] Vince Lattanzio, "Jim Kenney wins democratic bid for mayor in Philadelphia," NBCPhiladelphia.com, May 19, 2015, www.nbcphiladelphia.com/news/local/Jim-Kenney-Wins-Democratic-Bid-for-Mayor-of-Philadelphia-304342991.html.

but also toward the political actors who played a role (see, e.g., Campbell, 2003a; Mettler & Soss, 2004). In fact, attributions of blame are critical for ensuring that elected officials are held accountable to its citizenry. Since accountability is essential for democratic responsiveness, citizens must know where to attribute blame for poor policy and, more importantly, possess the power to do something about it.

While Chapter 1 demonstrated that the majority of Black and Latinx citizens affected by closure have negative attitudes toward the policy, this chapter explores how affected citizens translate their negative attitudes into attributions of blame, or approval in some cases, of related school and political officials. In particular, I show who citizens blame for closure the most and why. In doing so, I highlight how citizens engage in a process of political learning through their school closure experiences, specifically at community meetings, and, in turn, can make distinctions between those who do and do not have power over the resources necessary to influence the policy. In other words, I illustrate how citizens make strategic decisions about where to point the finger for what they are experiencing, particularly in a context where many leaders share their same racial identity *and* political affiliation.

Race, Blame, and Public School Closure

Most studies of political blame have focused on national-level issues, such as the economic recession of 2008; natural disasters that received national-level attention, such as Hurricane Katrina; or issues involving national-level leaders, such as the president of the United States (e.g., Gomez & Wilson, 2008; Malhotra & Kuo, 2009). These studies find that citizens either blame the incumbent or members of the opposite party and therefore do not exhibit a high level of political sophistication (e.g., Achen & Bartels, 2016). Yet, these same cues may not exist at the local level due to the homogeneous political landscape (e.g., Forgette, King, & Dettrey, 2008; Malhotra & Kuo, 2009). They may also be less relevant due to citizens' easier access to policy actors and policy information (Malhotra & Kuo, 2009). As stated by Christopher Berry and William Howell (2007), local level policy positions are "reasonably well defined ... which simplifies the task of evaluating their performance in office" (p. 9). Therefore, assessing issue agreement and attributing blame may be more efficient at the local level (Oliver & Ha, 2007).

Correspondingly, those targeted by a specific policy may know, or have previously worked with, the policy perpetrators. These more close-knit relationships can have significant impacts on citizens' attitudes toward political actors or policy bureaucrats (e.g., Arceneaux & Stein, 2006). While there is not much research on the effect of close-knit relationships with political leaders on citizen attitudes, one can hypothesize that they can be either more forgiving of these persons or hold them to a higher standard. In either case, these close-knit interactions might replace the role of race or party to act as cues for knowledge and/ or experience.

School closures represent a clear disruption at the local level that in most cases does not receive a great deal of national attention. The actors involved include the superintendent and school board, both of whom are empowered to make decisions on behalf of the school system, in addition to the city council, the mayor, governor, and state legislature, all of which play a critical role in appointing members of the school board and contributing to school funding decisions. These various actors, some of which are people of color from the affected communities, can complicate the ability of citizens to attribute blame to a particular person. For example, in the cases examined, school closures occurred in areas where a majority of those involved are Black people from the same political party. And yet, Black voters, just like Latinx and White ones, often support those of their same race or ethnic background, regardless of the performance of the official (Kaufmann, 2004; Tate, 2004). Thus, they may be more supportive of Black candidates even if they are associated with school closure.

Nonetheless, Black voters' support for Black candidates may wax and wane over time, due in part to concentrated poverty, social isolation, and/or specific policy events (Cohen & Dawson, 1993; Alex-Assensoh, 1997; Gay, 2002; Harris et al., 2005; Laird, 2019). In other words, determining who is to blame for a policy, at the local level, is likely to be conditional on the racial, social, and political context. Claudine Gay (2002), for example, demonstrates how Black residents support candidates who champion their policy preferences, regardless of race, thereby providing less support for representation that is purely descriptive as opposed to substantive. Melissa Marschall and Anirudh Ruhil (2007) find that Black perceptions of local government services improve when descriptive representation is accompanied by improvement in local government services. Further, Fredrick Harris and colleagues (2005) highlight how descriptive representation also has a positive influence on mobilization, but that these gains are constantly undermined by the harsh economic conditions Blacks experience.

Social isolation due to economic and racial segregation is known to undermine the political participation of Blacks. Still, low participation can be circumvented when citizens of these communities view their actions as remedying inequality – specifically through discussing politics with neighbors at community meetings (Alex-Assensoh, 2002). In this work, I find that the advent of community meetings related to school closures played an important role in providing opportunities not only for affected citizens to discuss political issues but also to form political opinions of political actors – especially those that looked like them.

Encounters with School Officials and Political Leaders at Community Meetings

During the school closure process, the official avenue provided for citizens to gain information and speak out are the community meetings required once closures are proposed. These community meetings are critical not only for providing a space to voice opposition but also for teaching those in attendance how the government works and who has the power and responsibility to control the closure policy. The political lessons derived from community meetings can also guide the mostly novice participants on how to accurately attribute blame when school closures occur.

The common political actors involved in creating and approving school closure policies include the superintendent and the school board in addition to, city council members, the mayor, and possibly even the governor. The behavior of these individuals at the community meetings and across the process has a direct impact on how participants view them after the fact.

One of the most frustrating aspects for participants at community meetings for school closures, particularly in Chicago, was that the spaces where the meetings were held were often overcrowded. With attendances ranging from 200 to 2,000, the large number of people made the facilitation of meetings difficult. In fact, many of those who desired to participate either had to wait outside of the door for space to open or participate with a smaller group in a separate room, typically away from the officials to whom they wanted access. Community members viewed the inattentiveness of officials to selecting spaces that would ensure all those who wanted to participate could, as an indicator of their insensitivity to the needs of the community. When an official would not allow more people into a meeting room in Chicago, one community resident received a round of applause after declaring,

> you knew it would be a big meeting. It's been huge all over the city, and now you're going to try to tell us no! We want to be in the same room! You're trying to divide us! (network meeting, Pilsen-Little Village, Chicago, February 2, 2013).

Failure by officials to address language barriers at meetings also agitated participants. Several persons I interviewed in Philadelphia recalled multiple meetings in which the only district officials in attendance did not speak or understand Spanish nor did they bring a translator to ensure that non-English speakers could participate. As stated by one community organizer:

> I remember one meeting in Kensington [where] three-quarters of the parents were Spanish-speaking. The [school district] sent a team but didn't have a single person who could speak Spanish, which to me said a lot. If it was an obligation they thought about it, they wouldn't have made these mistakes (interview, North Philadelphia, Philadelphia, October 22, 2014).

The lack of attention to the aspects of a community meeting, including a strict two–minute time limit, that would ensure that the people attending are, in fact, heard sends a message to citizens that officials do not value engagement with the community or that they have a lack of regard for its members' voices. These perceptions affect citizens' perceptions of fairness during the entire process as well as after.

The ways that citizens' meeting experiences shaped their perceptions about the fairness of the policy process is best exemplified by another parent I interviewed after a community meeting in Chicago:

PARENT: I mostly come to the meetings to see if they are going to answer questions, and they don't answer any questions. They just have them come up here ... and display a PowerPoint and make a case for what? They already know what schools they are going to close.

ME: How are you so sure?

PARENT: The last meeting was [two days prior] … They already put
           out a list today … How do you make a decision that fast if
           you just heard parents speak? I don't think you can crunch
           numbers and make an idea that fast and that quick (inter-
           view, Garfield-Humboldt Park, Chicago, February 5, 2013).

As illustrated in this interview, the quickness of the process
raises questions about the legitimacy of the process: "How do you make
a decision that fast if you just heard parents speak?" These questions
about the legitimacy of the process likely translate to feelings about the
policy purveyors, especially as they learn that those who are supposed
to have the power to make these decisions are not in fact present at the
meetings to receive their feedback. As said by two different community
members in Chicago:

> I have to ask one question, where are the members of the board of
> education? What about the leadership of CPS, where are they? The
> people charged with making the decisions are absent from these
> meetings. They've been absent from all the meetings (network
> meeting, Austin-North Lawndale, Chicago, February 13, 2013).

* * *

> My first question is where is the board of education? Where is
> Barbara Byrd Bennet? Where is Rahm Emmanuel? Who truly is
> the puppet master? We know that you all are not making these
> decisions over our community school and if they are not here
> what does this say about our input? (network meeting, Austin-
> North Lawndale, Chicago, February 13, 2013).

Participants in the school closure process determine that they
are being asked to submit feedback to powerless individuals and view
this as an indication of how their input is being valued. Yet, how do
affected citizens know who to blame for what they are observing? In
other words, do participants simply blame school officials for not
having Spanish translators or large enough meeting rooms? Or do they
translate that blame to the mayor, city council, or governor? Beyond
their poor meeting experiences, who do affected citizens ultimately
blame for the school closure policy? And, what role does the race of
the representative play in their decisions on who to blame and why?

Political Blame in Chicago

My study of political blame in Chicago began with the development of a data set that combines original data collected on schools closed in Chicago from 2012 to 2013 with the Cooperative Congressional Election Study (CCES). The CCES data include questions on attitudes toward schools and politics. Using these data, along with similar precinct–level data on political behavior from the Chicago Democracy Project,[2] facilitates an investigation of the relationship between race and living in or near an area where a school is threatened for closure on various political attitudes.

Using these data, in collaboration with the Chicago Democracy Project, we compare over-time changes in how citizens in Chicago with varying exposure to school closure policy view their local political leaders. In essence, we are approximating a quasi-experimental framework by comparing changes in attitudes before and after the wave of closures in 2013 across areas of Chicago that either did or did not experience the policy.[3] In particular, we analyze changes in the waves just before and after the biggest closure wave (2010 and 2014, respectively).[4] The aforementioned data are spatially merged (at the precinct – or zip code – level) with an original data set on public school closures in Chicago between 2012 and 2013. This data set provides the key information about which respondents or precincts were most likely to be directly affected by the closures. For the CCES data, respondents from zip codes in which schools were closed from 2012 to 2013 are compared to those from other areas. For the Chicago Democracy Project data, precincts near closures are compared to those farther away.

In this analysis, meeting attendance is also included – since I make the claim that it is at these meetings that affected citizens are

---

[2] The Chicago Democracy Project is an effort led by scholar and coauthor Thomas Ogorzalek. This section is reflective of a collaboration with this project and can be found in Nuamah and Ogorzalek (2021).

[3] Although not a tightly controlled experiment, the underlying logic of comparison is similar: I hypothesize that the "treatment" of school closures will be associated with negative attitudes toward related political officials. While the treatment was not random, no communities opted into it, so by observing changes that are theoretically linked to the policy, I can get close to estimating its effects.

[4] These years also have the advantage of being otherwise similar: Neither was a mayoral or presidential election year, so they are comparable in their models' overall level of nonlocal mobilization. We also use the 2016 wave, which included some local policy evaluation questions

engaging in the political learning necessary to accurately assign blame. Generally, my expectation is that citizens learn from community meetings to blame state and local political officials for the school closing policy, rather than district officials and administrators. Nonetheless, I also expect lower evaluations of public schools among those affected by closure, overall.

In previous collaborative work I conducted on New Orleans with Domingo Morel, we find racial differences in how Blacks and Whites viewed the quality of their public schools post-Hurricane Katrina. Following Katrina, New Orleans began to transform most of its traditional public schools into charters. Although studies show that test scores improved after the mass adoption of charters, surveys revealed that most Black citizens in New Orleans did not perceive New Orleans schools as having improved. A majority of White residents, however, perceived that the schools were better. To explain this difference, we argue that *local shifts in political power between racial groups* influence how citizens evaluate local government services. That is, the loss or gain of political power between racial groups at the city level can help shape how citizens view their local government and local government services. In this case, we suggest that Blacks' school attitudes are reflective of their interest in restoring political, economic, and social power that is increasingly being consumed by Whites in the post-Katrina era (Morel & Nuamah, 2019).

Given the racial differences in support for school closure found in Chapter 1, and the fact that school closure threatens to remove resources and thus power from Black communities, one should expect similarly lower evaluations of public schools among those affected (whether directly or indirectly) by them. And indeed, drawing on the case study of Chicago Public Schools I will show how poor meeting experiences in Chicago contributed to poor evaluations of schools and lower support for the mayor. Thereafter, I will draw on the case study of the School District of Philadelphia to show how experiences with the policy process taught citizens to blame the governor, as opposed to the mayor, for the policy. In both cases, I will make clear how citizens learn to attribute blame based on who holds the most political power, even as local school officials represent the public face of closure throughout the process.

Evaluating Schools in Chicago

The analysis first explores whether affected citizens give schools poorer evaluations post closure. It also accounts for the role of community meetings in providing affected citizens with the information needed to make these evaluations. All details are available in the Appendix. The following is the short version.

Like the case of New Orleans, the results present a contrast between Black Chicagoans and members of other racial groups: While Black respondents in neighborhoods with school closures rate schools lower, non-Black respondents in neighborhoods with school closures rate schools *higher*. More specifically, Table 2.1 estimates the relationship between living in an area with school closures, meeting attendance, and how respondents grade the schools.[5] Model 1 presents a limited analysis (bivariate) that does not account for other factors that may matter, such as income and education. Model 2 adds political and demographic information (for income, race and ethnicity, education, and interest in news) and finds basically the same outcome. Model 3 also accounts for political and demographic information as well as tests the possibility that attending meetings and living in a neighborhood with closure will contribute to changing citizens' evaluation of schools.

In each of these three models, neither living in an area with school closures nor attending meetings has a relationship with school evaluation, alone. However, there is a significant relationship between race and school evaluation: Blacks, on average, grade schools by about a half-letter grade less than non-Black respondents. Model 4 digs deeper to test a conditional hypothesis of living in a neighborhood with school closures, attending political meetings, *and* being Black. The relationship is statistically significant. In particular, being a Black person who attends community meetings *and* lives in an area where schools have been closed is positively associated with lower evaluations of schools post closure.

Taking a closer look at this interaction term, Figures 2.1 and 2.2 show the predicted school grades for different subgroups based on

---

[5] The raw averages in Table 2.2 are suggestive and basically consistent with what we would expect based on observation of the school closures in the press and in person, but we can look closer to explore the mechanism by which place-based experience ought to shape policy opinions.

Table 2.1. Determinants of school evaluations, 2016

	Model 1	Model 2	Model 3	Model4
	(No Controls)	(Controls)	(Controls)	(Controls)
Meeting attendance	0.183	0.216	0.211	0.081
	−0.15	−0.16	−0.2	−0.21
Living in neighborhood w/closure	0.004	−0.031	−0.034	−0.075
	−0.11	−0.11	−0.12	−0.15
Child in household	0.363**	0.374**	0.378**	0.341*
	−0.14	−0.14	−0.14	−0.14
Black	−0.302**	−0.424*	−0.434*	−0.476*
	−0.11	−0.18	−0.19	−0.24
Closure neigh*meeting			−0.031	0.621
			−0.34	−0.38
Closure neigh*meeting*Black				−2.345***
				−0.66
N	455	417	417	417
R-sqr	0.046	0.062	0.067	0.091

Data Sources: CCES, 2016; Chicago Democracy Project; NCES School Closure Data 2001–2013

Model 4.[6] Figure 2.1 shows the expected school evaluations among residents of closure areas by race and meeting attendance.[7] While residents of closure areas who did not attend a meeting tend to evaluate the schools about the same (around a "C"), meeting attendees diverge: Blacks who attended meetings are likely to grade the schools down to a D,

---

[6] Respondents answered the following: "How would you grade the schools: A–Excellent; B–Above Average; C–Average; D–Below Average; F–Poor?"

[7] Triple interactions are complicated (and graphically confusing) to interpret, so these figures break out predicted evaluations by different measures within the interaction separately.

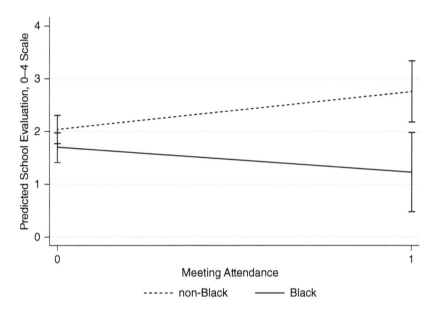

Figure 2.1 Effects of meeting attendance on school evaluations among residents of zip codes with closures, by race

while non-Blacks who attended meetings are likely to give the schools slightly higher grades (e.g., C+ or B–). Figure 2.2 shows a different way of interpreting the interaction. Among respondents who attended meetings, living in a neighborhood with closures is associated with an almost two-letter downgrade (e.g., a B to a D) for Black respondents.

The key observations to take away from Figures 2.1 and 2.2 have to do with race. Overall, neither living in an area with closures nor attendance at meetings have a significant relationship with school evaluations on their own; however, the factor of race does. Figure 2.3 shows the predicted relationship across Blacks living in different areas of the city. Those who did not attend meetings were likely to give schools a grade of C–, no matter where they lived; those who attended meetings in closure areas were likely to downgrade to a D; and those who attended meetings in non-closure areas were likely to give a much rosier B grade. In other words, after the mass closure of schools, *Black respondents were likely to give schools lower grades, particularly if they had attended political meetings **and** lived in neighborhoods with school closures.*

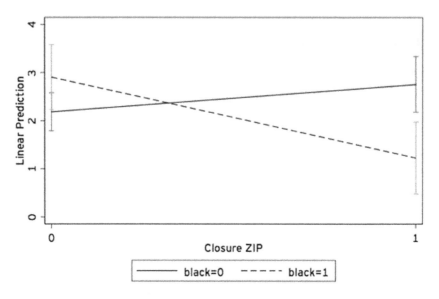

Figure 2.2 Effects of closures on school evaluations among meeting attendees, by race

Connecting Meeting Attendance and Evaluations of School Policy to Political Blame

The intersection of living in a neighborhood with school closures, attending a community meeting in areas where schools are closed, and identifying as Black combine to contribute to lower school evaluations. This finding is consistent with my expectation that residents of affected areas, especially those who have attended community meetings, give relatively disapproving evaluations of school systems, in part, because they associate the loss of their schools with the loss of political power. Yet, did respondents connect their school evaluations to blame of political officials?

Those affected by school closures in Chicago may have initially attributed blame to the school system for the process since the school board makes the final decision. However, in Chicago, the school board is appointed by the mayor, who citizens rightly judged as the political actor with the most institutional power. As one community member noted: "The mayor's office has too much power, and that's the problem, and that's why I am all for an elected school board" (interview, Englewood-Gresham, Chicago, February 18, 2013). Because the mayor

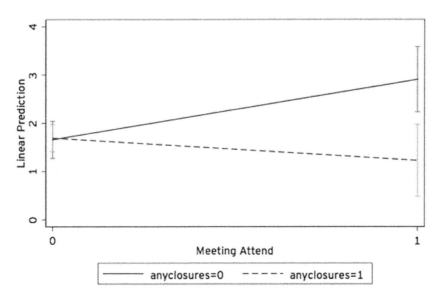

Figure 2.3 Effects of meeting attendance on school evaluations among Black respondents, by zip codes with closures

appointed the school board in Chicago, residents in closure areas, especially those who gave low grades to their schools, should have given relatively disapproving evaluations of the mayor. And, indeed, this is the case, as *the findings show a relationship between school closures, meeting attendance, and decreased support for the then Chicago mayor, Rahm Emanuel.*

The relationship is fairly straightforward: Negative evaluations of schools are directly related to negative evaluations of the mayor. Table 2.2 shows evaluations of the mayor (using the same report card–style grade scale). In each model, school evaluation is a significant predictor of the mayor's grade: a letter-grade drop in evaluation of the schools is associated with about a half letter–grade drop in evaluation of the mayor, even when including other theoretically related predictors. Results at the contextual level also demonstrate that Mayor Emanuel's change in support was greater in areas geographically closer to school closures: *His support declined about 13–16 percentage points more in precincts within 1.5 miles of closing than in similar precincts 5 miles away from any school closures.*

Collectively, then, these findings provide some evidence that those in proximity to school closures may develop political attitudes

Table 2.2. Determinants of mayoral evaluations, 2016

	Model 1	Model 2	Model 3
School evaluation	0.543***	0.546***	0.531***
	−0.05	−0.05	−0.06
Meeting attendance		−0.045	−0.028
		−0.14	−0.15
Neighborhood with closures		0.043	0.086
		−0.12	−0.12
Black		0.024	−0.147
		−0.12	−0.23
Years in city			0.001
			0
Family income			0.012
			−0.02
Education			−0.011
			−0.04
Child in household			0.048
			−0.12
White			−0.139
			−0.22
Latinx			−0.037
			−0.03
Political interest			−0.024
			−0.05
constant	0.414***	0.390**	0.611
	−0.1	−0.12	−0.4
N	446	446	409
R-sqr	0.215	0.216	0.21

* p < 0.05, ** p < 0.01, *** p < 0.001

that are both informed and consistent with their experiences as targets of the policy. Even though the community members most affected by school closures likely lack the formal political knowledge due to relatively lower incomes and lower education, the school closure process provides a political learning experience. Specifically, school evaluations and political attitudes are likely affected by the information gained and lessons learned about power from the participants' attendance at these meetings.

Studying Political Blame and Approval in Philadelphia

My study of blame in Philadelphia began with a different set of data thanks to the Pew Charitable Trust, who fielded a survey after the 2013 closings that asked both about attitudes toward education and political blame, directly. These surveys included responses from over 1,200 Philadelphians. These data were then linked at the zip code level to school closure data on Philadelphia from 2012 to 2013 and the 2009–2013 American Community Survey. All details are available in the Appendix.

Using this survey, the independent variables I focus on are being Black, living in an area with school closures, and working with others to solve problems (my proxy for meeting attendance). The dependent variables I focus on are political blame and mayoral approval. To examine how those affected by closure attribute blame, I construct a proxy variable for living in an area affected by a potential school closure. This variable is based on the number of schools closed or on the closure list per zip code. I then develop a dummy variable of whether one lives in an area that experienced a potential school closure.[8] It is important to note that, for the dummy variable, "neighborhood" is a substitute for zip code since it is the smallest geographic identifier available. While it would have been ideal to have a question on the survey that directly asks respondents whether their school was on the closure list, in the case of Philadelphia, I view the dummy variable as a strong proxy given the ways in which closure was concentrated within

---

[8] The other variable ranks the rate of closure based on whether one lives in an area that has a high, medium, or low rate of closures. High refers to more than six closings in a respective community since the adoption of the school closing policy, medium refers to between four and six closings, and low refers to between one and three closings. A community might also have no experience with closure.

the same zip codes. Accordingly, I expect zip codes to be especially useful for the analysis.[9]

To target the mechanism at work, participation at a community meeting, I rely on a question in the Pew survey that asks respondents whether they have worked with others in their community to solve problems in the past twelve months (1 is coded yes; 0 is coded otherwise). While the question does not specify the type of participation, it is time specific. Therefore, by interacting participation with closure, I can get closer to developing a proxy variable that measures those affected by closure who participated in their community during the same period as the mass closure of their schools.

The issue of safety is often directly tied to schools (e.g., data reveal that 26 percent of reasons raised against closure were related to concerns about safety). Accordingly, I created a variable for neighborhood safety based on a question that asks residents to rate how safe they feel in their neighborhood. Respondents who say they feel "a little safe" or "not safe at all" are coded 1, and those who state they "feel safe" or "somewhat safe" are coded 0. This variable also allows me to test the expectation that citizens believe that the safety of their neighborhood is a direct responsibility of the mayor as opposed to the governor.

The most important demographic variable is race, particularly being Black, although I also include being Hispanic and White in the analysis. If one self-identifies as Black, 1 is coded; 0 is coded otherwise. Other important demographic variables at the individual level include whether a person is a renter, earns an income of 50,000 USD and below, has a high school diploma, is employed, and has school-aged children. Additionally, I include a dichotomous variable that accounts for if the person pays a "great deal" or "some" attention to politics, which are each coded 1, and 0 otherwise. My intention was to find out if citizens that work with others to solve problems – in other words, participate – are already well informed about politics. If this is the case, then

---

[9] It is important to account for the possibility that the school closure variable may be acting as a proxy for race and/or poverty since areas with closures also have high levels of poverty and a large concentration of minorities. Yet, by using rate of closures, I can get variation in the types of neighborhoods affected. Furthermore, by including measures of race and poverty at the individual and contextual level, I can control for whether the inclusion of these variables influences the effects found for living in a neighborhood with closures. Finally, I examine the extent to which these variables coexist with one another and determine that there is variation between the two variables. Thus, the variables are not capturing/measuring a single item.

disapproval of Mayor Nutter has little do with participating in a community meeting and more to do with the fact that those participating are already informed. All details are available in the Appendix.

For the investigation, I begin by specifically examining the impact of race and closure on different variations of the political blame variable: the school reform commission, the teachers' union (Philadelphia Federation of Teachers), Mayor Michael Nutter, and Governor Tom Corbett, respectively.[10] Similar to Chicago, being Black and living in a neighborhood with schools on the closure list should be associated with blame and/or disapproval of major political actors, especially among those citizens who participate in community meetings.

Who Philadelphians Blame the Most: Governor Corbett and Mayor Nutter

While initially it may appear that Black residents blame political actors and the school board at similarly high levels, their attribution of blame to the governor and the union are the only statistically significant relationships in the analysis, at the .05 and .01 level, respectively (see Table A.2A in the Appendix). In particular, Black residents living in neighborhoods with school closures have the highest probability of blaming the governor and state legislature, at 86 percent, and the lowest probability of blaming the union, at 35 percent. In short, Blacks affected by closure blamed the governor the most for the educational crisis. As for the mayor, there are no distinct differences across race for blaming Mayor Nutter, in that all groups blamed him at similarly high levels but less than the governor. Further, these attributions of blame for Mayor Nutter are not statistically significant.

Blacks' high probability of blaming the governor is both plausible and consistent with my expectations. Given the power of the governor over public schools in Philadelphia since the state takeover in 2001, and the creation of the school reform commission, the mayor had the power to appoint only two out of five members of the commission (as opposed to three for the governor). As a result, the mayor could not propose, pass, or stop the state from doing what it wanted, including swaying the vote to keep any one school open.

---

[10] These models include both individual- and contextual-level controls and are reported as predicted probabilities and marginal effects for ease of interpretation.

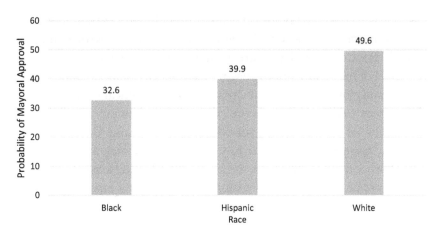

Figure 2.4 Probability of blame among Blacks living in neighborhoods with school closures

The qualitative data (i.e., interviews with parents) collected on Governor Corbett reveal that he received the most blame because affected citizens are aware that the governor had the most power to fund (or defund) school districts (Figure 2.4). In addition, they knew that he appointed a majority of the members of the school reform commission and other policy bureaucrats. After the school closings in Philadelphia, the governor was also the target of significant blame because – unlike the Mayor – he was eligible for reelection and thus could be "punished" at the ballot box.

As one community activist stated, "I don't want to give the mayor a pass, but he is the junior partner ... he has less appointees ... We are bound up in what happens to the state" (interview, North Philadelphia, Philadelphia, October 11, 2014). Additionally, and perhaps most important, the mayor could not be reelected in the November 2015 election as he had already served two terms. His inability to be reelected had direct consequences on affected citizens' decision to attribute blame toward him. As one union leader stated, "[the mayor] never put out publicity to support the community ... never made a statement. [But] no one mentions him because he can't be reelected. He is a lame duck. He has nothing to lose" (interview, South Philadelphia, Philadelphia, October 15, 2015). Mayor Nutter's inability to be reelected made it meaningless to expend energy and resources extending the most blame to him as he was unlikely to be responsive to these attributions.

So, the decision to blame the governor more than the mayor for educational crises was partially shaped by the particular electoral climate. This was reiterated in ads created by the teachers' union, as noted by one community member:

> [The] Mayor has been an abysmal failure; [Governor Corbett] is just not the only one. [In] September 2013, the union took shots and made a lot of ads toward the mayor. But [the governor] is in an election right now ... so they are focused on him ... But the school district, ... federal city council, and the mayor also has influence ... even the city's contribution can be better (interview, South Philadelphia, Philadelphia, October 15, 2014).

Altogether, while Mayor Nutter was perceived by affected citizens as not giving enough support to those who were fighting against school closures, they recognized that he did not have the capacity to take action that could make a significant difference in their lives.[11] The result is that affected citizens blamed the governor more than the mayor for the school closure crises.

Blame versus Approval for Mayor Nutter

Interestingly, I find that, while Blacks do not attribute more *blame* to Mayor Nutter for the educational crises than other groups, Blacks who live in neighborhoods with closures express the highest level of *disapproval* for the mayor relative to any other group. This is due, in part, to concerns about the effects of closure on neighborhood safety. More specifically, in the model that focuses on mayoral approval overall (not particular to education), the results reveal that being Black and living in a neighborhood with school closures are associated with the lowest probability of approving the mayor relative to any other racial group. In particular, Blacks who live in neighborhoods with school closures have a 32.6 percent probability of approving the mayor,

---

[11] Many who placed blame on Governor Corbett also compared him with previous Governor Ed Rendell. A sense of nostalgia for Governor Rendell was echoed across several interviews, and many community leaders lamented that the change of leadership in the governor's office played a critical role in the circumstances facing the Philadelphia public schools: "Ed Rendell ... understood that we have children with the most needs. When he left, the [school reform commission] stayed and then Tea Party [members] were being elected. So, even though we had a Democratic [mayor], they were able to put in laws to attack the teachers' union through the creation of the charter laws" (interview, North Philadelphia, Philadelphia, October 11, 2014).

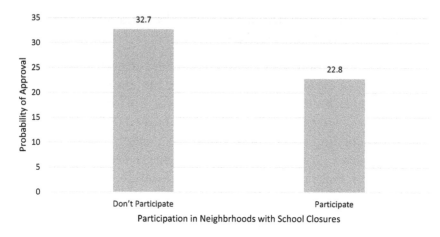

Figure 2.5 Probability of approval of mayor by race and living in a neighborhood with closures

compared to 39.9 percent for Hispanics and 49.6 percent for Whites (Figure 2.5).[12]

If we account for attendance at community meetings (or working with others to solve problems), the probability of approving Mayor Nutter for Blacks who live in neighborhoods with closures declines even further from 32 percent to 22 percent (Figure 2.6). This suggests that, for Blacks living in a neighborhood with school closures, participation in community meetings (i.e., working with others) plays a significant role in shaping perceptions of mayoral approval.[13]

While I do not have comparable data on governor approval, a closer investigation of data on mayoral approval is valuable for further teasing out these results. In particular, the analysis supports the claim that distinctions are made between mayoral blame and approval because citizens understand the institutional responsibility of the office and, thus, hold the mayor accountable based on these understandings. Regarding issues that are under the jurisdiction of the mayor, I find evidence of a clear relationship between neighborhood safety and

[12] In addition, the regression model output reveals that living in an unsafe neighborhood, working with others to solve problems, and living in areas that experienced medium to high concentration of closures have a highly significant relationship with disapproval of Mayor Nutter (see Table A.3).

[13] Working with others to solve problems remained significantly related to disapproval for Mayor Nutter even after a variable that measured political knowledge was added. Furthermore, the variation found between political knowledge and working with others to solve problems suggests that the two variables are not capturing a single attribute.

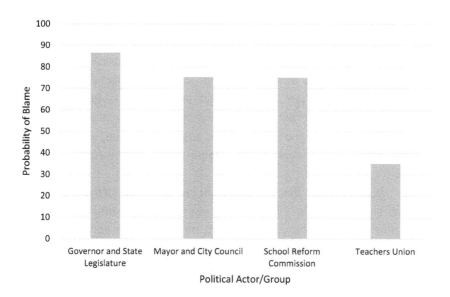

Figure 2.6 Probability of approval of mayor among Blacks who live in neighborhoods with closures by participation

disapproval of Mayor Nutter. In particular, living in an unsafe neighborhood is related to a 0.8-point increase in disapproval of Mayor Nutter at the highest level of significance.

Indeed, neighborhoods targeted for closure are often the same neighborhoods viewed as unsafe. Furthermore, citizens believe that these neighborhoods will become even less safe if schools are closed because schoolchildren will have to walk longer distances and possibly cross gang territory lines. As said by one parent at a community meeting in 2013, "if you send kids from one side of the community to another – you will put our kids in harm's way." (Garfield-Humboldt Park, Chicago, February 5, 2013) Accordingly, even if Governor Corbett may be the main person that affected citizens' blame for the educational crisis, Mayor Nutter *is* responsible for neighborhood safety. Thus, when schools are closed, that responsibility of keeping students safe likely affects citizens' approval of him.

How Race Affects Power

Racial representation must also be considered in the blame and approval of Mayor Nutter. In neighborhoods where schools are targeted for closure, the racial and ethnic makeup of the political actors often reflects the citizens they represent. Mayor Nutter is Black, like many of those targeted, and, historically, Blacks have associated political leaders of their same race with a number of positive outcomes, especially as it relates to efficacy, trust, and knowledge about politics (see, e.g., Bobo & Gilliam, 1990). In fact, across all racial groups, voters often support those of their same race or ethnic background, regardless of the performance of the official (Gay, 2001; Kaufmann, 2004).[14] This is likely related to perceptions that these positions will result in more power for their group.

Indeed, some Black Philadelphians were supportive of Mayor Nutter partly because of his race, especially in comparison with Governor Corbett, who is White. Yet, most residents appear to draw a distinction between racial representation and power. If we return to the case of New Orleans, for example, it is important to note that Black resident's poor evaluations of schools occurred at a time when Black citizens represented the majority of the population and had a Black mayor. Nonetheless, they still viewed their social and political prospects through a lens of political powerlessness. This is not uncommon: In 1992, Black Power founder and activist, Kwame Ture (Carmichael and Hamilton, 1992), observed that Blacks were "more integrated into the democratic party today than ever before; they have more elected officials than any other ethnic group, yet they have no power at all in the Democratic Party!" He went on to describe them as representing "powerless visibility" (p. 190). Nearly thirty years earlier Martin Luther King Jr. (1967 [2010]) expressed a similar concern, stating, "our political leaders are bereft of influence in the councils of political power ... He is accorded a measure of dignity and personal respect but not political power" (p. 156). The case of Philadelphia suggests that affected citizens shared these same sentiments.

One community resident noted, "the mayor? I mean everyone knows who has the power ... two White men, everything else is just smoke and mirrors" (interview, South Philadelphia, Philadelphia, 2015). Similar statements by others made it clear that some targeted citizens do not view an Black mayor as having the financial means or political power

---

[14] Although some studies conducted at the congressional level have contradicted this, these contradictory findings have been justified in that the empowerment associated with an Black holding office may wear off after the initial run and the candidate secures the position (Lublin & Tate, 1995; Gay, 2001, 2002; Tate, 2003).

to affect the closure decision because he or she must "play politics" with White politicians who have more power and resources.

For this reason, affected citizens often decide that being the same race as the policy maker should not play a part in who they support. As stated by one community resident and leader:

> There is a difference between having Black leaders and people with actual power. It's largely ... useless. I say that because a lot of folks in our leadership have been here so long that it's about what benefits them ... I don't care what color the person running the city is so long as you understand there are things that this community needs. [Black] Senator Vincent Hughes gets it, but he is far outweighed by the Blacks who have been there for thirty years and don't want to change (interview, North Philadelphia, Philadelphia, October 13, 2015).

Similar feelings were expressed by several persons interviewed and is consistent with Ture's observation that "when Blacks have had the choice to support a conservative Black or a liberal White, the choice invariably goes to the latter" (Carmichael and Hamilton, 1992: 215). As another community member stated, "we've had Black leadership for over twenty-five years so why are we in this position? We have Black leadership but still the same problems" (interview, Northwest Philadelphia, Philadelphia, 2014). So, while some Black Philadelphians affected by closure associate Mayor Nutter's lack of power with his race, others refuse to give him a "pass" *because* of his race. The result is that most Blacks affected by closure disapproved of his overall performance at the highest level when compared to any other racial group.

Assigning Blame the Right Way

Altogether, this chapter draws connections between the micro–level education policy experiences of affected citizens and the political officials responsible. More specifically, the survey analysis of Chicago and Philadelphia reveal that citizens blame major political leaders (e.g., the mayor and the governor) more than local bureaucrats (e.g., members of the school board) in some instances. I suggest that the experiences of affected citizens, particularly at community meetings, give them insights into who has control of the resources and power over schools.

In Chicago, the poor meeting experiences of affected citizens contributed to poor evaluations of schools *and* low support for the mayor following the high number of school closures in 2013. Their evaluations are logical, in that the mayor was the most responsible for the distribution of resources to public schools in Chicago. The analysis in Philadelphia reveals that most citizens, including Blacks, attribute more blame to Governor Corbett for the education crisis. My qualitative data suggest that this is also because of his power over resources critical to helping schools remain open. These data further suggest that, while Blacks do not attribute blame to Mayor Nutter for the education crises at a higher level than other groups, due to his lack of electability, they do disapprove of Mayor Nutter at the highest level overall, because of concerns around neighborhood safety. These varying patterns are indicative of the fact that Blacks attribute blame based on political leaders' policy positions, power, and institutional responsibility (as opposed to party identification, for example).

To be sure, these findings still do not tell us much about the role of race *and* gender in shaping political blame in Chicago and Philadelphia. But if we look at the case of Karen Lewis; a Black woman who led the Chicago Teachers Union during the bulk of the mass closure process, for example, we gain some insight into how race and gender might matter. More specifically, Lewis ran for mayor against Rahm Emanuel before having to step down due to an illness in 2014. If we accept the empowerment thesis of participation, her race and gender background should have had a positive effect on mobilizing Black women to participate and in shaping their political attitudes.

At the same time, while there appeared to be more participation by Black women, particularly in terms of organizing persons to attend community meetings on closures, there were no Black woman leaders at the level of mayor or governor to blame at the time that Lewis ran for office. Further, I observed differences by gender, particularly in the ethnographic observations of community meetings – which were central cites of political learning. For example, I observed that even as Black women participate at high rates as attendees and leaders, Black men appeared to still represent a disproportionate percentage of those who spoke at the mic (relative to their level of general engagement). While women in the context of school closures could be more comfortable speaking up (given that they represent the majority), they still must work with men who are present.[15] Thus, it is unclear how these gender dynamics may have shaped who affected citizens chose to blame for their experiences.

Nonetheless, it is important to consider why I maintain that meetings make such a difference – since citizens appear to blame those who they do not have direct contact with anyway (e.g., the governor as opposed to the school board). This is because, across multiple meetings, local education bureaucrats casted the closure issue as one they had no power to resolve as a result of their "inability to generate revenue" and, thus, their inability to provide additional resources necessary to keep schools open. Statements commonly made by school board members themselves included:

> The SRC is a weird political animal that does not collect its own taxes so the people who have [some] power to close cannot raise their own money (interview, board member, Philadelphia, November 12, 2014).
>
> [***]
>
> You don't have a school district that can tax so it goes down to the city council and they have to make these decisions ... so we bank on the passage of the cigarette tax. The process is inherently political (interview, board member, Philadelphia, October 15, 2014).

These statements leave affected citizens not only frustrated but also convinced that these persons were simply powerless agents or "puppets" of the actual policy makers: the politicians. Accordingly, even if their interactions at these meetings are with school board members, political actors become the individuals to blame for their experiences and, most important, the policy.[16]

Ultimately, the findings of this chapter are important for several reasons. First, they contribute to our understanding of how blame is

---

[15] As Kathlene (1994) argues, once women become the majority, men become more aggressive. Further, Karpowitz et al. (2012) reveal that men may use their minority status to exceed equality in a context where all participants must agree on a single solution. These differences are less observable using existing survey data. However, this may reflect how questions around engagement are asked and measured in ways that are not gender relevant (Dolan, 2011).

[16] And in the case of Chicago and Philadelphia, none of these politicians were Black women at the time.

attributed at the local level where traditional cues such as partisanship are not salient (almost everyone in both cities identifies as a Democrat). Second, they show how, once exposed to the political process through community meetings, citizens can become more sophisticated in understanding policy issues, evaluating their experiences, and logically attributing blame to policy actors. Finally, these findings contribute to our understanding of descriptive representation as they move us beyond determining whether people of color blindly support political leadership of their same race and explains how race matters more as a policy position. As stated by Carmichael (Ture) and Hamilton (1992), "[Black Power] does not mean *merely* putting Black faces into office. Black visibility is not Black power" (p. 46). Recognizing this, Blacks make informed determinations about the position they support and put their support behind the person who has the power to make changes. Inversely, they blame those who do not.

HOW TARGETED CITIZENS FIGHT BACK

3 Participating While Poor and Black in the Policy Process

In September 2015, a group of one dozen parents, teachers, activists, and community members engaged in a thirty-four-day hunger strike to demand that the city of Chicago reopen Walter H. Dyett High School on the city's Southeast Side. A parent involved in the strike described her rationale for participating:

> My three younger children are in elementary school, and my eighth grader will be starting high school in the fall. Mayor [Rahm] Emanuel closed ... schools in "low-income neighborhoods" for "underutilization." I'm no politician but I do know that schools underutilized are schools underfunded ... We will continue to fight ... until justice is served to our children on a platter (quoted in McDonald, 2015).

Dyett was shut down in 2013 as part of the single largest incidence of school closures by a district in a single year in US history. Due in large part to a years-long protest, including the hunger strike, the city agreed to reopen Dyett as an arts–focused neighborhood public school, making it the only school of the forty-nine closed to reopen (Eltagouri & Perez, 2016).

The extraordinary outcome for Dyett High School demonstrates the power of political mobilization that can take place when closures occur. It is one example that shows that citizens need not merely *experience* policies – they can take action and force a response.

Nonetheless, given that Dyett was the only school to reopen, it remains unclear whether it is in fact representative of typical school closure battles and their political consequences.

School Closures Shape Political Blame, but Do They Shape Political Action?

The previous chapters make clear that the groups most affected by closures are vehemently against them and know who to blame. Thus, one would expect that they would engage in multiple forms of political action to express their opposition. However, research has found that most people who participate in political and civic processes are only able to do so because they have the money, time, and experience needed: "The resources of time, money, and skills are ... powerful predictors of political participation in America" (Brady, Verba, & Schlozman, 1995, p. 285). Of the school closure policies discussed in this book, nearly 90 percent of the schools to be potentially closed were in resource-poor communities that traditionally participate at low levels, particularly around school issues (Henig et al., 2001). In fact, schools had been closing in Chicago since 2001, and although there had been some engagement, it was relatively low. Across many cities, participation in school board elections, for example, rarely surpasses 5 percent (Allen & Plank, 2005). Accordingly, it was unclear whether those targeted would participate in the public meetings organized by the district or other forms of political action. In other words, it was uncertain whether the case of the Dyett hunger strike, Sharon and Leslie's meeting participation (mentioned in Chapter 1), and Leanne's parent organizing (discussed in the Introduction) were mere anomalies.

At the same time, in Chicago, Mayor Emanuel faced a runoff election against Jesus Garcia in 2015, which he won; however, he decided not to run again in 2018. In Philadelphia, Governor Corbett lost his reelection bid in 2014, and both the mayor and governor were replaced in 2015 with elected officials more sympathetic to the cause of stopping school closures.[1] The aforementioned provides suggestive evidence that those affected by controversial policies such as school closure may not only determine who to blame, but also act to vote those

---

[1] In 2018, the SRC voted to dissolve itself. There is currently a mayoral-controlled school board in Philadelphia.

responsible out of office. Even Mayor Rahm Emanuel himself admitted that he suspected his actions would result in political blowback from those affected in 2013, stating "I will absorb the political consequences, so our children have a better future."[2]

In this chapter, I show that poor Black people affected by school closure *did* in fact translate their blame to formal political action, despite coming from backgrounds traditionally associated with low participation. In particular, I illustrate that these groups go on to participate in community meetings, advocating for an elected school board and voting for, or rather against, Mayor Emanuel at a relatively higher rate than any other group in the period immediately after the announcement of school closures. In the short term, affected participants interpret their experiences as contributing to their broader civil skills and positive perceptions of internal efficacy. In the long term? Well, that's another story to be addressed in Chapter 4. For now, let's discuss the short-term engagement and impacts on those affected by school closures.

Studying the Impacts of Participation

Between 2012 and 2015, I collected semi-structured interviews, observed community meetings, and analyzed community meeting transcripts in Chicago and Philadelphia. I collected semi-structured interviews with parents and community residents to understand citizens' reasons for participating and their feelings about their participation and politics. I then conducted semi-structured interviews with leaders of organizations to determine the methods they used to encourage citizens to participate in the closure process and to examine their perceptions of the utility of participation.[3] I observed community meetings and analyzed transcripts to learn how meetings were run and to investigate citizens' experiences with participation.[4]

---

[2] See article on the "political fallout" from school closings, at www.nbcchicago.com/news/local/rahm-emanuel-political-fallout-cps-closures/1952537.

[3] I also asked school officials about how they used the feedback to make decisions, but I was only provided with general answers, along the lines of the following: "we collect all the responses, they are put into a report, and then presented to school officials to be considered in the final decision."

[4] The intent of the investigation was not to develop a causal analysis of the impacts of school closure participation on political attitudes but rather to engage in an ethnographic analysis of citizen participation against a specific policy, followed by an interpretive analysis of

Selecting Interviewees

Given the large number of schools on the closure list, I focused my selection of interviews on members and/or supporters of schools that varied based on level of organization and outcome. For example, if a community meeting had relatively low attendance from one school, when compared to that of another school, I would select members from both – the low attendance and high attendance school – and then follow their outcomes. In addition, if one school evaded closure, while another school was closed, I asked members from both schools' questions about their perceptions of participation and political efficacy.

While members of schools threatened for closure were the primary persons selected for interviews, I used a combination of snowball sampling and purposeful selection to ensure variation among them. When using snowball sampling, no more than three people were interviewed per referral to reduce self-selection issues. In addition to personal referrals, parents and elites were identified at community meetings and asked to be interviewed either at the meeting site or at a future date, based on their preference. Semi-structured interviews with parents, community members, and elites lasted between twenty-five minutes to an hour.

Altogether, I collected transcripts of community responses from sixty meetings produced by the school districts in Chicago and Philadelphia. I attended twenty-four of these meetings in person (for sample coding of meetings see supporting information). Both during and after these meetings, I interviewed, recorded and transcribed 100 interviews with parents/community members and elites (i.e., local activists and district officials) in Chicago and Philadelphia.[5] With these data, I examine how those targeted for closure participate in the policy process, and their interpretations of its political consequences. Table 3.1

citizens' perceptions of the impacts of their participation. Qualitative interviews are most useful for understanding how citizens articulate their own experiences (Mettler & Soss, 2004; Walsh, 2012). Although surveys facilitate the ability to generalize from findings, and to some extent to determine causality, they rarely ask in-depth questions about policy experiences. In addition, because of my interest in examining community meetings as sites of political learning, ethnographic observations of community meetings were optimal for investigating community members' experiences with the school closure process and their interpretations of its impacts.

[5] Twenty-five parents/community members and twenty-five elites in Chicago; twenty-five parents/community members and twenty-five elites in Philadelphia.

summarizes the sample, approach, selection criteria, and purpose (see the Appendix for more info).[6]

Coding for Mobilization

To start, I coded the data collected into a set of categories based on the themes in existing literature on participation that includes resources (i.e., time, money), group cohesion, and political trust (for examples, see Miles & Huberman, 1994; Emerson, Fretz, & Shaw, 1995; Skogan & Hartnett, 1997). Based on observed patterns and themes that emerged in early interviews, I then re-coded them into an expanded and more refined set of categories that identified how parents, community residents, and elites described what enabled their participation (and what acted as a barrier to their participation). In addition to the shared target identity described above, the responses for what enabled their participation could be categorized into the theme of "resources" including transportation, meetings and civic partners.[7] One school administrator in Philadelphia, for example, said that the school had only three community organization partners prior to the closure announcement, but that number more than quadrupled after the school was put on the list of schools threatened for closure. In fact, across all neighborhoods examined except one,[8] the announcement of a potential closure contributed to an increase in the number of community partners available to assist in the fight against closure.

Additionally, the school district provided resources in the form of access to public officials through meetings that took place in the communities affected by closure. Prior to these meetings, parents made references to the "poor timing" of school-related events by the district, particularly for those who had to work double shifts at their places of employment. Furthermore, when meetings were not clearly within walking distance,

---

[6] From 2016 to 2017, I returned to both Philadelphia and Chicago and reinterviewed nearly one third of my original interlocutors, whom I had interviewed between 2012 and 2015. My aim was to document whether their perceptions had changed. From 2016 to 2017, I also interviewed other parents and community members who had been a part of the fight to save schools in 2013 but whom I had not interviewed earlier.

[7] I categorized both parents, school officials, and political bureaucrats by similar codes, when applicable, to examine how each group responded to the same set of issues.

[8] The work samples communities across fourteen neighborhoods in Chicago and eleven in Philadelphia. These neighborhoods largely represent those areas facing the threat of closure. Please note that all names are pseudonyms to ensure privacy unless otherwise noted.

Table 3.1. Number of participants, method, selection criteria, and purpose

Year(s) of Study	Number	Method	Selection Criteria	Purpose
2012–2015	60 meetings in total (attended or read transcripts): 28 *in Chicago* 32 *in Philadelphia*	Observed community meetings	Attended 24 meetings in person to capture a range of turnout and outcome possibilities (e.g., schools with low turnout *and* others with high turnout at meetings; schools that evaded round one of closure *and* schools that did not)	Learn how meetings operated and observe citizens' experiences with participation
	50 people in total: 25 *in Chicago* 25 *in Philadelphia*	Interviewed district and community leaders (elites)	Identified at community meetings and contacted via email	Identify methods used to encourage citizens to participate in the closure process and examine perceptions of the utility of participation
	50 people in total: 25 *in Chicago* 25 *in Philadelphia*	Interviewed parents and community members	No more than three people per referral	Investigate citizens' experiences with participation and perception of politics (e.g., efficacy)
2016–2017	26 people in total: 12 *in Chicago* 14 *in Philadelphia*	Reinterviewed parents and community members	Representative sample based on outcomes of meetings (closed vs. saved schools)	Investigate how citizens' perceptions of their participation may have changed (or not)
	6* people	Interviewed parents and community members who did not participate initially	Referral	Gathered perceptions of those who did not participate in the process

parents and community members raised issue with transportation options available to them. Yet, the advent of school closure facilitates new partnerships with community organizations and the provision of resources by the school district, which helped community members overcome traditional barriers to participation and engage in the policy process.

Providing Resources to Participate in the Policy Process

In both Chicago and Philadelphia, laws mandated a ninety-day window between the announcement of a school closure and the closing of a school building/program. These laws require public input on school closure decisions.[9] To facilitate public input, CPS developed an Office of Family and Community Engagement that appointed local officers across their fourteen established school networks. In addition, CPS developed a community engagement process and provided space, transportation, and financial support to encourage participation at community meetings and public hearings.

The School District of Philadelphia also developed a process "that provided multiple opportunities for public comment," in addition, "the mayor's chief education advisor hired a staffer whose focus [was] on community outreach" (Cucchiara, Gold, & Simon, 2011, p. 297) and developed an Office of Family and Community Engagement. District officials from this office reached out to community groups and residents nearly two years in advance of the final decision and created additional opportunities for students, school administrators, and community leaders to discuss alternative options in more intimate settings than the community meetings. As one of the teachers who held a leadership role in the campaign to save University City High School summarized, "to show the district was listening, they arranged a meeting with students and the deputy superintendent, I think, to discuss what options there were" (interview, West Philadelphia, Philadelphia, October 27, 2014). It became clear to community members that the district wanted to be perceived as responsive, due to their mandate, and,

---

[9] These mandate laws were reforms passed between 2010 and 2012 because of public demand. For Chicago, see, for example, "(105 ILCS 5/) School Code," Illinois General Assembly, http://ilga.gov/legislation/ilcs/ilcs4.asp?DocName=010500050HArt.+34& ActID=1005&ChapterID=17&SeqStart=184700000&SeqEnd=209000000; for the Pennsylvania law, see www.education.pa.gov/Documents/K-12/Safe%20Schools/Chapter% 2010%2042%20PaB%204574.pdf.

thus, provided resources to enable their participation. And indeed, these resources likely contributed to the participation of groups that typically are associated with low participation, particularly in the available school closure meetings (Bobo & Gilliam, 1990).

Across Philadelphia and Chicago, a record number of persons attended school closure meetings across their respective cities. In fact, many attended school closure meetings regardless of whether the policy directly or indirectly affected them, contributing to a united front in working to save all schools. This collective strategy was especially clear with Latinx citizens, who faced only one tenth of the closures and yet participated at similarly high levels and exhibited similarly high opposition to the policy as Blacks (Nuamah, 2019a). Chapter 1 makes clear that this shared perception of being a target of closure, particularly based on race, widened the pool of people who could participate in the process made available by the school districts. In the end, participation in community meetings related to closure ranged between 500 and 800 people (totaling about 30,000) in Chicago and between 200 and 500 (totaling about 5,000) in Philadelphia.

Learning Civic Engagement

Raising Awareness

From 2012 to 2015, I found that parents were not only active in the fight against closures but also that their participation in the fight enabled them to develop and strengthen their civic skills throughout the process. For those parents and community members that did participate, many got their first taste of civic engagement, initially in learning about the policy process and then in participating in it. For example, community organizations such as the Kenwood-Oakland Community Organization of Chicago (KOCO), which led the fight to reopen Dyett High School, and Parents United of Philadelphia began organizing affected citizens as soon as the list of schools targeted for closure was released in 2012. As one parent activist in Philadelphia explained, "here is the thing: Most of them didn't realize the school was up to be closed – and we rallied on the school steps and then people would come up and sign up" (interview, West Philadelphia, Philadelphia, February 18, 2015). Another teacher activist added, "you know, the average person doesn't really understand the fight. And so ... we have to make the story important to them so that we can have momentum" (interview, South Philadelphia, Philadelphia, March 4, 2015). After parents and the wider community were notified, usually through the school or a community group, they became part of the process. A parent in Philadelphia stated, "we found out at first there were threats ... and they were calling these meetings about the school and that was the first warning sign ... Then the letters came, then you would go to these meetings, call your politicians, write letters, do this and do that" (interview, South Philadelphia, Philadelphia, March 4, 2015).

The next step was typically for community organizers, including union leaders, to mobilize the local media to raise public awareness of potential school closures and the activities to protest them. A parent activist explained: "We had a meeting ... The radio stations were there ... a bunch of people ... a lot of community leaders ... Everybody came in. They agreed to give us three hours to talk about the Philadelphia situation with the school system" (interview, North Philadelphia, Philadelphia, January 23, 2015). Ultimately, the goal of these community organization efforts was to help parents and community members understand the importance of investment in the school closure issue before moving to help them defend against the closure of their schools (Cohen et al., 2018).

School Meeting Participation

Public meetings allowed community organizations discrete mechanisms to generate engagement among resource-poor groups, specifically. Resource-poor citizens needed to learn how to make a "good" argument so that they could save their school. As an organizer against the closure of University City High School in Philadelphia explained: "When people are at the mic and must present an argument, it's a learning experience. You have to figure out how do you get a response" (interview, West Philadelphia, Philadelphia, October 27, 2014). Getting a positive response from school officials was a central goal that community organizers conveyed to participants, especially parents. Participants also had to adhere to guidelines provided by school districts regarding how they should present their case. Because of their desire to keep their schools open, participants, many of them parents with limited civic engagement experience, willingly learned and implemented these strategies.

Most of the strategies taught to participants focused on the use of surveys and quantitative data. For example, I saw firsthand in

Chicago how participants' statements about school closings evolved over the process, from initially emotional responses – "I'm not a great speaker, but all I have to say is please don't close our school" (interview, Englewood-Gresham, Chicago, February 2, 2013) – to responses that used data particular to that school: "We have established a very strong and safe and supportive school environment, according to your My Voice/My School Survey" (interview, Englewood-Gresham, Chicago, February 18, 2013). As one parent observed, "you have to fight facts with facts. You can't just go up there saying anything" (interview, West Philadelphia, Philadelphia, October 27, 2014). Once the data piece was in place, parents could back the data with examples of personal experiences and the experiences of others. As a Philadelphian participant in the effort to save Beeber Elementary stated,

> we took those lessons from seeing [others] keep their school open … seeing some schools that were having traction … If I didn't go to some of the facility master plan meetings, I was watching it on livestream … But I went to all the West Philly meetings, I went to the North Philly meetings, because I really wanted to understand the complexities and the issues, and seeing how the district was handling that. And so, I think that gave us a lot of foundation, in terms of coming up with our strategy (interview, West Philadelphia, Philadelphia, November 13, 2014).[10]

Parents learned skills not only from participating themselves but also from watching how others faced the threat of school closure. And indeed, this strategy appeared to work. As stated by a parent in Philadelphia, "we went down to rallies, we blocked traffic, went to the SRC [meetings], marched to the school, what didn't we do?" Parents likely participated because there were already mechanisms available, such as community meetings, that organizations could use to get them engaged in the policy process. In sum, armed with a combination of data, personal experiences, and support from local community organizations, affected citizens participate in the process, whether in person or "on livestream," and fight to save their schools.

---

[10] This date reflects when I accessed the interview, not when it was conducted.

Does Participation in School Meetings Lead to Participation in Formal Politics?

While my analysis thus far suggests that the school district, the union, and community organizations provided citizens with the resources to participate and the civic skills to do so, it is unclear if that participation was limited to school-based community meetings, as opposed to traditional forms of electoral participation. To answer this question, for the second part of the investigation I use quantitative data from three sources cited in Chapter 2: the CCES, which includes data in the form of respondents' zip codes and questions about political participation and local government performance; a new data set, the Chicago Democracy Project, based on precinct-level results from the Chicago Board of Elections that is joined to census data that ties demography to electoral outcomes; and an original data set of schools closed in Chicago in 2012 and 2013. These data are used to compare changes in political behavior before and after the wave of 2012–2013 closures across areas of Chicago that either did or did not experience closures.[11] (See Table 3.2 and the Appendix for more details.)

Aggregate Data Set Construction

To create a small–area aggregate election and demographic data set, official data from the Chicago Board of Elections and US Census Bureau was used.[12] Because Chicago changed its electoral map just before the 2015 elections, thus changing most precinct boundaries, the over-time comparisons in this book rely on estimates of "precinct fragment" areas, created by a GIS intersect function of the

---

[11] These data (which are geo-coded using their addresses) are used to construct two measures of community-based experiences with public school closures in Chicago. For CCES analyses, I, along with Thomas Ogorzalek (director of the Chicago Democracy Project and political scientist at Northwestern University), link the schools' zip codes to respondents to estimate whether a respondent lives in a zip code with at least one closure. For electoral results analyses, we calculate the distance from the centroid of an electoral precinct to the nearest closed school. These measures allow us to analyze the concentrated geographic effects at the lowest level possible given the available data. Table 3.2 summarizes which data and measures we use in the analyses.

[12] Because of administrative incompatibility and change, these data require some processing for use in comparisons.

Table 3.2. Data sources for analyses

Data Sources	Year	Unit	Measure of Proximity to Closure	Measure of Participation	Measure of Attitude
CCEs	2010	Individual	zip co-location	Meeting attendance	n/a
	2014	Individual	zip co-location	Meeting attendance	n/a
	2016	Individual	zip co-location	n/a	School and mayor evaluations
Elections	2011	Precinct	Distance to closure	Turnout	Emanuel vote share
	2012	Precinct	Distance to closure	Ballot measure mobilization	n/a
	2015	Precinct	Distance to closure	Turnout, measure mobilization	Emanuel vote share

2013, 2014, and 2015 maps. Because these measures are in percentages, the electoral calculations are relatively straightforward: Each fragment is assigned the relevant percentage value from its precinct in each year.[13]

For demographic estimates, the analyses relied on five-year estimates from the 2014 American Community Survey. Because census geography and electoral precincts do not match, estimating precinct demography involves some data processing. To make these estimates, we collected ACS data for Block Groups (BGs) and used a GIS intersect function with the precinct-fragment map described in the previous section to create a new terrain of block-group-precinct fragments across the city. The ACS count for each measure (e.g., total population, or non-Hispanic White persons) was divided among each BG's fragments according to its proportion of the BG's overall area. After, these

---

[13] For precincts that did not change, the measurement and interpretation is clear. For precincts that did change, there is a modest risk of measurement error. The underlying logic holds as long as precincts are internally homogeneous in their behavior. A reasonable assumption for units of about 550 voters, on average.

proportionate counts were added up according to which precinct they were in, and the estimated percentages (e.g., percent non-Hispanic White) were created based on these newly estimated precinct counts.[14] For crime data, we relied on crime incident report data sets made available by the Chicago Police Department, which include point-level shape files. We include only felony incidents in our data and aggregate up by precinct-fragment within each year to calculate the estimates of local change between 2011 and 2015. These data are used as controls in some aggregate-level analyses. Using these data allows for an analysis of the relationship between proximity to closure and political participation.

Attendance at Political Meetings

First, this chapter investigates participation in political meetings by Blacks. The analysis reveals that the difference between Black respondents in and out of school closure areas is particularly key in identifying the role of closures in fostering participation.[15] Meeting attendance among Blacks who did *not* reside in closure areas declined after the closures, while attendance by non-Black Chicagoans stayed the same and Black residents of closure areas increased. The difference in changed probability of meeting attendance between Black respondents in and out of closure areas is approximately 10 percentage points.

Most significantly, before the school closure wave (2010), Blacks in closure areas were very unlikely to attend a political meeting, but after (2014) they were the most likely group.[16] In fact, before 2013 nearly 80 percent of closure-area residents, as well as most Blacks in Chicago, did not participate in *any* political actions asked

---

[14] Again, the key underlying assumption of this procedure is that persons in the categories of interest are evenly distributed within the BG. Because BGs are small (less than half a square mile on average in Chicago), the error potentially introduced by this procedure is outweighed by the advantage of being able to compare election results to demographic characteristics.

[15] Using a difference-in-difference analysis (in which school closures are the quasi-treatment), the net difference in change between Blacks within zip codes with closures and those within zip codes without closures is statistically significant at P < .05; the results are robust when accounting for other likely factors such as other participation, family income, education, and political interest (see the Appendix for these full results).

[16] However, intense participation, including meeting attendance, is not *particularly* common among any of the groups.

about in the CCES.[17] However, during and after the closure wave, Blacks became more likely to participate and non-Black Chicagoans became less likely to. In sum, during and after the closure process, overall political participation (defined, in this case, as political meetings) increased substantially among Blacks in areas with closures (Figure 3.1).[18]

Advocating for an Elected School Board

In addition to increased engagement in political meetings, affected citizens also demonstrate support for a nonbinding ballot measure advocating for an elected school board. This measure was proposed twice, in similar though not identical form, in 2012 and 2015 (Figure 3.2). Because of technicalities in Chicago's ballot rules, measures were not on the ballot across the entire city (signatures must be collected separately in each precinct to get the measure on the ballot). This procedural hitch makes analysis slightly trickier because we cannot just compare support for the measure before and after as it was not on the ballot in the same place. However, it affords an extra opportunity to gain analytical leverage because of the observed patterns in where the measure was considered may suggest that simply getting it on the ballot may be interpreted as a sign of sophisticated, organized reaction against school closure policy.

The locations in which these measures appeared on the ballot are shown in the maps in Figure 3.2. The areas of the city with the measure on the ballot increased and shifted, covering more of the city in 2015 than 2012 (1,489 precincts in 2015 as opposed to 327 in 2012) and including much more of the South Side, one of the areas where closings were concentrated. For the most part, these same areas on the South Side did not have the measure on the ballot in 2012. Yet, not only was the measure on the ballot in 2015 at a high rate, but support for the

---

[17] Note that the most common measure of political participation, self-reported voter turnout, is not among the measures included here. The levels of turnout reported by survey respondents was extremely high (over 80 percent in 2014) and is discussed later in the book.

[18] Again, participation declined among Black respondents from non-closure areas.

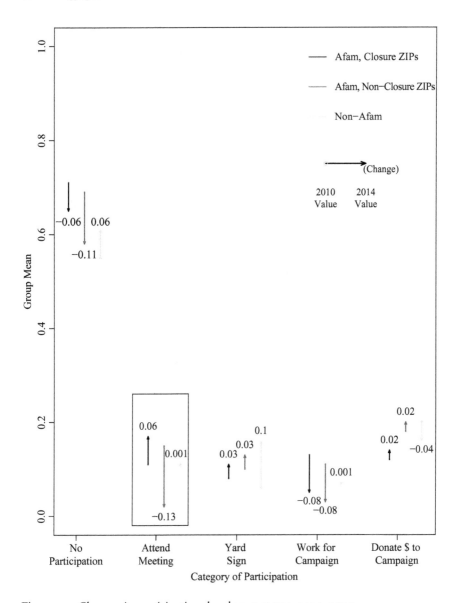

Figure 3.1 Changes in participation, by closure status, 2010–2014

measure where it was on the ballot was very high, ranging from 83 to 93 percent. Because of these two facts, the biggest change in the ballot measure vote was getting the measure on the ballot (referred to as "listing"): Many communities where the school board measure did

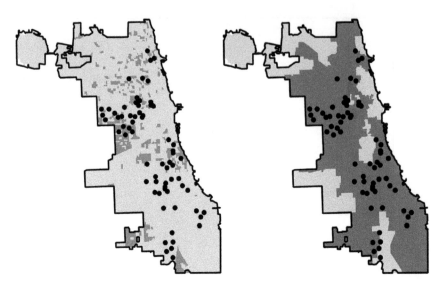

Figure 3.2 Precincts that voted in 2012 versus 2015

not seem important enough to consider in 2012 seem to have become more interested in the idea by 2015, after the mass closure of schools.[19]

In a given precinct, there are four possible patterns of ballot measure listing across 2012–2015 (Table 3.3). *Mobilizing* precincts did not have the ballot measure in 2012 but did have it in 2015 (most of the South Side is like this on the map). *Demobilizing* precincts had it on the ballot in 2012 but not in 2015, indicating a falloff in mobilization on the issue over time (see the far Northwest Side). *Always mobilized* precincts had it on the ballot in both years, indicating a higher level of interest in the first place, which was sustained (these precincts are mostly on the near Northwest Side). *Never mobilized* precincts did not have it on the ballot in either year, indicating low levels of mobilization in both years (the small areas near downtown fit this description).

Table 3.3 shows the relationship between ballot measure mobilization and proximity to school closures. The columns reflect a three-part division of the distance between a precinct and the nearest closed school: the closest third, middle third, and farthest third.

---

[19] This conclusion is supported when we compare whether precincts had the measure in each cycle.

Table 3.3. Total precinct fragments and percentages in each ballot measure category

Precinct Type	Total N	Near Closures (%)	Middle Distance (%)	Far from Closure (%)
Mobilizing	2,647	76.0	70.1	48.5
Demobilizing	63	1.4	1.6	1.7
Always mobilized	433	14.2	8.9	8.9
Never mobilized	923	8.4	18.8	41.0

Note: Proximity categories are top third, middle third, and bottom third of distance between precinct fragment centroid and nearest school closure.

Among the precincts nearest a closed school (the closest third), 76 percent were mobilizing precincts, meaning they added the measure to the ballot in 2015 after schools closed, and only 8 percent did not mobilize to put the measure on the ballot; among those farthest from a closure (the furthest third), only 48.5 percent were mobilizing, and 41 percent did not mobilize to put the measure on the ballot. This is a difference of nearly 20 percent when compared with areas closer to closures. In short: Those areas closest to where schools closed were nearly twice more likely to mobilize for an elected school board than those further away.

In an analysis of precincts that did not have the 2012 ballot measure, an additional mile of distance from a school closure is associated with an approximately 7 percent decrease in the likelihood that the precinct added the measure to the ballot by 2015. This finding holds even when accounting for precinct-level demographic measures including crime rates, poverty, and school populations. In other words, proximity to a school closure is positively associated with mobilizing to place an elected school board measure on the ballot in 2015 (Figure 3.3).

Mayoral Vote

In the final analysis, we turn to changes in mayoral elections. In addition to increased mobilization on school policy, the previous chapter demonstrates that voters experiencing school closures will decrease their support for the elected official with authority over the decision. In this case, Mayor Emanuel was elected in 2011 just before the closures

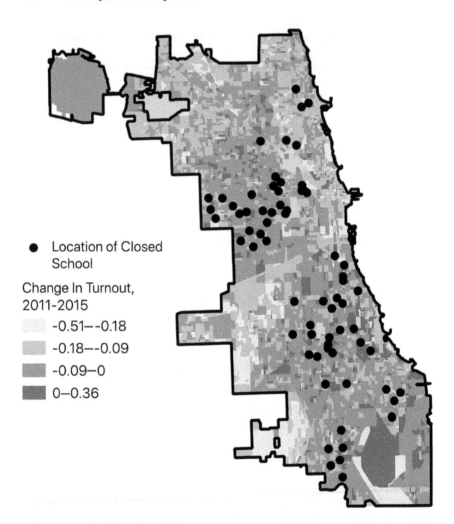

Figure 3.3 School closures and change in voter support for Rahm Emanuel, 2011–2015

and ran for reelection in 2015, just after the closures. As in the analysis of school board referenda, this before-and-after timing gives leverage for analysis. Unlike the school board referenda, Emanuel was on the ballot in every precinct in both elections. Figure 3.4 shows the location of school closures (represented as small triangles) and the change in support for Emanuel by precinct fragment from 2011 to 2015 (represented by shades of gray, with darker shades representing bigger decreases in support). This figure shows an apparent association between school closures and change in support for Emanuel in those two elections. Broadly, we can see that the relationship between

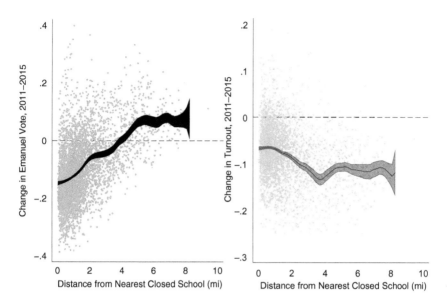

Figure 3.4 Location of school closures and the change in support for Rahm Emanuel, by precinct fragment, 2011–2015

distance and change in support for Emanuel appears to be strong, and that there is a small negative relationship between distance from a closed school and change in turnout.

While Emanuel's support fell in nearly every part of the city, the models show that Emanuel's change in support was larger nearer to school closures – his support declined about 13–16 percentage points more in precincts that were very near a closing than in similar precincts five miles away. Further, there was about a 1 percent greater decline in turnout for each mile from a school closure (Table 3.4). These twinned findings – that Emanuel's support fell more and turnout declined less near closed schools – provide support for the notion that citizens broadly impacted by the threat of closures translate their school level participation to formal political participation.

Did School Closures Positively Impact Civic Skills *and* Engagement?

Ultimately, after the unprecedented wave of school closings in 2013, several changes took place: Affected citizens' attendance at political meetings increased, they acquired civic skills, areas near closed

Table 3.4. Election changes in participation by race and distance to school closure, 2011–2015

	TO, Feb NW	TO, Feb	TO, Apr	RE, Feb NW	RE, Feb	RE, Apr
Miles to Closure	-0.014***	-0.005***	-0.009***	0.018***	0.026***	0.033***
	(0.00)	(0/oo)	(0.00)	(0.00)	(0.00)	(0.00)
% Black	0.022***	0.030***	-0.029***	-0.074***	-0.063***	-0.027***
	(0.01)	(0.00)	(0.00)	(0.01)	(0.01)	(0.01)
% Hispanic	0.027***	0.037***	0.048***	0.076***	0.066***	-0.118***
	(0.01) (0.00)	(0.00)	(0.00)	(0.01)	(0.01)	(0.01)
% Schoolkid		0.015	-0.023		0.035	0.051*
		(0.02)	(0.02)		(0.02)	(0.02)
HH MedInc		-0.000	0.000		0.000	0.000
		(0.00)	(0.00)		(0.00)	(0.00)
% in Poverty		0.027**	0.025**		0.005	0.031*
		(0.01)	(0.01)		(0.01)	(0.01)
% Renter		0.043***	0.019		-0.093***	-0.159***
		(0.01)	(0.01)		(0.02)	(0.02)
N	3,437	4,892	4,896	3,437	4,892	4,896
R-Sqr	0.050	0.109	0.108	0.343	0.377	0.296

Note: * $p < 0.05$, ** $p < 0.01$, *** $p < 0.001$

schools were more likely to mobilize for a ballot measure designed to support an elected school board, voter turnout increased slightly with proximity to a closure, and support for the incumbent mayor's reelection bid fell substantially in those same areas.

More broadly, the school districts in Chicago and Philadelphia agreed to several concessions by the end of 2013 including the removal from the closure list of high-performing schools (sometimes known as performance level 1 schools) and schools that had recently experienced a school action, such as consolidation. In Chicago, all high schools were also removed from the closure list, and in Philadelphia, a one-year moratorium on school closures or actions was passed via a city council vote of 14 to 2 (Limm, 2013) As one community organizer from Philadelphia explained:

> We thought it was a victory of sorts that the number of schools was descaled, and the year after they didn't close any. We felt it was because of us. The fact they didn't close any last year was a significant victory in the previous year (interview, North Philadelphia, Philadelphia, October 22, 2014).

In 2014, then CEO of CPS, Barbara Byrd-Bennett, also announced a moratorium that would limit the school district's ability to close schools over the next five years (Chicago Public Schools, 2014). Outside of the moratorium, the greatest triumph was that, in both Chicago and Philadelphia, some schools were saved from being closed: The 2013 school closure list in Chicago, which began at 330 schools, was reduced to 129 and finally narrowed down to 49, and the school closure list in Philadelphia, which began at 60, was reduced to approximately 40 and finally narrowed down to 24.[20] These reductions were presumably, at least partially, the result of evidence presented by parents and community members at school closure meetings.

The Efficacy of Participation

Parents, community members, and school staff members participated, in part, because they thought they could succeed at saving

---

[20] Some sources note the total number of schools closed in Philadelphia as 23. See, for example, John Hurdle, "Philadelphia officials vote to close 23 schools" *New York Times*, March 7, 2013, www.nytimes.com/2013/03/08/education/philadelphia-officials-vote-to-close-23-schools.html.

their schools. As one parent from Philadelphia's University City High School, which was not removed from the closure list and shuttered in 2013, stated, "it was a good lesson in civic engagement, but we weren't just fighting just because – we thought we could win" (interview, West Philadelphia, Philadelphia, October 27, 2014). The perception that one or they can impact the political process and that it is worthwhile to get involved (Campbell, Gurin, & Miller, 1954), known as *political efficacy*, is a fundamental component to overcoming the barriers faced by low-resource communities targeted by school closures. Political science literature has examined both *internal efficacy* (the extent to which citizens believe they have the capacity to influence the political process) and *external efficacy* (the extent to which citizens believe the government is responsive to their needs) over the decades (see, e.g., Lane, 1959; Craig & Maggiotto, 1982; Finkel, 1985; Niemi, Craig, & Mattei, 1991; Soss, 1999). The levels of political efficacy among different populations are often structured by their encounters with public policies, such as Social Security Disability Insurance and Aid to Families with Dependent Children (Schneider & Ingram, 1993; Soss, 1999; Mettler, 2007; Lerman & Weaver, 2014; Soss & Weaver, 2017; Bruch & Soss, 2018). The aforementioned findings also suggest that efficacy can be fueled by the victories secured from other closure meetings.

Indeed, efficacy can be fueled when parents and community members who are successful in their efforts support those fighting for other schools by passing along the strategies that worked for them. For example, when I asked how parents of students at Beeber Elementary in Philadelphia succeeded in initially keeping their school open, one parent responded, "we became a committee to stop the closing. We formed a committee to come together, and [after our success], we were able to save almost all the schools" (interview, West Philadelphia, Philadelphia, February 18, 2015). Parents and community members that witnessed other schools come off the closure list or a school district declare a temporary moratorium on school closures were initially encouraged to keep fighting for their schools to remain open.

Efficacy can also be inspired by the example of others who step up. Perhaps the most notable example of this is the case of then nine-year-old Asean Johnson, who in 2013 led the fight against closing Marcus Garvey Elementary in Chicago. Johnson, who was often referred to as "little Barack," became the center of the school closure debate when he began giving speeches across the state attacking CPS and Mayor Rahm Emanuel. Johnson was backed by multiple community groups, the Chicago Teachers Union, and, not surprisingly, his mother. When his school was saved from being shut down, Johnson became a compelling example of the power and value of political action (Clark, 2013). The experience provided Johnson with civic engagement skills he can use in the future to participate in other issues, and his success likely acted as an impetus for members of his community to become or continue to be active and involved.

In 2015, for example, I asked a group of parents if there was utility in participating in a school-related community meeting. Most answered yes, even if they themselves did not participate in the effort to stop the closings in 2013. As one parent stated, "if they had not done that, you can look at how many schools would have been closed" (interview, Northwest Philadelphia, Philadelphia, April 20, 2015). Most parents I interviewed at that time seemed to believe that they had the ability to make a difference if they tried. Another parent stated, "I believe there is something you can do if you do the work ... The support you need is out there. You just have to know where to go and what to do, but it's out there" (interview, Northwest Philadelphia, Philadelphia, April 20, 2015). In fact, even some school board members could see that many parents believed they could make a difference. As one school board member in Philadelphia stated, "parents go [to the closure meetings] thinking they are going to get through to someone" (interview, school board member, Philadelphia, November 12, 2014). While it is unclear whether these same parents had a sense of political efficacy before participating in the school closure process, these statements strongly suggest that many parents possessed a fair level of internal efficacy during and immediately after. It appears then, *at least in the short term*, that, even in a community whose members do not have many opportunities to be directly heard by policy makers, efficacy and civic skills can be fueled.

These findings, as I present them in this chapter, would seem to suggest that closures provided a perverse incentive to participate that worked because closures were followed by record levels of participation, increased political efficacy and civic skills. Further, the political participation of affected citizens resulted in some schools being saved from closure, and at least in the case of one school, Dyett, even reopened. Yet, it is important note that although the 2012–2013 school-closure process may have taught parents some positive lessons and led to record participation, several of the parents interviewed – even those parents who succeeded in defending their children's schools from closure – expressed a disinterest in continuing to participate in education-related actions thereafter, between 2016 and 2017.

If community members affected by closure had the civic skills and internal efficacy to participate (and in some cases saved their schools), why did they have such negative attitudes toward future participation? Chapter 4, the final empirical chapter, answers this question.

4 WHO WINS AND WHO LOSES IN THE ERA OF MASS SCHOOL CLOSURES
Toward a Theory of Collective Participatory Debt

Let us circle back to the beginning of this book to learn more about how Leanne Woods and her community fared in their fight to save Steel Elementary in Philadelphia in 2013. Once word got out that Mastery Charter planned to take over the school, nearly 200 parents organized themselves to contest the proposal and won the vote by 75 percent, forcing the superintendent, Dr. William Hite, to withdraw his proposal in its entirety. The parents, and the school community, won the battle to stop the school district from turning Steel into a charter yet to all involved in the fight to save traditional public schools, keeping Steel open was indeed a victory for them as well. Philadelphia parents, whom school board leaders had long viewed as "unwilling to show up," were vindicated.

Nonetheless, when I returned in 2017, things had changed at Steel. As Leanne informed me, before the closure threats the average tenure for teachers had been close to twenty years, and the principal had been there for eight years – a record in a district where principals are often replaced every three years. But by 2017, the school had a new principal who had no administrative experience and lost 80 percent of its original teaching staff. In turn, overall academic results had declined by 50 percent, and Steel was once again placed on a school action list, this time for schools that would be "turned around." One parent recalls the outcome as follows:

> After the vote, our principal was forced out ... and then the
> first year we lost 50 percent [of our teachers], ... we got a
> brand-new principal ... then the next year we lost another
> 30 percent [of our teachers] ... As soon as they made the
> announcement [that they were firing the principal], teachers
> left, so whether we won or not, we lost a lot of the
> teachers ... Teachers don't leave schools, they leave
> principals ... Once you broke up the family, the commitment
> wasn't there (interview, North Philadelphia, Philadelphia,
> February 2017).

In addition to losing their principal and teachers, the school lost their
parent community, which the school had heavily relied on. The
school subsequently struggled to rebuild that community while dealing with other challenges. As Leanne stated four years later in 2017,
"the problem is that we did not have the same connectivity ... and
this time I didn't have the same energy... this is not what we
fought for."

The Steel community is reflective of the many institutions
observed in my research that seemingly won their battles to remain
open and yet still felt a sense of loss as their efforts failed to materialize
as expected. In this chapter, I illustrate the anticlimactic nature of saving
a school and how it negatively shapes perceptions, not only of the policy
process but also of future participation.

I label the lack of interest in future participation as indicative
of what I call *collective participatory debt* (CPD) – a type of mobilization fatigue that transpires when citizens who are engaged in the
policy process are met with a lack of democratic transparency and
responsiveness, despite high levels of repeated participation. This
concept, which I explain in more detail later, recognizes that each
effort to participate in an unfair policy process is remembered by
those who engaged and believed in it to start. With each negative
experience, it becomes more difficult to justify future participation,
even when securing policy "wins" was successful. This is because
citizens' mistrust of government deepens based on how they are
treated during the process. They also experience mobilization

fatigue, precipitated by the recognition that what they have won "is not what [they] fought for."

But Even When We Win, We Lose?

This feeling of loss, following short-lived victories, is not new for Black Americans. In fact, it is the precise subject of Martin Luther King Jr.'s 1967 (2010) book, *Where Do We Go from Here: Chaos or Community*. The context was one in which some of the nation's most significant legislation had been passed only a few years before, and yet the tenor of the civil rights movement had changed from hope to despair.

Take, for example, the 1965 Voting Rights Act. When it was passed, the federal government promised that there would be – in King's words – "hundreds of registrars and thousands of federal marshals to inhibit southern terror" (1967, p. 35). Yet, as King himself acknowledged, "instead, fewer than sixty registrars were appointed and not a single federal law officer capable of making arrests went into the South. As a consequence, the old way of life ... continued unabated" (p. 35). The fate of the Voting Rights Act provides a historical, and parallel, example of the subject of this book: securing apparent victories, only to learn that they were not quite what was promised. This tension between promise and praxis forms the basis of CPD theory.

Collective Participatory Debt

In 2014, and again in 2017, I asked affected citizens to assess the benefits or disadvantages of their participation in the closure process. For example, did they feel that attending the meetings was valuable and/or that the meetings went as they had expected? Did they feel that policy makers were responsive? What did they learn from their experiences? Through these questions, I sought to understand their perceptions of the impacts of their participation, particularly related to the responsiveness of public administration.

In 2013–2014, as detailed in Chapter 3, affected citizens viewed their experiences through the civic skills they gained (e.g., learning how to make an effective argument). In addition, they expressed belief in

Table 4.1. Quotes on issue classification over two sets of interviews

	Sample Quotes
Interviews 2012/2015	
Civic Skills	You have to fight the facts with facts.
Internal Efficacy	They had to go back and change because of us.
Mistrust	I can't tell if ... these meetings are a sham.
Interviews 2016/2017	
Fatigue and Disillusionment	[We were] worn out.
Deepened Mistrust	I don't have any more trust in government.

Note: Data collected from original interviews.

their ability to get policy makers to respond to their concerns (internal efficacy) even though they maintained general negative perceptions of the policy process and policy makers.

From 2015 to 2017, I found that a few parents transformed into activists and formal political leaders. However, most people I talked to – surprisingly, many of those who had won the battle to save their school – were far less participatory and, in fact, were further disillusioned by the policy and political process. Many used the terms "fatigue," "tired," and "worn out" when answering my questions. Furthermore, citizens expressed a deepened distrust of the government; one Philadelphian stated that "[the school board] had to go back and change based on our actions, but [even so] I don't have any more faith in government" (interview, West Philadelphia, Philadelphia, April 2017). My findings from these later interviews appeared to show that the policy wins of affected participants did not necessarily contribute to positive attitudes toward government or future participation. Instead, their experiences appeared to do the opposite and contributed to what I call CPD, which combines the deepened distrust, fatigue, and disillusionment that results from negative experiences with high levels of participation in processes that essentially "have no bite on policy decisions" (Besley et al., 2005, p. 649).[1] See Table 4.1.

---

[1] For more on the coding process, see the Appendix.

Returning to the Steel case, the community ties that sparked the fight against the district later broke down, thus impacting future participation. As explained by another parent, "when you win, you want to walk away ... you want to win and go on with your life ... you don't want to win and be back ... you don't always want that pit in your stomach" (interview, Philadelphia, 2017). Parents who win the fight against closure expect that they will be able to leave the memory behind and work toward building the school they deserve, only to find that their participation did not result in the outcome they expected.

CPD is about realizing that the battle is unending. To put it differently, if the battle was succinct, I would venture that they may continue fighting. Yet, it is both the high cost and the notion that they must pay the cost again, potentially in perpetuity, that is untenable. Accordingly, when the next battle arises, parents choose acceptance over advocacy since they were never really given an opportunity to recover from the first round.

Indeed, this became the problem for Steel when it was placed on a school action list for a second time. The school district's use of similar austerity measures (e.g., firing the principal) prevented the parents and community members, who had fought for and saved Steel, from benefiting from their success. It also raised serious questions about the efficacy of their engagement. While these same parents have often been blamed for lack of participation in the past, what did their participation actually achieve this time around? And if the result is nothing but additional disinvestment, what is the utility of participation at all? Why does democratic theory hold participation as so important if those who win ultimately lose? Because for the Steel community, even though they won the battle to remain a district school in 2013–2014, they lost everything that enabled them to win in the first place, which they needed to fight the bigger battles that came in 2016–2017.

Steel is not alone in this. In many of the cases examined in this work, I find that the number of groups that once supported a school affected by closure dropped by almost half as they redirected their resources to new battles. In addition, the structure that the school district put in place (e.g., making school officials available to meet with community members and parents in their neighborhood via community meetings) was removed after the final closure list was established. Thus, the community's lower interest in participation after one school closure process was likely shaped by the fact that most of those affected by the policy no longer had access to the conditions that facilitated their participation in the first place. Read this way, one would expect a decreased interest in participation when the resources that facilitated engagement are reduced or removed.[2]

My observations make clear, however, that the removal of resources alone does not explain the lower interest in participation among those affected by closure. One must also account for affected participants' experiences with the actual policy process and their interpretations of its impacts. In the long term, the analysis reveals that affected citizens express a combination of deepened distrust, fatigue, and disillusionment with the policy process and future participation. I label these negative attitudes as indicative of CPD.

The source of this CPD is twofold: It begins with negative experiences with the policy process and is exacerbated by the lack of substantive policy response once the policy process concludes. More specifically, CPD accrues because of the nondemocratic way that participation is organized (e.g., overcrowded meetings, lack of language translators, strict two-minute time limits for each participant to speak to officials) and because of the nondemocratic responsiveness that results from that participation (e.g., a lack of preferred outcomes in the long term, and by short-lived victories). *My expectation is that, under any circumstances where marginalized citizens are repeatedly participating at a high level in the democratic process but failing to receive an adequate democratic response, CPD can result.*

Deepened Distrust

Regarding the school closure process, specific directives, such as dividing participants into separate rooms and sending them "here and there," contribute to negative feelings toward it. Data from both cities show that participants made similar claims about the closure process, stating that it sought to "isolate people ... separate them," in similar ways to *The Hunger Games* (community meeting, Pilsen-Little Village, Chicago, March 4, 2013).

---

[2] Research shows that both material incentives to participate in collective action and peer pressure play powerful roles in encouraging participation, even among individuals who would not typically participate (Leighley, 1996).

Despite these negative experiences, these same persons continued to participate in the process because they were hoping to "work together" to "not step on each other's toes" and save their schools (community meeting, Pilsen-Little Village, Chicago, March 4, 2013). What citizens eventually learn through their repeated participation in the community meeting process is that the undemocratic nature of the process contributes to a policy outcome that is also not democratic. For example, community members come to realize that even if they do save their school from closure, it will be at the expense of others, because there is no plausible reality under which *all* schools can be saved. In the words of one parent in Chicago: "The board is not asking whether [closing schools] is a valid option, they are asking which schools" (Austin-North Lawndale, Chicago, February 13, 2013). Consequently, participants learn that even if they "win" the battle to keep their school open, this will not ensure that they do "not step on each other's toes," as initially hoped. Evidence of this is best illustrated in the case of Philadelphia, two years after mass school closures:

PARENT: I think the people were in denial. They didn't know that this could possibly happen, so we all attended the meetings and went along and thought we would win, and it turned out we didn't win – we lost our school.

ME: But didn't many people save their schools?

PARENT: I don't think those people actually won. There was a number ... say it was 120; we are going to close 120, hypothetically speaking. Parents were outraged, so the district gave in and said that is too much to close at one time, so we will just close 100. So, they had to pick which 100, and they got that small margin of twenty, and it just happened to be [their] school.

ME: How are you so sure?

PARENT: Because they are not telling us the truth about the future of education. Just tell us the truth about education and what we need to actually do to save our schools ... What do we need to do? What is the real picture of the funding? ... Just tell the truth instead of having all of us fight over the limited resources (interview, Southwest Philadelphia, Philadelphia, March 4, 2015).

As illustrated in this interview, the key components of people's experiences with the process raise questions about the policy that were left unanswered by the district. These experiences confirm citizens' suspicions of the futility of their participation as they move from "denial ... that this could possibly happen" to attendance and a belief that they could win to, finally, a complete reevaluation of whether any schools had "actually won."[3]

Public hearings and community meetings on school closures are, in theory, offered by the government in order to solicit input on a specific policy issue. These forums are necessarily short term and are disbanded once a policy decision has been reached. They function in contrast to cases of deliberative democracy that are commonly cited, such as community beat meetings in Chicago or participatory budgeting exercises in Porto Alegre, Brazil, where ordinary citizen participation is a central and routine part of local government. According to Archon Fung and Erik Olin Wright (2003), empowered deliberative democracies have the following: "(1) a focus on specific, tangible problems, (2) involvement of ordinary people affected by these problems and officials close to them, and (3) the deliberative development of solutions to these problems" (p. 17). With participatory budgeting, for example, citizens have the power to vote for representatives and make decisions about where a certain amount of money is allocated. There is a focus on the equitable distribution of power between citizens and the government. With community meetings on school closures, citizens attend in order to defend a position in hopes of reversing a decision that has *already been made* by the state.

Accordingly, while school districts in both Philadelphia and Chicago claim that the meetings represent the "greatest source of community input" and that the input from the meetings will "inform recommendations that [they] make" (interview, school district leader, Chicago Public Schools, 2012), those affected learn that these meetings represent a type of democratic responsiveness in themselves: one in which accountability is measured simply through participation, rather than by the democratic outcome of that participation. In other words,

---

[3] In contrast to commonly cited examples of participatory budgeting (where citizens have the power to vote for representatives and make decisions about where a certain amount of money is allocated), community meetings on school closures exhibit an inequitable distribution of decision-making power between citizens and the government. In these meetings, citizens participate in a process where the impacts of their efforts are less clear.

"everyone gets an equal opportunity for input into a decision, not an equal opportunity for impact on a decision" (Polletta, 2012, p. 49). Ultimately, then, affected citizens determine that their policy "wins" do not reflect the type of democratic responsiveness they want the most: "The truth about the future of education ... and what [they] need to actually do to save [their] schools" rather than a "fight over the limited resources."

Fatigue and Disillusionment

Over time, it becomes more difficult for citizens to justify their participation, not only due to mistrust of the system but also due to mobilization fatigue, which leaves them disillusioned with the policy process. The feeling of fatigue is a critical, distinguishing aspect of CPD, because it recognizes that the poor likely pay a higher price (relative to high-resource individuals) for their repeated participation when there is little responsiveness from government.

Returning to the case of Beeber Elementary in Philadelphia, featured in Chapter 3, one parent explained why she stopped participating after successfully defending the school against closure:

> The parent involvement is like ... I think they were tired, we fought to ... keep the school open. It was one [school] right after the other ... It wore me out, it took me three months to get myself together[4] (interview, West Philadelphia, Philadelphia, February 18, 2015).

Another parent from the same school added, "and so now ... you say, we're spared ... [But] when the budget hit the fan ... it was like, whoa! So, now it's like we moved to the point where ... we are fatigued" (interview, West Philadelphia, Philadelphia, November 13, 2014). References to fatigue and disappointment continued as each year passed and long-term outcomes of their efforts failed to be realized. In the case of Beeber, although parents and community members were technically successful in defending their school against closure, the school district decided to colocate the school with a new independent school. Theoretically, the two schools would work together to improve Beeber's overall academic

---

[4] Parents who successfully fought to keep their children's school open made similar statements about being worn out.

performance, but, in the end, the school district decided to slowly integrate the two schools by phasing out Beeber. When I returned in 2017,
Beeber no longer existed, and the parents and community members
involved in the original battle were too exhausted to fight against
the decision.

Regarding the role of organizations, they also benefit from the
community meeting apparatus set up by the district because it is necessarily time constrained; there is a clear start and end time by which they
need to mobilize their resources to influence a policy outcome. Yet, once
that structure is removed, several community organizations remove
their support, because it is essentially ineffective to continue when
resources are constrained. The result is that community members stop
receiving as much support, at the point where they are most fatigued,
and therefore lessen their participation in the policy process as well.[5]

In summary, while many of those affected by the previous
actions now have the civic skills to fight against school closure policies,
as well as the internal belief that they can, many lacked the energy and
resources to do so the next time around, thereby contributing to their
CPD. The result is that many parents and community members do not
participate in new fights against school actions that arise, and the few
who do continue to fight report negative feelings toward the government and participation. As one parent in Philadelphia remarked at a
community meeting in West Philadelphia, "people were here, and they
were lied to. They are not going to keep coming out when they are being
lied to" (interview, West Philadelphia, Philadelphia, April 22, 2015).

The Damaging Effects of Being Targeted for Closure

The negative impacts of closures on children, their families, and
the surrounding community begin to take effect long before a school has
actually closed. As a CPS official who is involved in the closures explained,

---

[5] While Hahrie Han (2009, 2014) and others may view CPD as indicative of the difference
between organizers and mobilizers, of which the former builds power and the latter resists it,
it is also important to note that this work is based on observations of relatively well-
resourced organizations. In the contexts that I study, affected neighborhoods are dealing
with declining populations and perpetual disinvestment. As established in the literature on
neighborhood poverty, this has a direct impact on citizens' access to community
organizations and the capacity of community organizations to provide skills and services
(Alex-Assensoh, 1997, 2002). Accordingly, while I acknowledge and observe the potential
power of community organizations, I also acknowledge and observe their limits.

"the minute you tell a teacher that their school is closing in a year is the minute that school becomes unstable because teachers immediately begin looking for jobs ... and it becomes a chaotic school environment ... extended across a whole year ... You see a huge uptick in a need for substitute teachers" (interview, school district leader, Chicago Public Schools, 2015). Indeed, the period between announcement and closure contributes to vacated positions by teachers, due to the fear of job loss, and lower academic performance by students, due to the emotional trauma associated with losing their school (De la Torre & Gwynne, 2009; Deeds & Pattillo, 2015). These adverse effects are seen once a possible school closure is announced and last long after decisions are made.

Citizens learn this lesson not only through their experiences of school closures but also the closures of other institutional safety nets, such as hospitals. For example, in June 2019 the Tenet Healthcare Corporation announced that the Hahnemann University Hospital (HUH) of Drexel University in Philadelphia, which served a population made up of close to 70 percent Black and low-income individuals, would be closing within ninety days. Yet, within thirty days, the hospital had already begun to unravel. As stated by the department chair of emergency medicine, Richard Hamilton,

> [w]ithin a few days of the announcement, the Accreditation Council for Graduate Medical Education (ACGME) began the displacement process for 570 residents and fellows. Within a week, the owners filed for Chapter 11 protection. Unable to purchase supplies or retain key personnel such as cardiothoracic surgeons, HUH was designated as a trauma center and began to divert critical patients. Soon thereafter, ... inpatient volume declined so precipitously that little in the way of clinical education remained for the trainees. Within 24 days, anticipating unprecedented financial losses, [Drexel University College of Medicine] terminated all its clinical faculty (Hamilton, 2020, p. 494).

Despite an effort by Drexel University to halt the closure and various protests, the hospital had effectively closed before these efforts materialized. Therefore, even before being given the chance to save institutions from closure, the damage had already been done.

The case of one Chicago school illustrates this point well. After a five-year moratorium on school closings in Chicago was lifted, the school district proposed that another round of schools should be closed in 2018. The National Teachers Academy (NTA), an elementary school with an Black majority in the South Loop neighborhood, was one school impacted by the decision.[6]

The NTA was a high-performing (level 1) school that was formed partly due to discriminatory efforts that would not allow Black students the opportunity to attend South Loop Elementary School only a few blocks away from where they lived. NTA was placed on the closure list in 2018, not because of low performance or under-enrollment but because CPS wanted to build a high school for families in the South Loop and decided that NTA's location and building would be the best fit. After closing NTA as an elementary school, the district would allow current NTA students to attend South Loop Elementary, which they were previously barred from attending due to boundary changes.

NTA families protested the decision, attending all the meetings and fighting hard to oppose closure. Nonetheless, they technically lost the battle to stay open when it was voted that NTA would be phased out and integrated into the nearby elementary school that had a White majority.

The NTA, with the help of the Legal Assistance Foundation, filed a case with the state court to request an injunction on the basis that closing the school would be damaging to its students. The suit cited the fact that school closure has dramatic impacts on the emotional stability, academic achievement, and economic health of students and the surrounding community, leading to lasting negative impacts on socio-emotional health and long-term declines in academic performance (Gordon et al., 2018). In the end, the case of the NTA versus the CPS became the first in which a state court intervened in a school closure, by placing an injunction on the decision by the CPS. As of the writing of this book, the NTA remains open.

As with Steel Elementary, the NTA community fought for its school to remain open and won. Yet, like Steel, NTA parents and teachers admitted to the anticlimactic feeling of winning and then trying to get things back to normal. Teachers and staff had spent significant and valuable instructional/educational time fighting the decision to close. Once the school was saved, however, recruiting students to attend a school that was once targeted for closure became a difficult task.

---

[6] In full disclosure, I was involved in a legal case to impose an injunction on the closure of this school.

How do potential families know for sure that it is worth the effort to reinvest in the school? What if they end up in the exact same situation again – particularly when it seems the goal post keeps moving (e.g., low performance to under-enrollment) (Nuamah, 2019b). The NTA's case followed the trajectory of so many other schools that faced closure and fought to stay open. But not every school followed this path when put on a closure list.

Indeed, on the other side of the spectrum is the case of Jenner Elementary School, also in Chicago. In 2013, Jenner was threatened with closure by the CPS, due to low enrollment. While the school had the ability to serve almost 1,000 students, its enrollment had declined to only one third of its capacity. The community fought back, citing improved test scores and strong networks to evade the closure process, and won. However, the enrollment of the school continued to decline thereafter, in part due to parents' and teachers' fears that the school could be closed again and due to changing neighborhood patterns: The school was located a few blocks from the infamous Cabrini-Green housing projects that had been closed only a few years earlier, thereby contributing to dramatic population changes. Given that CPS schools are funded on a per-pupil basis, the low enrollment affected the school's ability to obtain the resources it needed to serve its students. At the same time, a nearby elementary school, Ogden, faced the exact opposite problem: over-enrollment. The school was less than a mile from Jenner but served a growing middle- and upper-class population moving into the area. Ogden did not have a way to serve all the families seeking to enroll their kids. However, potential Ogden families refused to enroll their kids at nearby Jenner despite its proximity.

In 2015, the principals of Ogden and Jenner decided to work together to determine possible resolutions to the dilemmas at their respective schools. Eventually, they came up with a proposal to merge both schools into a single school: JOLT (Jenner and Ogden Learning Together). The Jenner building would be used for the middle school (grades 5 to 8), and Ogden would be used for elementary and high school. The outcome would ensure Jenner remained open, provide Jenner students with a high-quality education, and allow Ogden to accept more students over the years. A steering committee that included both Jenner and Ogden community members was formed in 2016 and engaged the school and neighborhood community to determine the feasibility of a merger.

When the CPS announced another round of closures in 2018, the steering committee decided to propose the merger of Jenner and Ogden as an alternative to traditional closure, in which case Jenner would lose its building, and its students and staff would be sent to similar nearby schools. The CPS agreed to let the committee bring the proposal to the broader community via a series of meetings held in January 2018. The majority of those who participated appeared to be highly supportive of the merger. With the CPS' approval, the schools began to integrate in the fall of 2018.

At the time, it appeared that the Jenner community had figured out a way to hold off closure for the second time and actually improve its students' future experience – something that had not been accomplished by most previous schools that had "won" the fight against closure. Yet, a series of events – both unexpected and engineered – occurred to threaten the positive outcome. First, Jenner's principal, Robert Croston, who initiated the merger, passed suddenly before he could steer the process. Next, less than six months after the merger began, the principal of Ogden, Michael Beyer, who had taken leadership on the merger, was unexpectedly removed by the CPS. The CPS also stopped any evaluations or studies of the merger, thereby removing the ability to accurately gauge if the merger was effective. Therefore, it remains unclear whether this alternative to closure was any less damaging than the trauma many of Chicago's Black and Brown students had already endured.

A year after the merger, in June 2019, the interim principal of Ogden, Rebecca Bancroft, announced during the last week of school that she was also leaving, calling it a "fractured" community. Furthermore, contrary to what was expected, Jenner's name was never added to the school, students from Jenner were disciplined at twice the rate of students from Ogden, and the outspoken Jenner parents stopped coming to local school council meetings because they "got tired and overwhelmed" (Emanuel, 2019). The stories of both the NTA and Jenner/Ogden demonstrate how just the action of putting a school on a closure list can induce setbacks even if the school ultimately achieves the desired outcome of staying open. Once this occurs, the same persons that fought the hardest often become too tired and overwhelmed to fight again, contributing to the CPD of those communities. In the words of one parent that won the fight against closure, "I feel like we won the battle, but we lost the war" (interview, North Philadelphia, Philadelphia, November 2017).

"Failing" Public Schools

While many people are sympathetic to the stories I chronicle in this book, I know a key question always arises: Why are parents striving to hold on to schools that are "failing"? I have been asked this question often, mostly from those unaffected directly by the issue of public school closures. The short answer is best stated by Journey for Justice director and Dyett community organizer Jitu Brown: "We don't have failing schools, brothers and sisters, we have been failed."[7] The long answer follows.

Let us look at Steel Elementary again as an example. During the time of my research, the school was treated for mold while classes were in session. Nearly one third of the population was made up of foster children who required individualized education plans. It also lacked the resources it needed to serve its extremely disadvantaged population: "We have a teacher who for the past year or so has quietly been meeting with students to take their uniforms with her to wash ... because they don't have running water," a staff member informed me (interview, North Philadelphia, Philadelphia, 2015). The school had a nurse, librarian, or counselor present only once a week. And, not surprisingly, Steel students scored extremely low on their annual standards-based assessment tests (an 11 and then a 12 out of 100) during the time of my research.

On paper, these things appear to fit the criteria of a failing school, especially the latter fact, because schools are traditionally rated based on standardized test scores. But designating Steel as a school that is failing is indicative of the problem with the use of such terms, as it assumes a shared belief in a single way of measuring success by standardized test scores even in an environment where academics are competing regularly with students' needs for food, water, shelter, and heat (Ewing, 2018; Nuamah, 2019a).

During my time at Steel, many parents opted their children out of taking the standardized tests due to their belief in their ineffectiveness. "What our parents have learned over time is the [standardized test] is not a positive representation of our children's education ... You have 25 to 30 percent opt out, and that is the reason the score is down," a parent volunteer told me (interview, North Philadelphia, Philadelphia, November 2016). So, it is not surprising that the Steel community

---

[7] See Public Education Forum Speech, 2020 at http://schottfoundation.org/blog/2020/03/09/message-presidential-candidates-we-want-sustainable-community-schools.

questioned the entire notion of the term "failing" when, in their view, it was measured by tests that their students did not take. Instead, many Steel parents and staff members referenced the need to record growth as a measure of progress and cited purposes to education entirely different than scoring well on standardized tests. As one parent noted, "the purpose of education [is] to make better human beings ... We measure that with how we interact with others: Are you a whole, productive, and healthy being?" (interview, North Philadelphia, Philadelphia, November 2017). This definition of education, and its measurement, marks a stark contrast from the one currently used to evaluate schools.

The consistent reality is that schools such as Steel have never been given the required support to succeed in the first place. Therefore, when parents act to keep a public school open and develop a transition plan to improve it, they are fighting for the opportunity for their kids to finally get the resources they need. As Leanne Woods said to me, "we need stability ... we need to ensure that we have a safe school ... [We need a] curriculum that is socially relevant ... and to use adaptations of what is already there ... [we need] trauma-informed education ... To me that is what is important ... those are the things we are fighting for ... and need to be implemented district wide."

Because they continue to be deprived of these basic resources, schools such as the ones featured in this book have a difficult time putting the focus on academics. As one parent commented, recalling a meeting where parents were asked to raise and discuss topics to improve schools,

> school safety was first ... When we got through the whole list, someone had to remind us to talk about education and curriculum. Parents can't get to the point [of worrying] about education when they are worried about bullying, fights, bugs, safety, things that prevent education from happening ... We have to hold the education of our children as sacred ... We have to hold the fundamentals close to heart ... It's a moral way of looking at education ... We understand what human beings need, so don't measure my performance on how many times I get to school on time when I don't have heat at home or [when] I have to wake myself up at 8 a.m. [because] my mom works (interview, North Philadelphia, Philadelphia, November 2017).

This parent raises the important question of how to evaluate a school that lacks the necessary tools to ensure the fundamentals of human decency, for example, how much academics matter when kids do not have basics, such as heat. This connects to a moral problem of how children and their education are viewed. If a kid lacks many of life's basic necessities, is it not incumbent on democratic institutions to provide those first?

As discussed in recent work I conducted in collaboration with other scholars of school closure, the unprecedented closure of school buildings due to the COVID-19 pandemic has further revealed the role of schools in filling the gaping holes in America's social safety net: Closed school buildings result in a loss of routine childcare that makes going to work every day possible for the 11 million parents with school-aged children who live in poverty. For the nearly 1.5 million students experiencing homelessness, school closures remove an important source of stability and access to social workers and healthcare providers. For the 13 million children experiencing hunger, school closures disrupt a critical source of food that students rely on to maintain a nutritional diet.

To be sure, the fact that our most vulnerable communities are reliant on schools for meeting basic physical, social, and emotional needs makes clear that our social safety net is unable to mitigate the consequences of the escalating inequality in this country. Nonetheless, it also makes apparent that this is a role that schools play even now – and that they will continue to play when the most acute threat has passed. Accordingly, new threats to permanently close schools, especially in the face of post-pandemic budget cuts, should perhaps be confronted with an accurate understanding of what schools actually provide. Rather than an evaluation of schools with a narrow focus on academic performance, enrollment, or building capacity, which often perpetuates inequities, districts and the public should judge schools instead on their broader civic and social purposes (see Nuamah et al., 2020).

The Allure of Charter Schools

Based on the accounts in this book, it would appear that, in general, parents and communities feel strongly that public schools are essential to the betterment of students. However, if people do not want their traditional public schools to close, why are charter schools in such high demand? I think there are many reasons for this, most of which are related to neoliberalism (as discussed in the Introduction).

While schools have taken on more responsibility in recent years, they have also been increasingly subjected to neoliberal reforms – changes based on market principles – that intensify racial inequality. As mentioned in the Introduction, Lester Spence (2015) describes this shift as the *neoliberal turn*, and argues that these "neoliberal policies kill the welfare state," thus reproducing the need for them (Spence, 2015).

There is perhaps no better example of this neoliberal turn than the contemporary way that philanthropic organizations distribute funding for education. As stated by Margaret Kohn (2020) in her observations of public parks, "philanthropy often exacerbates inequality because it's not subject to democratic control" (p. 106). For instance, in a comprehensive investigation of the fifteen largest foundations in the United States, Sarah Reckhow and Jeffrey Snyder (2014) found that, between 2000 and 2010, "most major education foundations increasingly support[ed] jurisdictional challengers—organizations that compete with or offer alternatives to public sector institutions" (p. 187). The authors argue that this approach represented a shift from previous times when more funding was awarded to support the growth and development of traditional public education institutions. As one might expect, once public institutions receive less external support – in the name of competition – they begin to falter. Their "failure," due in large part to this decrease in support, contributes to growing perceptions that traditional public schools are incapable of providing students with what they need to succeed. At the same time, charter schools – which are now receiving more support – are framed as the only viable solution to improve education.

In this way, neoliberalism's proponents frame policies as if they are technical, common-sense responses to problems, as opposed to reflections of capitalistic values. For example, closures are justified as a common-sense solution to population decline, rather than a perverse response to the chronic disinvestment in Black and Latinx communities that preceded it. Similarly, the proliferation of charter schools is framed as a response to public demand to improve education quality, rather than an indicator of the inequitable funding of traditional public schools. In sum, a direct consequence of neoliberal reforms is that they "disavow the structural problems facing Black and Latinx working class communities," thereby effectively displacing Black and Latinx people and their institutions – housing, schools, community centers – in favor of capitalist-based alternatives (Lipman, 2011, p. 3).

Returning to the school closures examined in this book, parents leave their experience with the process feeling betrayed, both by the district that seemingly welcomed their participation and by the local activists who convinced them their participation would have an impact. In the words of Tieken and Auldridge-Reveles (2019), "[c]losures mostly happen to, not with, students, families, and communities" (p. 938). This is, in part, directly related to the neoliberal turn as well. For example, Pauline Lipman (2011) describes how "neoliberal versions of participation take the form of appointed advisory boards with no decision-making power or regulated public hearings with no response from persons responsible and no clear sense of the process of which that feedback will be used" (p. 13). And yet, this participation occurs within a context where mobilization at the neighborhood level has already been, and likely will continue to be, disrupted because the "neighborhood schools that can help cement those community ties are replaced by non-geographically bound charters" (Spence, 2015, p. 79). The neoliberalization of schools and the closure process together undermine the democratic possibilities of participation. It is therefore unsurprising that, in the long term, many parents feel their participation was essentially meaningless and, in turn, become less invested in the district and in subsequent fights to save their public schools.

Concerns over being betrayed again may make parents more willing to abandon the traditional public school system and opt for the same charters they fought against. In other cases, enrolling one's children in a charter may be parents' only choice, because some neighborhoods eventually only have charters available to students (Logan & Burdick-Will, 2016). For example, nearly thirty-nine new schools, mainly belonging to a handful of charter organizations, were opened in Chicago during the five-year period following the forty-nine closures in 2013. A parent leader in Philadelphia explained a similar dynamic, stating:

> When we had school closures, we also had an explosion of charter schools ... [But] they are still not doing what they said they were going to do for our community ... If you have a special education need, because you might require more service

then they are willing to provide they won't take you ... But if [the charter school] is the only option in your neighborhood, what are you to do? ... One parent ... had no public school [in the neighborhood] to take her kid so she did the process of [charter] selection, and no one selected her, and they were like how is that possible? ... [But] her son had autism, so they did not have to take him (interview, Northwest Philadelphia, Philadelphia, November 2017).

Even when charter schools may seem to be the better option in some communities, and the only option in others, they come with a new set of constraints. As stated by a youth organizer in Philadelphia, "whoever is the principal answers to the president, or if it's a for-profit, [the principal] answers to whoever owns the company ... In public schools, at least, we know where the chain of command goes" (interview, Northwest Philadelphia, Philadelphia, November 2017).

It is true that communities have a difficult time keeping charter schools accountable in the same way as public schools. One major reason is the potential consequence of a child not being accepted – or being removed. As one youth organizer in Philadelphia explained, "six out of ten times people know that the charter has better resources ... and I think charter advocates use that [to their advantage] very well. Folks [end up] saying 'I am not going to rock the boat, because I don't want my kid to be kicked out'" (interview, West Philadelphia, Philadelphia, November 2017).

Among those considering enrolling, or who are currently enrolled, in charter schools, the reality of not being kicked out, or rather ever let in, came up multiple times as disincentives for holding charter schools accountable. While public schools as institutions must accept *any* student who comes into the building, charter schools are viewed as engaging in tactics that enable them to select only who they want to accept. Even parents who are essentially forced to apply to charters because they are their only option may still struggle to get their children admitted. Yet, without a clear regulatory body or union holding them accountable, charter schools may face no consequences for their decisions.

Consider the case of one charter school in Philadelphia, founded and run by Walter D. Palmer, that fell under scrutiny after the school district discovered that it had been reporting a higher enrollment number than the actual enrollment: 1,300 vs. 675. The district asked the school to reimburse them for the nearly 700 students on behalf of whom they had made payments and began withholding future payments to the school. Additionally, it was discovered that the school was chartered to be a K-8 and yet was operating as a K-12. It was announced in October 2014 that Palmer ran out of the necessary funds to operate the school, thus forcing parents to find another school for their children to attend in the middle of the school year. It officially closed its doors in December 2014.

This situation raised important questions: How did the school get to the stage that it needed to close suddenly in the middle of the year? Were any accountability structures in place from the start? At the time of the closure, Philadelphia's charter regulation office only employed three people to serve dozens of charters in the city. Furthermore, the office was relatively new. In an interview with two of the staff members in 2015, they admitted that they simply did not have the manpower or regulations in place to avoid this situation from occurring: "We had not done a substantive amount of work in terms of the annual monitoring system ... This office had as few as two or three people assigned to work on charter school issues, other cities had more people" (interview, charter administrator, Philadelphia, January 20, 2015). It appeared, then, that closure of charter schools became a blunt tool used by the district as a consequence of this lack of regulation.

Indeed, multiple cities that initially embraced the expansion of charter schools, such as Philadelphia and Chicago, are now closing them at increasing rates, perhaps suggesting that many of these schools should not have been opened at all. While their closures suggest some level of accountability after the fact, it ultimately does not represent the full accountability necessary to avoid these situations from occurring. Most importantly, the closure of charter schools year after year acts as a serious disruption to students' education and stability – and many of these students are already underserved.

So where do the students go when charter schools close or turn them away? Back to traditional public schools. As stated by a parent activist in Philadelphia, "I still believe in public schools. At public schools, you *have* to teach my children ... any other schools can put them out" (interview, West Philadelphia, Philadelphia, February 18, 2015). It is this role of savior, which public schools continue to fulfill, that ultimately keeps disadvantaged communities tied to them. In these communities, public schools will always accept their kids. If allowed to stay open, they will always work to educate and provide for the larger social and emotional needs of their students and the broader community.

The reality is that public schools give most disadvantaged groups their first and, in many instances, last experiences with public accountability. As stated by one youth organizer, "if my experiences are disenfranchised, schools are the one place where I can experience any kind of accountability" (interview, North Philadelphia, Philadelphia, February 2017). Public schools are critical pillars in enabling disenfranchised communities to feel fully human, as one parent elaborated: "If you look at schools as a human right and an obligation of our government to its citizens, or even as an obligation of one human to another, you will see that education encompasses every aspect of life. It's just an extension of human socialization" (interview, Northwest Philadelphia, Philadelphia, November 2016). It is through public schools that people see their humanity – and their future.

When districts close schools, they are also undermining the broader function of schools as reducers of inequality and, ultimately, anchors of political equity. Accordingly, when schools close, so do the only mechanisms that can potentially give disadvantaged citizens access to the promises of "life, liberty, and justice for all." As stated by organizer Jitu Brown, "this is not about simple policy change. This is about a violation of ... human rights."

Referring to the fight to save Dyett (discussed in Chapter 3), Brown remarked, "this is bigger than Dyett. This about who deserves public services." Said another way, that fight was never about just saving one school from closure, or even multiple, it was about disrupting racist policies that construct some groups as less deserving than others of state resources. The fight was to ensure that "justice is served" to Black and Brown children.

In Our Democratic Future, Can We Win?

In 2017, I asked Leanne Woods what she wishes for those who are poor and disadvantaged, who are Black or Brown, to which she responded:

> When you have kids and grandkids, you have no choice but to have hope, ... you have no choice but to hope that things have

to be better ... No matter what type of parents you are, your hope is engrained in your children to have a better future ... That's why you send your kids to school every day ... All parents have hope ... because if you don't, then what are you fighting for or rooting for? ... There is hope in me that I will continue to fight (interview, West Philadelphia, Philadelphia, 2017).

I also asked Leanne if she sees hope in the election of anti–school closure advocates to the city council: Do they represent political victories in the fight for an equitable education? Do they represent hope? She described their elections as a "win and a loss ... because we won a voice in politics, but we lost their voice in the community."

To be sure, the idea that democratic politics is characterized by winners and losers is a fact as old as democracy itself. For instance, the peaceful transfer of power, which is a cornerstone of democracy, requires the acknowledgment that one party has won and the other has lost. Democracy requires reciprocity to survive.

Theoretically, democratic losses are randomly distributed. At some point, every group in the polity should experience them. Yet, in America, who wins and who loses is not arbitrary. Instead, losses are disproportionately distributed to the same groups. Still, these same groups are expected to deal with their uneven experiences with loss as if they bear no costs. They are expected to persist. To be resilient, or in the words of King (1967, 2010) to "stand firm, move forward nonviolently, accept disappointment and cling to hope" (p. 48).

The ability of this same group to consistently react to their loss with grace and acquiescence is in some ways necessary for American democracy to function. But this raises questions about the sustainability of such an approach. Or rather, as Juliet Hooker (2016) asks, at what point "does asymmetric democratic vulnerability not become political martyrdom?" (p. 455).

As stated by Melvin Rogers (2014), in this book's Introduction, "Blacks are perpetually losers in American democracy." He explains: "Allegiance and respect in any civic community is based on reciprocity —the idea of a mutual exchange for mutual benefit. Where Blacks are concerned the exchange has historically been one-sided—a fact that continues to dog the integrity of democratic life." He points to the fact that, "in all relevant areas—health, education, personal security, and economic security—Black Americans endure the greatest harm and are at the greatest risks."[8]

Hooker (2016) expands on this notion, arguing that "the absence of reciprocity thus calls into question not only the integrity of US democracy, but also the kinds of democratic obligations that can be fairly placed upon Black citizens as a result" (p. 450). Departing from the idea of Black people as virtuous political heroes for enduring racial violence for the sake of democratic sacrifice (Allen, 2009), Hooker concludes, "[i]f formulations of Black politics as democratic sacrifice create a trap whereby any deviation from submission, respectability, and non-violence serves to render Black grievances illegitimate, perhaps we should instead consider instances of 'rioting' as a form of democratic redress for Black citizens, even if in and of themselves they cannot transform the prevailing racial order" (p. 464).

Indeed, if we return to the signing of the 1965 Voting Rights Act, America would come to witness one of its largest rebellions in Watts, Los Angeles, only a few days after. The uprising was marked by striking differences compared to those that had been displayed through the nonviolent actions led by King. Nonetheless, civil rights activist Vincent Harding recalls a specific story of King rushing to Watts following the rebellion to engage the youth involved, and then hearing the youth say, "we won ... we made them pay attention to us" (King, 2010). To the youth, being heard was winning.

But it was of course not just the youth who thought this. Within the movement itself, there was conflict erupting because Kwame Ture (then known as Stokely Carmichael), leader of the Student Nonviolent Coordinating Committee, had begun to shift his position on nonviolence, championing the idea of "Black Power" and liberation instead (Carmichael, 1967). Ture explained this shift during an address to the Organization of Latin American Solidarity in 1967, saying, "for four years [the Black masses] watched to see if any significant changes would come from the non-violent demonstrations. It became clear to us that nothing would change." Thus, the Black Power movement would take a different approach focused on self-definition, pan-Africanism, and

---

[8] It is important to note that even as Rogers recognizes the losses that Black people have endured, he nonetheless expresses opposition to the perception of struggle that suggests White supremacy and racism cannot be escaped (see, for example, his review of *Between the World and Me* by Ta-Nehisi Coates (2015) at www.dissentmagazine.org/online_articles/between-world-me-ta-nehisi-coates-review-despair-hope.

rebellion to "change the power base of the world." King understood the basis of this shift, at least intellectually, stating, "cries for Black Power and riots were not the causes of White resistance, they are the consequences of it" (1967, p. 12). Yet, he did not agree with it as a philosophy that could be translated into a mode of action, or rather a program, because he viewed it as rooted in a belief that "we cannot win." He explained that it required "the view that American society is so hopelessly corrupt and enmeshed in evil that there is no possibility of salvation from within," and that "although this thinking is understandable as a response to White power structure that never completely committed itself to true equality... it nonetheless carries the seeds of its own doom" (1967, p. 45). He acknowledged that even though changes in the daily bread of Black people had been "sluggish," they had gained values such as hope, laws that eliminated cruel injustices, and "manhood in a nation that had always called him 'boy'" (1967, p. 17). Thus, he asserted that "the fight is far from over, because it is neither won, as some assert, nor lost, as the calamity ridden declare" (1967, p. 17). In other words, the fight for freedom is ongoing, or perhaps, in the words of Angela Davis (2016), "is a constant struggle."[9]

If this is the case, then what do we make of those who directly refer to their experiences as a short-term win and a long-term loss? More importantly, what do we make of the CPD concept within this longer history that King describes? More specifically, is CPD a submission, or rather admission, in the words of King, that Black people "cannot win"?

---

[9] More specifically, when asked explicitly whether "the struggle is endless," Davis (2016) responds: "I would say that our struggles mature, they produce new ideas, new issues and new terrains on which we engage in the quest of freedom. Like Nelson Mandela, we must be willing to embrace the long walk toward freedom" (p. 11).

CONCLUSION: CLOSED FOR SCHOOL, CLOSED FOR DEMOCRACY
Why Closing Schools Undermines Democracy

In 2019, two historic events took place in Chicago: Its first Black woman and openly queer mayor, Lori Lightfoot, was elected, and the Chicago Teachers Union held an eleven-day strike to demand a fair contract. In Philadelphia, something historic happened as well: The people elected the first third-party candidate for a city council at-large seat in 100 years: Leanne Woods.

As it turned out, Leanne decided to follow in the footsteps of other anti–school closure advocates and join the political establishment, theoretically leaving her community organizing roots behind. Leanne's decision to run for office raises questions worth exploring further – specifically, whether community activism and protests are more effective than engagement in formal politics. Indeed, if we look back to the 1960s, some of its most ardent activists, such as the late John Lewis (D-GA) and Rev. Jesse Jackson, made conscious decisions to move from grassroots mobilization to formal politics following the civil rights movement. In contrast, many of the members of the Black Lives Matter movement have expressly admitted their hesitation with even meeting formal political leaders, let alone running for political office.

Ultimately then, where does Leanne fit in all this? Is her story just another example of a protester turned politician? Or rather did she

decide, if she couldn't beat them, she would join them? Was her collective participatory debt assuaged?

My guess is that none of these theories fit her case. When
Leanne decided to run for office, after all, she ran not as a member of
the Democratic party, but rather as a member of the Working Families
Party. In other words, while she formalized her political engagement by
running for office, she did so in an unprecedented way, with a grassroots political party. Perhaps then, Leanne's win has opened a new
pathway to politics that could shift the ways in which citizens move
between activism and political office. Only time will tell.

In Chicago, it is important to note that, while the city celebrated
the election of Mayor Lightfoot, the Chicago Teachers Union did not
place their support behind her, endorsing Toni Preckwinkle (also, a
Black woman) instead. And as mentioned, the union decided to engage
in an eleven-day strike in Lightfoot's first year to demand that nurses
and social workers be put in every school within five years, and to
reduce class sizes. Through their actions, the union proved once again
the power of protests while at the same time showing the limits of race
and gender identification and representation for supporting who is
sitting in the electoral office.

A future investigation would benefit from more directly assessing the effects of having Black women representatives on the political
actions of affected citizens. Indeed, as people like Lori Lightfoot in
Chicago and Leanne Woods in Philadelphia become incorporated into
the political system, whether via traditional political parties or through
third-party grassroots mobilization, we will get to see how people who
were subjected to targeted policies and practices make decisions about
politics, government, and democracy now that they are on the other
side. The hope is that their efforts will enable those who have long been
disaffected and underserved – in this case, poor Black women – to
believe in the power of participation again.

For now, it remains the case that, in Chicago and Philadelphia,
more public schools have been closed since 2013 than in all the years
before. Further, affected citizens now have similar experiences with loss
that extend beyond schools, including housing, hospitals, and community centers. Between 2018 and 2020, for example, at least six hospitals
in Chicago and Philadelphia were threatened with closure. The majority
of these served low-income racial minorities from the same communities

where schools had been shuttered between 2012 and 2013.[1] By drawing these connections between the closings of schools and other safety-net institutions such as hospitals, we can see how the experiences of those targeted for closure act as a microcosm for the inequitable treatment of racial minorities in America in general. Perhaps, most important, it illustrates the unsustainability of this uneven relationship for our democratic future.

Throughout the book, I document how school closure policies target certain communities and, through the process, make those targeted feel excluded from the public goods afforded to equal citizens under the law. Targeted groups participate to make their voices heard, and some even attain policy gains. But their negative experiences with the policy process translate to negative perceptions of government and politics, which in turn further diminishes participation (via their Collective Participatory Debt) in American democracy by an already marginalized group.

Affected citizens take the closure of their schools seriously, in particular, because they play a critical role in their daily experiences with government and, by extension, one another. Yet, the lack of substantive response from the government once schools are threatened for closure undermines their belief in the power of political participation to elicit democratic responsiveness more generally. Put more directly, when schools are shut down, affected citizens' access to and belief in American democracy also shuts down.

This conclusion raises serious normative questions: Given the experiences of those affected by closure, should civic participation (as a mechanism for enabling material change) play such an important role in conceptions of liberal democracy? In the long term, can resource-poor minority groups gain collective – rather than individual – structural changes from their participation in the policy process? Or rather, should other means for demanding democratic responsiveness be considered, expected, or even privileged in such a situation?

Indeed, the initial provision of resources from government to citizens should, and likely does, instill a sense that, maybe this time, democracy will be different. And undoubtedly, citizens are always looking

---

[1] As I write this book, Black and Brown Chicagoans have been fighting to save a safety-net hospital, Mercy, on the South Side of the city. Only a year earlier, a hospital of the same name (and same owner) was threatened for closure in West Philadelphia. Thus far, both hospitals have been saved from closure, although under new leadership.

for opportunities to give democracy a second chance. But then they repeatedly fail to receive satisfactory responses to their participation, and eventually lose the resources that enabled them to participate in the first place.

When democracy continually disappoints them, the distance to reinvest and believe again grows. The result is that poor racial minorities appear to be less trusting of the government as well as tired of trying to make this relationship with democracy work. Together, these negative experiences contribute to their collective participatory debt. In other words, democracy's good credit runs out.

The findings of this book have significant empirical and substantive implications for research such as this across multiple modes of inquiry. First, it contributes to research on the subfields of urban politics and race, ethnicity, and politics (REP) by fundamentally expanding our understanding of the political attitudes and engagement of low-income racial minorities to include the temporal dynamics of participating while poor and Black in American democracy. In particular, the book demonstrates how citizens' experiences with policies are not static but rather dynamic as they become short-term winners and long-term losers in the quest to save a public good and attain racial justice. In addition, this work recenters the importance of education in studies of Black politics, thus highlighting the fundamental role that education policy experiences can play in upholding or undermining the democratic citizenship of Black Americans. Second, and related, it illustrates how measures of *perceived* contact with a policy is critical for expanding the way in which one defines experience to include meanings beyond direct formal encounters with a policy to an embedded contextual engagement through one's community. In doing so, it also extends the race and geography literature by using both qualitative and quantitative data to demonstrate the behavioral changes that result after a concentrated policy change is implemented within a racially and economically segregated community. Third, these findings contribute to literature on race and descriptive representation by demonstrating the role of citizens in making strategic decisions about who to blame for policies they oppose based on the leader's relative resources and *power* to change decisions – more than their shared racial and political identification.[2]

---

[2] These decisions are intrinsically related to, and affected by, racial identity due to white supremacy – meaning a white politician is more likely to have more power and resources over a Black politician in the modern American political system.

Finally, *Closed for Democracy* contributes to work on policy feedback by demonstrating how education policies related to race have broader consequences for electoral and non-electoral participation, thereby expanding the political outcomes of interest examined beyond the ballot box (e.g., ballot listings and community meetings). The reality is that the field's focus on federal-level policies, and the use of bureaucratic agencies as sites of research, often limits and obscures the location by which the mobilization of marginalized communities can be observed. Instead, this book adds to our understanding of how targeted groups mobilize toward *specific local policy* decisions (e.g., closures, land distribution), thereby moving the literature beyond its traditional focus on federal programs (e.g., Supplemental Security Income, Aid to Families with Dependent Children) to those issues closest to home.

Through an investigation of community participation toward issues closest to home, we learn not another story of uninformed, unengaged voters, but rather of rational citizens doing their part to hold democracy accountable to all it promises. We also learn, however, that despite their best efforts, these citizens get very little in return[3] and that this lack of democratic responsiveness contributes to their fatigue and disillusionment with the policy process. From this research, one might be able to deduce, then, that the collective action of poor Black people in the political process, and its material impacts, continues to be elusive. This conclusion, of course, brings us back to the fundamental question of whether this means "we cannot win."

Making the Juice Worth the Squeeze: The Power and Promise of True Democracy

In a democracy, winning is deeply connected to government responsiveness. Citizens participate in elections in an effort to translate their values into policy, and thus bring about changes in their conditions. The same can be said about why citizens protest or rebel: They are seeking a substantive response to their demands in the form of concrete changes to their collective reality. Citizens do not just want to

---

[3] Indeed, even as Morel (2018) found that Black people were able to effectively mobilize to gain representation on the school board and increased funding in Rhode Island, this was quickly followed by a state takeover of the school system, which thus neutralized the power they have achieved.

feel like they are heard in the symbolic sense; they want to know that they are heard in the material sense.[4]

Regarding school closures, this book demonstrates that the opinions and participation of marginalized groups are largely overlooked. In the face of resistance by those affected in the form of protests, attendance at community meetings, listings of ballot measures, and voting at the ballot box, policy makers proceed with their actions anyway, supported by a dominant White majority that has been nearly universally excluded from the experience of involuntary school closure. In doing so, policy makers further relegate marginalized groups to the sidelines of society, thus contributing to their negative interpretations of the policy's impact as well as their collective participatory debt.

When citizens experience CPD, however, they are not saying they cannot win or that their votes or protests will never matter. Let me be clear: They are acknowledging that they are not winning and that these losses have costs that affect them, because if Black people are to be treated like the humans that they are (as the civil rights, Black Power, and contemporary Black Lives Matter movements advocate), then this requires not only fighting against tropes that view Black people as animals or less worthy but also tropes that expect Black people to be superhuman. It requires dismantling conceptions of democracy that expect Black citizens to provide "a kind of civic sacrifice ... that is not expected of other citizens," even as they see no equivalent changes in their material conditions (Hooker, 2016, p. 455).

To be sure, Martin Luther King Jr. argued that, by being morally virtuous and illustrating the barbarity of White racial terror, the humanity of Black people would be revealed, thereby forcing a response by the state. And, in contrast, Kwame Ture argued that Black people must remove themselves from efforts that require the sympathy of White people and focus instead on building Black power (e.g., Carmichael, 1967). More recently, Angela Davis (2016) has emphasized political change by using electoral forums "as a terrain for organizing" (p. 4), specifically around the development of an independent party that is feminist and anti-racist. Each of these views provides a valid pathway for continued political resistance, but they largely place the burden on the already burdened.

---

[4] I should note that when referring to material and concrete changes, I am not referring to changes in individual success but rather collective conditions.

Black people may engage in protests, voting, and other civic actions, as they recognize that "justice arrives slowly, for oppressed people" (Carmichael & Hamilton, 1992, p. 256). But they may also disengage as they become too tired to fight and/or too disillusioned with the slow progress of change. When this occurs, it is unclear if the path forward for Black people is to try again.

At the same time, one could argue that even though the struggle was not *won*, it was *eased* (Carmichael and Hamilton, 1992), thus creating the conditions for securing substantive wins in the future. One could go a step further and make the case that the disillusionment and fatigue following loss are unwarranted and that Blacks "can't afford despair" (Rogers, 2014). In the words of Ghana's first president, Kwame Nkrumah, feelings such as disillusionment may be rooted in a selfish and egotistic idea that those who fight for change "must be the one[s] to bring it about." For example, in an interview Ture conducted right before his death in 1997, he recalls a conversation with Nkrumah following his ousting from the presidency:

> Nkrumah sat me down and asked me why I was so impatient. I told him because I see my people suffering. "Well," he asked, "if I saw a boat coming while I was on land, would I wade out and meet it?" I said, "Yes." He said, "You'll only get wet, and the boat won't come in any faster." "The revolution is going to triumph," he told me. Then he asked me if I thought the revolution would triumph. I said, "Yes, sir." "Oh, I see," he said. "It's just that you want to be the one to bring it about. All impatience is selfishness and egotism" (Cobb, 1997, p. 37).

Future investigations should try to reconcile the idea of being patient with the reality of fatigue that may follow repeated disappointments with political participation.[5] Future investigations should also determine the actions required not only to distribute the costs of participation more evenly but also provide the type of compensatory and reparative justice needed to make up for past harms (see, for example, Darity and Mullen, 2020). A compensatory justice framework acknowledges that a social debt is owed to those who have had to take on these

---

[5] Just as there is emerging research addressing the uses of anger and other emotions in Black political behavior (e.g., Phoenix, 2019), so should there be work on the role of exhaustion on political attitudes following participation.

uneven burdens, and that this compensation should be provided in the form of collective goods, such as equitable investments in public schools, as opposed to symbolic gestures (e.g., Bourgeoise, 2013). But it also recognizes that compensation alone is insufficient for ensuring equality (Kohn, 2020).

A society that takes seriously the idea of repair through compensation and equality through democratic responsiveness, must find ways for all its members to be made whole and then elevated. The spirit of this sentiment is best captured in an interview with community organizer and voting rights activist Fannie Lou Hamer, at the 1964 Democratic National Convention. A reporter asked her if she was looking for equality with the White man. Hamer responded, "[n]o. What would I look like? . . . I don't want to go down that low. I want the true democracy that'll raise me and the White man up . . . raise America up."

Like Hamer, this book recognizes that a democracy that is unwilling to treat Black people as equals – even in civic participation – is not the kind of democracy for which we should be invested. It acknowledges that we should be fighting for a democracy where uneven work is not required of Black folks – or any folks, for that matter – if we are to raise America up. The goal, then, is not just to thank Black people for engaging despite loss, thereby upholding democracy, but to create conditions such that they no longer must bear the brunt of democratic sacrifice. Perhaps most importantly, it is to push us to think past definitions of winning that require losing, so that we might instead enjoy a true democracy rooted in total *liberation* for all.

EPILOGUE: CLOSE TO HOME

I am a native of the inner city of Chicago. I grew up in a low-income, government-subsidized housing complex, of which 99 percent of the residents were Blacks, called neighborhood commons, or "Orchard" for those who are from there. My mother still lives in this neighborhood today.

Attending public high school in Chicago, I remember feeling like policies were always happening *to* us. Regularly, we would hear that we no longer had gym class or that a teacher had left. There were always some crises that we did not create but that we were directly affected by. So, after learning about the policy process firsthand in school, I became deeply committed to trying to change it.

I applied to college in Washington, DC, hoping to get closer to the policy makers, and was admitted to The George Washington University (GWU), where I studied political science with a public policy focus.

Going to GWU was a great experience, but it reminded me that I knew that I wanted to study communities like the one where I grew up. So after college, under the encouragement of Dr. Traci Burch, I returned to Chicago where I began a Ph.D. in political science at Northwestern University. I had no clue what I was I getting myself into so it was the only school I applied to.

When I returned for grad school, I moved in with my mom on Orchard and saw that the neighborhood I grew up in was changing a great deal. The now infamous Cabrini-Green housing projects, which had housed nearly 20,000 families before I left, were largely closed and replaced by condo buildings. The rundown gas station closest to me was now the second Apple store in the entire city.

As you would probably expect, most Cabrini families were pushed out of the neighborhood, but for the families that remained, there were several questions raised about what to do about these now under-enrolled schools that the children of Cabrini once attended. One major proposal on the line was to close them.

Growing up, I never thought there would be a time in my life when I would write about Cabrini, and it would no longer be around. But, here I was again, seven years after graduating high school, seeing policies happen *to* people and seeing people feel like they couldn't quite control the situation. And yet, it remained the case that, even if their schools did shut down, they still would not be able to attend the good schools right across the street.

It was not until attending the various community meetings that I realized how different groups talked about the issue and thus responded. Those at the meetings would talk about schools as not only places to learn – so you could get into college and eventually get a job – but also as second homes, safe havens, and community centers.

As a budding political scientist, I found it especially interesting that I would hear parents at these meetings say things like, "we are being closed because of politics," or "I blame everyone from Barack Obama on down for this."

I saw community members drawing connections between school and politics often. I observed them raise questions about whether the ways schools were closed were democratic, and yet I had learned almost nothing about the politics of school closure in my own education.

So, I became interested in studying how these connections were being made. I wanted to really think about how an educational issue like school closure that affects a relatively small and targeted group of people can be used to understand larger structural issues around race, politics, and democracy.

I began exploring these issues not only in the United States but in countries in Africa such as Ghana, the homeland of my parents. From this work, I have come to believe that there are very few issues more important than public education for improving access to social, economic, and political equity for the most marginalized.

Undoubtedly, public schools have had a profound impact on my ability to be in a position to write this book, despite the background that I come from. I hope that through this book I contribute not only to advancing scholarship but also to aiding the policy change necessary for providing the same opportunity I had to many others.

So, to those who put their bodies on the line to defend their schools from closure in Chicago and Philadelphia, I hope that this book might contribute to the longer journey for justice.

To the students who have been impacted by closure, I pray that your triumphs outlive your trauma, even if they may never repair them.

To my neighborhood, Orchard, I hope this book makes you proud of little "Sal Wal." I promise never to be ashamed or afraid to study those important issues that hit close to home.

APPENDIX

Note: All meeting transcripts can be found publicly at the following web locations: http://cps.edu/About_CPS/Policies_and_guide lines/Pages/qualityschools.aspx and CPS, School Quality, meeting notes and transcripts, https://cps.edu/About_CPS/Policies_and_guidelines/Pages/ qualityschools.aspx (Chicago) http://webgui.phila.k12.pa.us/offices/f/facil ities-master-plan/community-forums and WHYY. December 13, 2012. https://whyy.org/articles/meetings-list (Philadelphia)

The rest of the data was generated from work conducted in the field and range from observations of meetings and qualitative interviews. Relevant excerpts that exclude identifying information are made available in this appendix, as are additional instructions for how the data was coded.

Chapter 1

Data and Variables

For this investigation, I construct a data set on school closings in Chicago. The data set includes information on the address and the free/ reduced lunch level of each school closed, on the closing list, or disrupted by another CPS action from 2012 to 2013. The zip codes of the schools are then linked to zip code–level census data collected from the American Community Survey's 2009 to 2013 estimates. The linked data are then merged by zip code with the 2013 survey data on educational attitudes of parents conducted collectively by the Joyce Foundation, the *Chicago*

Table A.1A. Average attendance across two meetings in 2013

Group	Austin	Englewood	Fulton	Pilsen	Garfield	Ravenswood	Total
Speakers							
Parents	26	30	30	16	28	18	148
CPS officials	9	5	8	10	6	9	47
Teachers	12	30	18	30	20	8	118
Politicians	5	7	3	3	4	2	24
Total speakers	52	72	59	59	58	37	337
Total attendance	1,000	1,200	800	800	850	500	5,150

Table A.1B. School closures, charter school openings, and crime rankings across five networks in 2013

Network	School Closures	Charters	Crime Ranking
North Lawndale/Austin	8	13	7, 15
Englewood/Auburn Gresham	12	15	3, 9
Pilsen/Little Village	1	7	33
Garfield/Humboldt Park	16	6	2, 6, 20
Ravenswood/Ridge	4	4	28, 55
Total across these networks	41	45	
Total across Chicago	105	95	

Note: Estimates derived from multiple sources and represent minimums. Numbers are not exact. Crime rankings are per neighborhood within the network (i.e., 7 is the ranking of North Lawndale, while 15 is the ranking of Austin), with a possible ranking of 1–77. Source: CPS. edu, Chicago Tribune Crime Report, Illinois Charter School Network.

Tribune, and the National Opinion Research Center (NORC) at the University of Chicago. The survey sampled 1,010 individuals, more than half (520) of whom are parents in CPS, and featured multiple questions about education reform, two of which ask specifically about public school closure. The survey also over-sampled Black respondents, enabling a more reliable and robust analysis of Black attitudes (NORC, 2013). Additional demographic data on the survey population are shown in Table A.1C.

The majority of the analysis relies on a single dependent variable asking about attitudes toward closure. This question basically outlines the official explanation for school closures in Chicago. That is, the question echoes the dominant narrative, which makes it a conservative test for my hypotheses related to Blacks and Latinx. The specific question asked is:

> Chicago Public Schools recently announced plans to close some schools that are serving less than half the number of students that the school was built to serve in order to help balance its budget and free up resources to support the remaining schools more efficiently. Would you agree or disagree with a policy that would close these under-enrolled schools in order to balance the district's budget? (NORC, 2013, p. 15).

The question gives respondents the option to select one of the following: (1) strongly agree; (2) somewhat agree; (3) somewhat disagree; (4) strongly disagree; and (5) neither agree or disagree. (The respondents can also opt to say they don't know or refuse to answer.) I code the variable as a dummy (1 for agree).

It is important to note that the survey examined does not include a question about experiences with public school closure. Thus, I develop multiple proxy variables that aim to capture the characteristics of a potential school closure target in order to test my expectations.

According to CPS data, more than 85 percent of public school children qualify for free or reduced lunch. Furthermore, a majority of closures occurred in neighborhoods that had median incomes ranging between $20,000 and $50,000. Therefore, I construct a dummy variable at the individual level for earning an income of $50,000 or less. In short, I use one's low-income status as a proxy for one's experience as a target of closure.

Given that parents, in particular, have strong attitudes toward education and are the adult stakeholders most directly affected by closure decisions, I include a dummy variable in the analysis on whether the individual is a parent or not. Since race is closely linked to probability of being selected for closure, I also develop dummy variables for Black and non-Black, White and non-White, and Latinx and non-Latinx. Additionally, I construct a variable that measures whether a person lives within a zip code that had a school on the closure list. In this way, I am using one's status as resident of an area in which a threat of school closure occurred as a proxy for one's experience as target of closure. Finally, I construct additional individual level controls, including a dummy variable for gender and whether the individual is affiliated with the school district (outside of being a parent).

At the contextual level (zip code), I construct controls based on factors that can potentially confound the results if left unobserved. One such variable is the percentage of school age children in a zip code. Indeed, if an area has a high percentage of school-age children, this may bias residents' attitudes toward education. Thus, I include a variable for school-age children, measured as the percentage of population in a zip code that is fifteen years of age and younger. Furthermore, given that education level has been found to strongly correlate with political knowledge, engagement, and participation, I construct a variable for education that measures the percentage of individuals age twenty-five and older who have completed high school or less.

Given the population I am focusing on, there is a need to control for factors such as poverty and out-migration. I control for poverty through the inclusion of a family poverty level variable that measures the percentage of persons in a zip code that are under the poverty level. In addition, I control for percentage of rented or owned homes per zip code. For population shifts (out-migration), I construct a variable that measures the percent of vacant housing in a neighborhood. According to Lee and Lubienski's (2016) work on school closures in Chicago, "the school closures in 2013 were mostly clustered around two areas with high vacancy rates" (p. 7). Since school closures are framed as a response to an under-enrollment issue caused by population shifts, this variable aims to account for these shifts in the analysis.

Tests and Analysis

Given the dichotomous dependent variable as well as the multiple individual and aggregate level independent variables, the analysis is primarily based on logistic regression models. Using these data and measures, I test my expectation that being a target – whether direct or indirect – of school closure should result in negative attitudes toward the policy. For the analysis, I begin with a bivariate regression between the independent and dependent variable of interest. I then construct a multivariate logistic regression that includes individual-level variables, specifically race (Black, Latinx, or White), gender, income of $50,000 or less, parental status, affiliation with a school, and being on the school closure list. The next models include individual- and aggregate-level variables, together. The aggregate variables are from census zip code–level data and include percentages of school-age children, those with a high school education or less, those earning an income of $50,000 or less, those who are foreign born, those under the family poverty level, and vacant homes and rental units. Given the difficulty in interpreting coefficients in logit models, I report marginal effects as they enable a calculation of a select independent variable, relative to other independent variables, on the dependent variable.

As previously stated, the tests should reveal a strong relationship between being a target (operationalized as being any of the

Table A.1C. Descriptive data on survey respondents by race, level of closure, and income

Race	Total # of Parents	Income < $50K	Attended School That Closed	Attended School Not Closed	% < $50,000 All	Closed
Black	347	176	128	47	50	73
Latinx	184	111	21	90	60	19
White	423	96	26	70	23	27

Source: NORC, 2013

Table A.1D. Demographic data of interviewees across Chicago and Philadelphia interviews

Groups	Parents/Community Members Chicago	Philadelphia	Community Activists/ District Elites Chicago	Philadelphia
Female	75%	80%	56%	60%
College graduate	30%	22%	75%	70%
Low-income	76%	76%	35%	40%
Democrat	99%	97%	100%	100%
Parent	87%	90%	N/A	N/A
Total number of interviews	25	25	25	25

Note: Collected from original data.

following: Black/Latinx, low income, a parent, and/or on the list of schools threatened for closure) and negative attitudes toward closure. In particular, being a target should have an independent effect on attitudes toward closure across all models in a positive direction. Since being Black or Latinx acts as a critical proxy for actual and perceived targets of school closure in this study, it should be the case that being Black or Latinx should have the most negative attitudes toward closure.

Table A.1E. Predicted probabilities of opposing closure

	Coefficient	Probability	Confidence Interval	(N)
Parent	0.444722825	44.5	0.4931384–0.3829555	330
Closed list	0.424159933	42.4	0.4695417–0.3536070	200
Parent on closed list	0.456829458	45.7	0.6040412–0.4012646	172
Black	0.563513724	56.4	0.7140974–0.4796438	51
Black parent not on closed list	0.590444283	59	0.6202569–0.4624661	59
Black parent on closed list	0.609431793	60.1	0.6690352–0.5069446	111
Hispanic	0.572367571	57.2	0.6244097–0.4098705	59
Hispanic parent not on closed list	0.599140454	60	0.6709147–0.5787790	86
Hispanic parent on closed list	0.617985645	61.8	0.7494210–0.4264781	27
White	0.297967583	29.8	0.3506174–0.1596618	162
White parent not on closed list	0.321556636	32.1	0.3856644–0.2335780	185
White parent on closed list	0.314778531	31.5	0.4932467–0.2978145	62

Chapter 2

Data

Chicago Public Schools

In the following analyses, in collaboration with the Chicago Democracy Project, we compare over-time changes in how citizens in Chicago with varying exposure to school closure policy view their schools and local political leaders. In essence, we are approximating a quasi-experimental framework by comparing changes in political behavior and attitudes before and after the wave of closures in 2013 across areas of Chicago that either did or did not experience the policy.[1]

We rely on three innovative data resources that connect measures of attitudes and behavior to time and space to see the contrast between those who live in communities with school closure and those who do not. First, to evaluate individual-level relationships and mechanisms, We use the waves of the CCES, which include spatial location data in the form of respondents' zip codes as well as questions about political participation and local government performance. These CCES measures, which include hundreds of Chicagoans drawn from all parts of the city, allow me to test the hypotheses at the individual level and examine fine-grained shifts in attitudes related to the spatial policy change. In particular, I analyze changes in the waves just before and after the biggest closure wave (2010 and 2014, respectively).[2] I also use the 2016 wave, which included some local policy evaluation questions.

The aforementioned data are spatially merged (at the precinct- or zip code–level) with an original data set on public school closures in Chicago between 2012 and 2013. This data set provides key information about which respondents or precincts were most likely directly affected by the closures. For the CCES, respondents from zip codes in which schools were closed from 2012 to 2013 are compared to those from other areas. For the Chicago Democracy Project, precincts near closures are compared to those farther away.

There are three measurement caveats for this CCES analysis that we should mention. First, our measure of closure experience is based on the lowest-level geographical indicator available in the CCES, the zip code. This is a noisy measure. Students are not assigned to schools based on zip codes, nor are schools closed or left open on that basis; in zip codes with closures, some schools remain open and some closed. But this issue should ostensibly make it harder to detect effects of closures on opinion, since not every member of the closure zip is directly affected by closures (although every member of a non-closure zip is

---

[1] Although not a tightly controlled experiment, the underlying logic of comparison is similar: I hypothesize that the "treatment" of school closures will be associated with negative attitudes toward related political officials. While the treatment was not random, no communities opted into it, so by observing changes that are theoretically linked to the policy, I can get close to estimating its effects.

[2] These years also have the advantage of being otherwise similar: Neither was a mayoral or presidential election year, so they are comparable in their models' overall level of nonlocal mobilization.

unaffected by those closures). Second, while the meeting attendance analysis used data from just before and after the closings (in 2010 and 2014), the CCES did not ask questions about local government evaluations until 2016. That time lag is also probably a source of error in this analysis. Finally, meeting attendance is another noisy measure. There are lots of political meetings that respondents might attend, not all related to school closures – especially in areas where schools did not close. This may help explain in part why meeting attendance is not related to school evaluation outside of closure areas.

Table A.2A. Evaluations of schools and mayor by race, parental status, and school closure among Blacks

	Closure Neighborhood	Non-closure Neighborhood
No Children under 18		
Schools	1.770	1.769
Mayor	1.433	1.631
N	61	39
Children under 18		
Schools	1.769	2
Mayor	1.083	1.2
N	26	10

Table A.2B. Evaluations of schools and mayor by race, parental status, and school closure among non-Blacks

	Closure Neighborhood	Non-closure Neighborhood
No Children under 18		
Schools	1.873	1.974
Mayor	1.37	1.410
N	63	194
Children under 18		
Schools	2.8	2.297
Mayor	2.48	1.676
N	25	37

Data and Variables

School District of Philadelphia

For the Philadelphia case study, I rely heavily on a survey conducted by the Pew Charitable Trust in 2013 following the proposal to close sixty schools in Philadelphia. The survey collected data from more than 1,200 Philadelphia residents and asked questions about education, political blame, and mayoral approval, directly. These Pew survey data are linked to US Census data at the zip code level in the 2009 to 2013 American Community Survey. These data are then linked to an original data set on school closures in Philadelphia to develop a proxy variable for experience with school closure, also at the zip code level. The data are not only being used to test the claim that citizens affected by closure attribute blame to political actors but also to examine who targeted citizens blame the most.

My analysis of the data focuses largely on the attitudes of Blacks, who make up over 80 percent of those affected by school closures in Philadelphia, and rely on two central dependent variables. The first variable asks respondents the following question:

> As you may know, the Philadelphia school district has been struggling with a major budget crisis. I'm going to read you four groups of people and ask you how much each is to blame for the problem. Please tell me if each should get a great deal of the blame, some blame, just a little blame, or none.

a The Philadelphia school administration and school reform commission
b Mayor [Michael] Nutter and the city council
c Governor [Thomas] Corbett and the state legislature
d The unions representing the teachers and other school employees

The other variable the analysis will rely on is the following:

> Overall, do you approve or disapprove of the job Michael Nutter is doing as mayor?

a Approve
b Disapprove

These questions are coded dichotomously. Those that blame the individual/group, "a great deal" or "some" are coded as 1, whereas those that attribute "just a little blame" or "none" are coded as 0. Approval is also coded dichotomously (1 is equal to approval).[3]

To examine how those affected by closure attribute blame, I construct a proxy variable for living in an area affected by a potential school closure. This variable is based on the number of schools closed or on the closure list per zip code. I then develop a dummy variable of whether one lives in an area that experienced a potential school closure.[4] It is important to note that, for the dummy variable, "neighborhood" is a substitute for zip code since it is the smallest geographic identifier available. While it would have been ideal to have a question on the survey that directly asks respondents whether their school was on the closure list, in the case of Philadelphia, I view the dummy variable as a strong proxy given the ways in which closure was concentrated within the same zip codes. Accordingly, I expect zip codes to be especially useful for the analysis.[5]

To target the mechanism at work – participation at a community meeting – I rely on a question in the Pew survey that asks respondents whether they have worked with others in their community to solve problems in the past twelve months. While the question does not specify the type of participation, it is time specific. Therefore, by interacting participation with closure, I can get closer to developing a proxy variable that measures those affected by closure who participated in their community during the same period as the mass closure of their schools.

---

[3] I also run the analysis as a categorical variable; there are no differences in the outcomes.

[4] The other variable ranks the rate of closure based on whether one lives in an area that has a high, medium, or low rate of closures. High refers to more than six closings in a respective community since the adoption of the school closing policy, medium refers to between four and six closings, and low refers to between one and three closings. A community might also have no experience with closure.

[5] It is important to account for the possibility that the school closure variable may be acting as a proxy for race and/or poverty since areas with closures also have high levels of poverty and a large concentration of minorities. Yet, by using rate of closures, I can get variation in the types of neighborhoods affected. Furthermore, by including measures of race and poverty at the individual and contextual level, I can control for whether the inclusion of these variables influences the effects found for living in a neighborhood with closures. Finally, I examine the extent to which these variables coexist with one another and determine that there is variation between the two variables. Thus, the variables are not capturing/measuring a single item.

The issue of safety is often directly tied to schools (e.g., data reveal that 26 percent of reasons raised against closure were related to concerns about safety). Accordingly, I create a variable for neighborhood safety based on a question that asks residents to rate how safe they feel in their neighborhood. Respondents who say they feel "a little safe" or "not safe at all" are coded 1, and those who state they "feel safe" or "somewhat safe" are coded 0. This variable also allows me to test the expectation that citizens believe that the safety of their neighborhood is a direct responsibility of the mayor versus the governor.

The most important demographic variable is race, particularly being Black, although I also include being Hispanic and White in the analysis. If one self identifies as Black, 1 is coded; 0 is coded otherwise. Other important demographic variables at the individual level include whether a person is a renter, earns an income of $50,000 and below, has a high school diploma, is employed, and has school-aged children. Additionally, I include a dichotomous variable that accounts for if the person pays a "great deal" or "some" attention to politics, which are each coded 1, and 0 otherwise. My intention was to find out if citizens that work with others to solve problems – in other words, participate – are already well informed about politics. If this is the case, then disapproval of Mayor Nutter has little do with participating in a community meeting and more to do with the fact that those participating are already informed.

Finally, I add aggregate-level control variables at the zip code level to account for contextual factors that may affect the analysis. Indeed, it could be the case that when these variables are added they wash away the effects found at the individual level. These variables include neighborhood-level partisanship, proportion of households living below the poverty line, proportion of the neighborhood with vacant properties, proportion of households with an education level lower than high school, and proportion of population who are foreign born. The analysis is based on logistic regression models. I regress each of the independent variables described on different variations of the political blame variable: the school reform commission, the teachers' union (Philadelphia Federation of Teachers), Mayor Nutter, and Governor Corbett, respectively. These models include both individual- and contextual-level controls. I assess predicted probabilities for ease of interpretation.

Table A.2C. Predictors of opposition to charter schools versus closure

	Union	SRC	Mayor	Governor
	(1)	(2)	(3)	(4)
(Individual)				
Black	−0.084*	0.003	0.031	0.068*
	(0.037)	(0.027)	(0.026)	(0.026)
Hispanic	−0.184***	−0.033	−0.003	0.047
	(0.053)	(0.039)	(0.036)	(0.029)
Parent	−0.022	−0.020	0.081***	0.011
	(0.035)	(0.023)	(0.020)	(0.023)
Income below 50K	−0.004	0.056***	−0.000	0.002 *
	(0.005)	(0.004)	(0.004)	(0.004)
Follow politics	−0.013	−0.001	0.057	0.003
	(0.007)	(0.006)	(0.059)	(0.005)
Solve problems	0.091	0.004	0.031	0.0104
	(0.031)	(0.02)	(0.002)	(0.023)
Closed list neighborhood	0.130	0.049	0.068	0.046
	(0.062)	(0.037)	(0.034)	(0.040)
(Aggregate)				
High school education or less	−0.003	−0.002	0.004	0.001
	(0.004)	(0.003)	(0.003)	(0.003)
Rent	−0.003	−0.002	−0.004	−0.001
	(0.004)	(0.003)	(0.003)	(0.001)
Family poverty	0.003	−0.002	−0.004	−0.001
	(0.004)	(0.003)	(0.003)	(0.001)
Foreign born	0.003	0.001	−0.002	−0.003
	(0.004)	(0.002)	(0.001)	(0.002)

Note: Stars denote level of statistical significance (confidence in results from highest to lowest) ***0.001 (highest), **0.05, *0.010 (lowest); the coefficient of the independent variable is the value without parentheses; the standard error is the value within the parentheses.

Table A.20. Predictors of mayoral disapproval

	(1)	(2)
(Individual)		
Black	0.100**	0.97***
	(0.036)	(0.038)
Hispanic	0.004	0.002
	(0.050)	(0.051)
Income	−0.002	−0.002
	(0.006)	(0.006)
Education	−0.030	−0.030
	(0.014)	(0.014)
Unemployed	0.093	0.094
	(0.037)	(0.037)
Parent/Guardian	0.032**	0.029
	(0.034)	(0.034)
Information	0.007	0.007
	(0.008)	(0.008)
Solve problems	0.089	0.091
	(0.31)	(0.031)
Safe neighborhood	0.080***	0.079***
	(0.016)	(0.017)
Rent	0.059	0.054
	(0.033)	(0.033)
< 4 Closings (low)	0.028	0.037
	(0.042)	(0.045)
4 to 6 Closings (medium)	0.114*	0.108*
	(0.042)	(0.050)
> 6 Closings (high)	0.118**	0.130**
	(.048)	(0.062)
(Aggregate)		
% Education less than high school		−0.003
		(0.004)

Table A.2D cont'd

	(1)	(2)
% Renting		−0.002
		(0.00)
% Family poverty		0.004
		(0.004)
% Foreign		0.002
		(0.002)

Note: Stars denote level of statistical significance (confidence in results from highest to lowest) ***0.001 (highest), **0.05, *0.010 (lowest); the coefficient of the independent variable is the value without parentheses; the standard error is the value within the parentheses.

Predicted probabilities of blame and approval on Blacks living in neighborhoods with school closures (Table A.2E–A.2J).

Table A.2E. Probability of Blacks blaming the governor by level of closure

	Coefficient	Confidence Interval
0	0.8234464	0.9007261–0.7056663
< 3 Closings	0.8640403	0.9474932–0.8145209
4 to 6 Closings	0.8667053	0.9260603–0.7714617
> 6 Closings	0.8774554	0.9288278–0.7971024

Table A.2F. Probability of Blacks blaming the mayor by level of closure

	Coefficient	Confidence Interval
0	0.7528818	0.8537384–0.6139282
< 3 Closings	0.7740144	0.8615120–0.6534714
4 to 6 Closings	0.8536245	0.9326782–0.8106671
> 6 Closings	0.8857085	0.9326782–0.8106600

Table A.2G. Probability of Blacks blaming the school board by level of closure

	Coefficient	Confidence Interval
0	0.751593	0.8543389–0.6094991
< 3 Closings	0.7286619	0.8310906–0.5944306
4 to 6 Closings	0.7771091	0.8592695–0.6656468
> 6 Closings	0.760355	0.8343254–0.6665576

Table A.2H. Probability of Blacks blaming the union by level of closure

	Coefficient	Confidence Interval
0	0.4039091	0.4997113–0.5860051
< 3 Closings	0.421461	0.4202401–0.5114617
4 to 6 Closings	0.458413	0.4553878–0.5324571
> 6 Closings	0.4888249	0.4772694–0.5840540

Table A.2I. Probability of Blacks mayoral approval by level of closure

	Coefficient	Confidence Interval
0	0.392	0.5135369–0.2704306
< 3 Closings	0.378	0.4666650–0.2887251
4 to 6 Closings	0.3	0.3721178–0.2271508
> 6 Closings	0.4695	0.6006082–0.3391342

Table A.2J. Probability of Blacks approving the mayor by level of closure and participation

	Coefficient	Confidence Interval
0	0.3274219	0.4966443–0.19367364
< 3 Closings	0.2476597	0.3446121–0.17087221
4 to 6 Closings	0.1625739	0.2332046–0.11025912
> 6 Closings	0.2731736	0.3704288–0.19522152

Chapter 3
Data, Methods, and Strategies for Analyses

Qualitative interviews, in particular, are most useful for under-standing how citizens articulate their own experiences (Mettler & Soss, 2004; Walsh, 2012). Although surveys facilitate the ability to generalize from findings, and to some extent determine causality, they rarely ask in-depth questions about policy experiences. In addition, because of my interest in examining community meetings as sites of political learning, ethnographic observations of community meetings act as optimal methods for enabling an investigation of community members' experiences with the school closure process and their interpretations of its impacts (Fung, 2004).[6]

Accordingly, between 2012 and 2015 I collected qualitative inter-views, observed community meetings, and analyzed community meeting transcripts in Chicago and Philadelphia. I also collected and analyzed semi-structured interviews with parents and community residents to gain an understanding of how citizens developed reasons to participate and their feelings about their participation and politics. I then conducted semi-structured interviews with leaders of organizations to determine what methods they used to encourage citizens to participate in the closure process and examine their perceptions of the utility of participation.[7] I observed community meetings and collected transcripts to learn how meetings were run and investigate citizens' experiences with participation. In 2016 and 2017, I returned to both Philadelphia and Chicago and reinterviewed nearly one third of those initially interviewed between 2012 and 2015. My aim was to document whether their perceptions had changed.

The Content of My Qualitative Data

To start, I coded the data collected into a set of categories based on the themes in existing literature on participation that includes

---

[6] It is important to note, then, that the intent of the investigation was not to develop a causal analysis of the impacts of school closure participation on political attitudes but rather to engage in an ethnographic analysis of citizen participation against a specific policy, followed by an interpretive analysis of citizens' perceptions of the impacts of their participation.

[7] I also asked school officials about how they used the feedback to make decisions but was provided with general answers along the lines of the following: "We collect all the responses, they are put into a report and then presented to school officials to be considered in the final decision."

resources (i.e., time, money), group cohesion, and political trust (for examples, see Miles & Huberman, 1994; Emerson, Fretz, & Shaw, 1995; Skogan & Hartnett, 1997). Based on observed patterns and themes that emerged in early interviews, I then recoded them into an expanded and more refined set of categories focused on **their reason for participation, their method,** and their perceptions of the **impact** of their participation.

Their Reason (Why): Defining Shared Policy Targets

On the question of why, the following themes stood out: concerns that school closures would increase neighborhood crime and overcrowding in classrooms, disrupt family ties and community stability, increase the number of charters that are opened, lead to the unfair distribution of public goods, disproportionately affect Black and Brown schools, and increase mistrust between the school district and the community.

Next, I wrote memos summarizing the aforementioned observations, and took notes on questions that remained unclear (Feldman, 1995). Borrowing from the categories mentioned, for example, I developed a memo that grouped community responses into personal and societal concerns related to the consequences of closure. Personal concerns included a person's self-interest as a teacher or parent. An example of a personal concern in the data is articulated in this quote: "Each time you close a school I have to find a new job." Social concerns were articulated in statements about the implications of public school closure for larger bodies such as unions, the government, the school system, and race relations. A typical example of a statement that articulated a social concern includes statements such as the following: "They [are] not trying to close those schools on the North Side, it's only the schools on the South Side where the kids are Black and Brown." In this quote, the interviewee expressed a concern that the policy targeted people of color concentrated in specific areas of the city.

From this exercise, *it appeared the experience of being targeted by the school district's policy motivated many poor people of color to participate in the school closure process.* Many of these interviews included statements such as, "it's not a coincidence that these closings are only happening in Black and Latino neighborhoods." Like the quote, this statement illustrates an awareness that potential school closings affected some communities more than others and suggests that these differential impacts were intentional. Most important, they were indicative of broader claims related to a person's racial group rather than a person's position as a parent, teacher, or staff member, which appeared to contribute to the construction of a shared identity as a target of school closure based on race.[8] Data from interviews suggest that the development of a shared identity as targets of closure, or what I label as, "shared policy targets," united otherwise disparate groups, and contributed to their greater engagement with the school district and community groups (see also, Anderson, 2009).

Their Method (How): Mobilizing Resources

While such concerns identify a central reason for the participation of those affected by closure, they do not explain *how* people participated in practice. Accordingly, I returned the data and divided it into categories that identified how parents, community residents, and elites described what enabled their participation (and what acted as a barrier to their participation). In addition to the shared target identity described, the responses for what enabled their participation could be categorized into the theme of "resources," including transportation, meetings, and civic partners.[9] One school administrator in Philadelphia, for example, said that the school had only three community organization partners prior to the closure announcement, but that number more than quadrupled after the school was put on the list of schools threatened for closure. In fact, across all neighborhoods examined except one,[10] the announcement of a potential closure contributed to an increase in the number of community partners available to assist in the fight against closure. Additionally, the school district provided resources in the form of access to public officials

---

[8] It is also true that group consciousness works differently for different ethnic/racial groups. The literature indicates that Blacks tend to demonstrate the highest levels of group consciousness, followed by Hispanics and then Asians (see McClain et al., 2009)

[9] I categorized both parents, school officials, and political bureaucrats by similar codes, when applicable, to examine how each group responded to the same set of issues.

[10] The work samples communities across fourteen neighborhoods in Chicago and eleven in Philadelphia. These neighborhoods largely represent those areas facing the threat of closure. Please note that all names are pseudonyms to ensure privacy, unless otherwise noted.

Table A.3A. Summary statistics, aggregate precinct-fragment measures

VARIABLES	N	Mean	SD	Min	Max
Miles to Nearest Closure	4,066	1.463	1.174	0.00994	4
% Black	4,066	0.397	0.420	0	1
% Hispanic	4,066	0.253	0.292	0	1.000
% in school	4,066	0.266	0.0844	0.0194	0.901
% in poverty	4,066	0.230	0.156	0	0.900
% Unaffordable rent	4,066	0.153	0.108	0	0.678
Δ Turnout, 2011–2015	4,062	−0.0803	0.0685	−0.447	0.358
Δ Emanuel Vote, 2011–2015	4,062	−0.0937	0.115	−0.421	0.415
Δ # crimes	4,066	−0.262	0.0728	−0.441	0.253
Med. HH Inc. ($10K)	4,066	2.463	2.353	0.00292	42.67
ΔPresidential turnout, 2012–2016	4,090	−0.0476	0.0809	−0.327	0.238

through meetings that took place in the communities affected by closure. Prior to these meetings, parents made references to the "poor timing" of school-related events by the district, particularly for those who had to work double shifts at their places of employment. Furthermore, when meetings were not clearly within walking distance, parents and community members raised issues with transportation options available to them. Yet, the advent of school closure facilitates new partnerships with community organizations and the provision of resources by the school district, which helped community members overcome traditional barriers to participation and engage in the policy process.

Aggregate Regression Results

Table A.3B includes full regression results of the precinct-fragment-level analysis of change in turnout and change in support for Emanuel from 2011 to 2015.

Table A.3B. Multivariate regression results, change in turnout and support for Rahm Emanuel in mayoral race, before and after school closings

	ΔTurnout	ΔTurnout	ΔTurnout (Maj. Afam Precincts)	ΔEmanuel Vote	ΔEmanuel Vote	ΔEmanuel Vote (Maj. Afam Precincts Only)
Miles to nearest closure	-0.02***	0.01***	0.01**	0.05***	0.01***	0.00
	(0.00)	(0.00)	(0.00)	(0.00)	(0.00)	(0.00)
% in school		0.04**	-0.00		-0.04**	-0.01
		(0.02)	(0.02)		(0.02)	(0.02)
Change, # Crimes		-0.03**	-0.01		0.09***	-0.01
		(0.01)	(0.02)		(0.02)	(0.02)
% Black		0.04***	-0.01		-0.12***	-0.03*
		(0.00)	(0.02)		(0.01)	(0.02)
% Hispanic		-0.01***	-0.10***		-0.14***	-0.10***
		(0.00)	(0.02)		(0.01)	(0.02)
Med. HH Inc. ($10K)		-0.00	0.00		0.00***	0.00
		(0.00)	(0.00)		(0.00)	(0.00)
% in poverty		-0.05***	-0.06***		-0.01	0.00
		(0.01)	(0.01)		(0.01)	(0.01)
% Unaffordable rent		-0.02	-0.04***		-0.03*	-0.02
		(0.01)	(0.01)		(0.01)	(0.01)

Table A.3B cont'd

	ΔTurnout	ΔTurnout	ΔTurnout (Maj. Afam Precincts)	ΔEmanuel Vote	ΔEmanuel Vote	ΔEmanuel Vote (Maj. Afam Precincts Only)
Change, Presidential Turnout, 2012–2016		0.12***			−0.10***	
		(0.02)			(0.03)	
Turnout, 2011		−0.40***	−0.43***			
		(0.01)	(0.02)			
Emanuel Support 2011					−0.61***	−0.86***
					(0.02)	(0.02)
Constant	−0.06***	0.07***	0.13***	−0.17***	0.33***	0.38***
	(0.00)	(0.01)	(0.02)	(0.00)	(0.01)	(0.02)
Observations	4,062	4,006	1,599	4,062	4,006	1,599
R-squared	0.08	0.39	0.30	0.26	0.61	0.52

*** p < 0.01, ** p < 0.05, * p < 0.1

Note: All models are OLS estimates with dependent variable and pool of precinct-fragments listed at top of column and covariates at left. Robust standard errors in parentheses

School Board Mobilization

In Table A.3C, we provide evidence that areas closer to school closures were more likely to mobilize for the second ballot referendum supporting a new school board structure in 2015. These regression results support that observation, estimating the relationship between distance to the nearest closure and mobilizing for the 2105 ballot measure among areas that did NOT have the ballot measure in 2011.

Alternate Specifications of Individual-Level Participation Change

Figure A.3 estimates changes in the mean rates of engagement in various forms of political participation among different groups of Chicagoans. The figure presented makes these estimates using population weights to correct for the fact that subnational samples of the CCES are not necessarily representative. These two figures present the same measures, using different techniques to make the estimate. The results in each figure vary slightly but are substantively the same, especially on meeting attendance, which is the key mode of participation for our analysis.

The figure at left uses the raw, unweighted responses. The figure at right displays regression-based predicted probabilities of engagement in each category for each group, based on a probit model of each outcome including measures of income and education.

Statistical Tests of Group Differences in Participation, Individual-Level Measures from CCES

In Figure A.3, we present evidence of changes in meeting attendance among Black respondents near closed schools based on analysis of a re-weighted sample population of CCES respondents from Chicago. This appendix section provides raw numbers for these groups, as well as results from regression, nearest-neighbor matching, and difference-in-difference analyses, providing evidence that these group differences are statistically significant.

Tablec A.3C. Multivariate linear probability model estimates of model of school board "mobilization," 2015

	DV: 2015 Ballot Areal Not 2011 Ballot Area	DV: 2015 Ballot Areal Not 2011 Ballot Area
Miles to nearest closed school	−0.132***	−0.102***
	(0.00386)	(0.00515)
% of population in school		−0.200**
		(0.0876)
% Black		0.200***
		(0.0301)
% Latinx		0.328***
		(0.0340)
Household median income		−0.0176***
		(0.00385)
% in poverty		0.192***
		(0.0516)
Change in serious crime		0.0669
		(0.0998)
Constant	0.954***	0.812***
	(0.00827)	(0.0425)
Observations	3,570	3,570
R-squared	0.202	0.262
N	3,570	3,570
r2	0.202	0.262

*** p < 0.01, ** p < 0.05, * p < 0.1
Robust standard errors in parentheses.

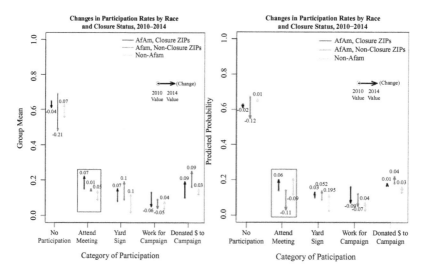

Figure A.3 Unweighted CCES sample (left) and regression-adjusted estimates of predicted participation in each area (right)

Regression Model

The theory predicts that differences in response to the race-place targeted policy will be concentrated among Black respondents in areas with a school closure. Given observations from before and after the coefficient of interest is a triple interaction of indicators for Black identity, proximity to schools, and 2014 measurement. The coefficient is highlighted for clarity in this model.

Aggregate Analysis: Comparing Precincts within Areas of the City Based on School Attendance Area Footprints

In this analysis, we compare changes in precincts directly within the attendance area footprint of closed schools versus the footprints of schools that were not closed. To conduct this analysis, we gathered spatial information about the attendance zone footprints before the

Table A.30. Regression estimates of model of participation in political meetings, Chicago respondents to 2010 and 2014 CCES. Weighted.

DV: Meeting Attendance

Covariates	Coef.	Std. Err.	z	P > z
Black	0.38	0.28	1.33	0.183
Closure	0.15	0.33	0.46	0.648
BlackXClosures	−0.45	0.44	−1.02	0.307
Time	0.069	0.21	0.32	0.752
BlackXTime	−0.56	0.38	−1.43	0.152
Closures#Time	−0.43	0.42	−1.01	0.311
BlackXClosuresXTime	1.24	0.58	2.12	0.034
Family income	0.13	0.049	2.57	0.01
Education	0.084	0.045	1.85	0.064
_cons	−1.92	0.26	−7.39	0

N = 645, Pseudo-R squared = 0.04

wave of closures in 2010–2011 from the Chicago online data portal: https://data.cityofchicago.org.

See shortly the footprints of "neighborhood" elementary and high schools in Chicago from that year, with schools that were closed in 2012–2013 shaded gray. The dark black lines are the unofficial "sides" of the city, which we use to compare precincts in closure school attendance areas to comparable nearby precincts. Elementary footprints are at left, and high school footprints are at right.

We then overlaid these maps with the map of precincts fragments from 2011 and 2015 described earlier in this appendix. A precinct was scored as "1" if it was within a closed school's attendance zone footprint, and a "0" if not. We then compared changes in the

Table A.3E. Difference-in-difference analysis of changed meeting attendance among Black residents of closure zips versus others, 2010–2014 CCES

Difference-in-difference, estimated using "diff" command in Stata.

	Before	After			
Control (either no closures or non-afam or both)	167	363			
Treated (Afam, w Closures)	86	111			
Outcome	Meeting Attendance				
		Mean	SE	|t|	P > |t|
Before	Control	.144			
	Treated	.093			
	Difference	.051	.044	−1.15	.251
After	Control	.116			
	Treated	.162			
	Difference	.046	.036	1.29	.198
	Diff-in-Diff	.097	.057	1.70	.089

political outcomes of interest – mobilization on the school board referendum,

We report the differences for the West, South, and far South Sides, the areas of the city where closures were concentrated.

Matched Comparison within Neighborhoods

Table A.3F reports the average differences between closure and non-closure precincts' outcomes in column 1 for closure versus non-closure precincts within the same area in column 3, and matched on racial composition, median household income, and percent of

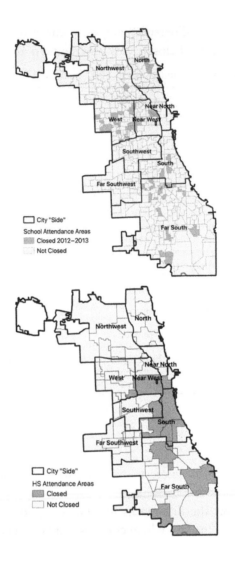

population in school in column 4. Only precincts from the West and far South Sides are included in these analyses.

Perhaps because elementary footprints are smaller, the differences were more precisely estimated when comparing precincts with elementary school closures to those without. Thus, the estimated differences reported and in the body of the paper may be conservative estimates of the magnitude of this effect.

Table A.3F. Pooled and match differences in mobilization

Change Variable	Raw Pooled Differences (Closure-Non-Closure)[a]	Area-Matched Differences (Closure-Non-Closure)[b]
Δ Turnout	.007	.008
	(.003)	(.003)
Δ Mayor support	−.14	−.017
	(.005)	(.005)
Δ Mobilization for referendum	.050	.06
	(.019)	(.017)

[*]Significant at p < .05
[a] Pooled precincts from West and far South Sides. Estimates are mean differences and SE based on student's T-test.
[b] Estimates are differences from matching algorithm with Abadie-Imbens robust standard errors.

Chapter 4

Data and Strategies for Analysis

In 2014 and again in 2017, I asked citizens to assess the impacts (benefits or disadvantages) of their participation in the closure process. Did they feel that attending meetings was valuable and/or that the meetings went as they expected? Did they feel that policy makers were responsive? What did they learn from their experiences? Through these questions, I sought to understand their perceptions of the impacts of their participation, particularly related to the responsiveness of public administration.

In 2014, affected citizens referred to their experiences of "seeing other schools win" and "learning how to make a case." I categorized these factors as "civic skills." In addition, they expressed belief in their ability to get policy makers to respond to their concerns even though they maintained generally negative perceptions of the policy process and policy makers. I classified the former responses as "affirmations of internal efficacy" and the latter as "negative interpretations of the policy's impact."

Table A.4A. Quotes on issue classification over two sets of interviews

	Sample Quotes
Interviews 2012/2015	
Civic skills	You have to fight the facts with facts.
Internal efficacy	They had to go back and change because of us.
Mistrust	I can't tell if ... these meetings are a sham.
Interviews 2016/2017	
Fatigue and disillusionment	[We] was worn out.
Deepened mistrust	I don't have any more trust in government.

Note: Data collected from original interviews.

Loss: Collective Participatory Debt – Deepened Mistrust, Fatigue, and Disillusionment

By 2017, I found that, while a few of those who were new to participation in the early years of the school closures had been transformed into activists and formal political and civic leaders, most people, even those who won the battle to save their school, became much less participatory and further disillusioned by the policy and political process. In particular, there were multiple references to the term(s) "fatigue," "tired," and "wore out." I label this "fatigue and disillusionment." Furthermore, citizens expressed a *deepened mistrust* for government (e.g., one Chicagoan stated that "[the school board] had to go back and change based on our actions, but [even so] I don't have any more faith in government"). From the reinterviews, it appeared that the policy wins of affected participants did not necessarily contribute to positive attitudes toward government and/or future participation. Instead, their experiences appeared to do the opposite and contribute to collective participatory debt. See Table A.4A.[11]

---

[11] Through snowball sampling and focus groups I was also able to speak to citizens who did not participate in the meetings. Most of the nonparticipants I spoke with said they believed that those who did participate made a difference in the outcomes, but they were not sure whether they would participate in the future. The only difference I identified among those who participated and those who did not was related to class. While several Black and low-income individuals participated across the community meetings, most middle-class Blacks who participated did so if they were already established activists, particularly in Philadelphia. It was clear that both groups had similarly negative perceptions of the policy

Coding for Reasons Raised in Meeting Transcripts (Instruction)

For community meeting transcripts, I engaged in an iterative process of coding and recoding (2x) the ethnographic observations taken across the meetings (see Skogan & Harnett, 1997, p. 120 for similar process). The first set of codes were developed after attending the first set of community meetings and then recoded and finalized at the second set of meetings attended. The coding was based on the key concerns citizens raised for their position on school closure. In particular, concerns were counted by the number of mentions per issue and then categorized. For example, violence and gangs were both issues that were included under the crime category. Therefore, if violence was mentioned 100 times and gangs 200 times, each of these issues were added together, thereby resulting in a total of 300 mentions for the crime category. The purpose of counting issue mentions is to gauge which concerns were most commonly raised in relationship to one's policy attitude, in this case, opposition to school closure, before determining how citizens are activated to participate.

I continued this type of coding with the use of transcripts across sixty meetings. By doing this, I am able to develop a fairly exhaustive set of coding categories. These categories include crime, family, fairness, politics, mistrust, charter, safe havens, resources, stability, race/race coded, disregard (lack of listening), community, special needs, and overcrowding. I then group them according to which issues were raised the most by those against school closings in order to shorten the list. I come up with the following final codes: crime, community, mistrust and charter schools, politics, and race/race coded. These codes/categories reflect the issues that were most salient across all networks.[12] The codes were then triangulated through additional interviews, and local media sources. Most important, all of the transcripts are publicly available on the CPS website and, thus, can be used to verify the coding scheme.

The **crime** category received one of the highest percentage of mentions of any other category – 26 percent. Crime mentions included

process and its outcomes. More importantly, while I included middle-class participants for the sake of comparison, they are not the focus of this study.

[12] Certainly, decisions had to be made, as often one comment can include references to three different issues. In this case, judgment calls were made based on how much of the comment referenced one issue over another

any reference to gangs, violence, guns, safety, and similarly related themes. A typical example of what would go into the crime frame includes statements such as the following:

> You are talking about sending those kids from this side of Austin, I mean, we got to admit, we got wars in the community, we got gangs in our community. They don't become gang bangers in high school. They start from somewhere else. So, these kids are about to go from here to here. So, we're talking about tearing our kids' life. We have the big thing about them being senselessly murdered. So, why we're going to add fuel to the fire and put our kids in harm's way? (community member).
>
> (Man stands up and shows gang map) If you send kids from one side of the community to another – you will put our kids in harm's way. Our kids safety and education (parent activist).
>
> It is the safety of our children. The safety of our children is a primary concern. Barbara Byrd-Bennett said this during a conference call with reporters, according to the *Sun Times*. She also said for children to travel farther, or to put children in the danger of crossing a gang barrier, [which] does not make sense to me (grandparent).
>
> I'll give you an example. We just had an incident where a young man was killed on ... [the] street, and he was killed by somebody from the ... side of the community, and he killed somebody on the [other] side of the community, and these kinds of tensions are going on. So, I'm saying that to say if you put these two schools together, it's not going to work. It won't work in our community. You give us some years to work on it, it will work, but it won't work (community member).

In this statement it is clear the person is arguing that because of the possible safety concerns related to gangs, the school should not be closed down.

The **community** category tied with crime at 26 percent and included referrals to schools as safe havens, or places of stability, family, and overall pillars of the community. Yet, this category also included references to special needs students. This is because many of the schools spoke of how closing the school would affect their special needs populations by disrupting the relationship built with these students, thereby stagnating progress. A few typical examples of sentiments that were placed in the community category, including one specific to special needs students, are:

> Goodlow is not just a school, it's a family, it's a home, it's an environment, it's a community. Their passion just runs deep, and I really, really wish that I could say something that would help you truly understand that you can't close this school (parent).
>
> My daughter is safe, this school is safe haven, if I'm late, I can call the parents. This impacts the whole community (parent).
>
> You need to realize, one out of every three kids in the schools at North Lawndale are special-ed children … So, we have created public schools that are really therapeutic schools. We have to realize that before we make our decisions (community member).

As we can see, particularly in the latter statement, even if the word community was not used, the overall statement is expressing concern for the impact closings will have on an established community at that school.

The **charter** category was the second most popular category and included any references to the term "charter" and any general mentions of charter school operators such as UNO, Noble, and KIPP. An example of comments made against school closings using the charter issues include:

> I'm here today to bring you a message. Stop our school closings. Stop the proliferation of charter schools. You cannot say you are going to close even one of our public schools; and in the same breath, say you're going to use our resources that belong to our schools to fund privatized schools. Private schools that will be funded with public monies, our money (parent activist).
>
> 120 new schools, many of which are charter, were open while 100 CPs schools were closed. Why are we here? (community member).
>
> This is about destabilizing communities. This is about failed charter schools. Charter schools are failing, but they want to sell Black people and Latino people a dream that charter schools are doing better than the neighborhood schools (community member).

We are here to say "no" to school closings, not in [Chester], not anywhere. We are here to say "no" to charters, turn-arounds, and military schools where they are not wanted (community members).

In this statement, the speaker is associating the closing of public school with the funding of charter schools, and privatized schooling more generally. The participant is thus using Charter schools to explain opposition toward school closings.

The **trust/politics** category received 15 percent of all mentions and included any referrals to suspicion, transparency and accountability, or the political mistrust A few examples of the various statements that were included in this category are:

We don't trust you. If you're going to try to start building trust, you got to tell us the truth (parent).

It's amazing to me how you can find a billion dollars, I don't know if you heard about that, to refurbish Grant Park, but we can't find money to better our schools. It's amazing to me how you can find money to get all these raises to all the politicians, but we can't find money to better our schools (parent).

In both statements, the speakers are expressing their suspicion of the reasons put forth by CPS for closings school – to reduce the budget, and general mistrust for CPS more generally.

The **race/race coded** category received 7 percent of all mentions and included any direct references to *race*, such as racism," in addition to *race-coded* sentiments, which instead used non-explicit referrals to race such as apartheid, and genocide, and comparisons to non–majority Black/Hispanic neighborhoods like Lincoln Park, or the suburbs. An example of the latter concern includes:

In reading through the history of the schools that you guys want to close, why is it that there's a disproportionate amount of schools that [are] on the South Side and the West Side that are closing, and then there are not that many schools in, if any, on the North Side that's closing? This is hitting the South Side and the West Side the hardest of anybody (community member).

Table A.4B. Direct and indirect mentions in community meetings and interviews attended by parents, community activists, and school officials

	Chicago		Philadelphia		
	Direct	Indirect	Direct	Indirect	Sample Quote
Type (Reason: Group Cohesion as Shared Policy Target)					
Crime (stability)	25.7	22	15	12.4	It is the safety of our children. The safety of our children is a primary concern.
Increased number of Charters (unfair)	21.5	17.3	27.4	33	Stop our school closings. Stop the proliferation of charter schools.
Politics/Mistrust	27.2	30	33	34.7	We don't trust you. If you're going to try to start building trust, you got to tell us the truth.
Race/Race coded	25.6	24.7	24.6	19.9	Why is it that there's a disproportionate amount of schools that [are] on the South Side and the West Side that are closing.
Type (Method: Mobilizing Resources)					
Meetings (also protests)	85	53.2	85	53.2	To show the district was listening, they arranged a meeting with students and the deputy superintendent.
Transportation (busses)	15	17.9	15	17.9	We went down to rallies, we blocked traffic, went to the

Table A.4B cont'd

	Chicago		Philadelphia		
	Direct	Indirect	Direct	Indirect	Sample Quote
					SRC [meetings], marched to the school, what didn't we do? All supported by the district or community organizations.
Radio, Newspapers, T-shirts, Stipends	10	28.4	10	28.4	The radio stations were there ... a bunch of people ... a lot of community leaders ... Everybody came in to get us the supports we needed.

Note: Data collected from community meeting transcripts and in-person observations.

> This is about the decline of Black and Latino teachers. Black children – Black teachers teach[ing] Black children. When you close schools that are 99 percent black, you are saying, "Black teachers, we don't want you. You are not good enough" (community member).

In this typical example, though the term race was not used, the concern has racial undertones given its implicit comparison between the South and West Sides, which are majority Black, and the North Side, which is not.

Participant Details (Tables A.4.1–A.4.4)
*Indicates reinterview between 2015 and 2017

Table A.4.1. Parents interviewed by neighborhood and income in Chicago[13]

	Income Classification (High, Med, Low)	Neighborhood/ Network
1	Low	Austin
2*	Low	Austin
3	Middle	Austin
4	Low	Englewood
5*	Low	Englewood
6*	Low	Englewood
7	n/a	Fulton
8	n/a	Fulton
9	n/a	Fulton
10	n/a	Fulton
11*	Middle	Kenwood
12	Low	Kenwood
13*	Low	North Lawndale
14	Low	Garfield
15*	Middle	Garfield
16	Middle	Garfield
17	Low	Garfield
18	Middle	Pilsen
19	Low	Pilsen
20	Low	Pilsen
21	Low	Pilsen
22*	Low	Pilsen

[13] No names were collected to ensure anonymity.

Table A.4.1 cont'd

	Income Classification (High, Med, Low)	Neighborhood/ Network
23	Low	Pilsen
24	Middle	Ravenswood
25	Middle	Ravenswood

Table A.4.2. Parents interviewed by neighborhood and income in Philadelphia

	Income Classification (Self-Reported)	Neighborhood
1	Low	Germantown
2	Middle	Germantown
3[*]	Middle	Mt. Airy
4	Middle	Mt. Airy
5[*]	Low	Northeast
6	Low	Northeast
7	Low	Northwest
8	Low	Northwest
9	Low	Northwest
10	Low	Northwest
11	Low	Northwest
12[*]	Low	Northwest
13[*]	Low	Northwest
14	Low	Southwest
15	Low	West Philly
16	Low	West Philly
17	Middle	West Philly
18[*]	Low	West Philly
19[*]	Middle	West Philly
20	Low	West Philly

Table A.4.2 cont'd

	Income Classification (Self-Reported)	Neighborhood
21	Low	North Philly
22	Middle	North Philly
23*	Low	North Philly
24	Low	North Philly
25*	Low	South Philly

Table A.4.3. Elites interviewed by position and organization in Chicago

	Position	Organization
1	Activist	Action Now
2	Program Development Team	AUSL
3	Senior Leadership	Chicago Public Schools Office of Special ED
4	School Board Member	Chicago Public Schools
5	Activist	Chicago Teachers Union
6	Activist/Lawyer	Chicago Teachers Union
7	Alderman	City of Chicago
8	Ward Committeeman	City of Chicago
9	Senior Leadership	CS Foundation
10	Senior Leadership	Chicago Urban League
11	Program Development Team	Educational Fund
12	Regional Leader	E4E
13	Senior Leadership	FACE, CPS
14	Senior Leadership	KOCO
15	Program Development Team	Illinois Charter School Network
16	Senior Leadership	Stand for Children
17	Senior Leadership	Teach for America, Chicago
18	Community Activist	Unaffiliated

Table A.4.3 cont'd

	Position	Organization
19	Community Activist	Unaffiliated
20	Scholar Activist	Unaffiliated
22	Legal Activist	Unaffiliated
23	Youth Member	KOCO
24	Activist	AAPS
25	Activist	Parents for Teachers

Table A.4.4. Elites interviewed by position and organization in Philadelphia

	Position	Organization
1	Activist	Action United
2	Member	ATAC
3	Parent Activist	Stonewall
4	Senior Leadership	Blaine Elementary
5	Education Committee Team	City of Philadelphia
6	Former Mayor	City of Philadelphia
7	Senior Leadership	Bridgetown Neighborhoods Association
8	Activist	Lea Elementary
9	Education Committee Team	NAACP
10	Senior Leadership	PCAPS
11	Senior Leadership	Philadelphia Federation of Teachers
12	Activist	Sayre Elementary
13	Program Development Associate	School District of Philadelphia – Charter Office
14	Program Development Team	School District of Philadelphia – Charter Office
15	Senior Leadership	School District of Philadelphia – Facilities

Table A.4.4 cont'd

	Position	Organization
16	Senior Leadership	School District of Philadelphia – Parent Engagement
17	Member	School District of Philadelphia – School Reform Commission
18	Member	School District of Philadelphia – School Reform Commission
19	Journalist	SUN Newspaper
20	Senior Leadership	Universal Charters
21	Activist	University City
22	Senior Leadership	Youth United for Change
23	Senior Leadership	Philadelphia Student Union
24	Youth Coordinator	Philadelphia Student Union
25	Youth Member	Youth United for Change

Table A.4.5. Facilities master plan meetings on school closures in Philadelphia, 2012–2013

Round 1: December (Citywide)	Round 2: January (Community Level)	Round 3: February (Community Level)
15: South Philadelphia High School	8: Temple University	5: Temple University
17: Sayre High School	9: Edison High School	6: Edison High School
18: Edison High School	15: Martin Luther King High School	12: Martin Luther King High School
19: Martin Luther King High School	16: Bartram High School	13: Bartram High School
	22: Overbrook High School	19: Overbrook High School
	23: University City High School	20: University City High School
	29: South Philadelphia High School	26: South Philadelphia High School

Table A.4.5 cont'd

Round 1: December (Citywide)	Round 2: January (Community Level)	Round 3: February (Community Level)
	30: Northeast High School	27: Northeast High School
Total: 4	**8**	**8**

Note: The location represents where closure meetings were held not necessarily where they were closed.
Source: WHYY. December 13, 2012 https://whyy.org/articles/meetings-list

Table A.4.6. Community meetings and hearings on school closures in Chicago, 2012–2013

January	February	March	April – Community Meetings	April – Public Hearings
28: Ravenswood/ Ridge	2: Englewood– Gresham Village	2: Midway	11: Amundsen High School Prosser High School Kenwood High School Harlan High School Lindblom Young High School Manley Austin Total: 8	16: Board Chambers Board Chambers Room 1500 Room 1500 Room 1550 Room 1550 Total: 6
29: Midway O'hare	4: Burnham Park	4: Pilsen– Little Village	13: Amundsen Dunbar Harper Harlan Raby Manley Total: 6	17: Board Chambers Board Chambers Room 1500 Room 1500 Room 1550 Room 1550 Total: 6
30: Lake Calumet	5: Garfield Humboldt Park		15: Schurz Harlan Lincoln Park Dunbar Kenwood CVS Harper Raby	18: Board Chambers Board Chambers Room 1500 Room 1500 Room 1550 Room 1550 Total: 6

Table A.4.6 cont'd

January	February	March	April – Community Meetings	April – Public Hearings
			Austin Total: 9	
31: Austin–North Lawndale	6: Austin–North Lawndale Pershing Pilsen–Little Village		16: Dunbar CVS Kenwood Harper Raby Austin Total: 6	19: Board Chambers Board Chambers Room 1500 Room 1500 Room 1550 Room 1550 Total: 6
	7: Skyway		19: Harper High School Total: 1	20: Board Chambers Board Chambers Board Chambers Room 1500 Room 1500 Room 1500 Room 1550 Room 1550 Room 1550 Total: 9
	9: Rock Island			22: Board Chambers Board Chambers Room 1550 Room 1550 Total: 4
	11: Fullerton Fulton			23: Board Chambers Board Chambers Room 1550 Room 1550 Total: 4
	13: Austin–North Lawndale 14: Lake Calumet			24: Board Chambers Board Chambers Room 1550 Room 1550 Total: 4
	16: Ravenwood–			25: Board Chambers Board Chambers

Table A.4.6 cont'd

January	February	March	April – Community Meetings	April – Public Hearings
	Ridge			Room 1500
	18: Englewood			Room 1500
	Gresham			Room 1550
	19: Burnham			Room 1550
	Park			Total: 6
	20: Skyway			26: Board Chambers
	21: Pershing			Board Chambers
	23: O'hare			Room 1500
				Room 1500
				Room 1550
				Room 1550
				Total: 6
	25: Rock Island			29: Board Chambers
	26: Fulton			Board Chambers
				Room 1500
				Room 1550
				Room 1550
				Total: 5
	27: Garfield-Humboldt Park			30: Board Chambers
	28: Fullerton			Room 1550
				Room 1550
				Total: 3
Total: 5	20	2	31	65*

Source(s): CPS, School Quality, Meeting notes and transcripts, https://cps.edu/About_CPS/Policies_and_guidelines/Pages/qualityschools.aspx

Questions for Community Members and Parents

1 Do you identify with being from a particular neighborhood in the city, if so, which one?

2 How you describe your income? *Income Classification (high/low/middle)*

3 What race and ethnicity do you identify with? *Race identification (Black/non-Hispanic White/Latinx/Asian)*

4 What gender do you identify with? *Gender identification (m/f)*

5 Are your currently employed? If so, where? *Occupation*

6 *Do you have a child in the public school system? Is that school threatened to be closed (or has it been in the past)?*

7 (original) Internal efficacy (political effectiveness) Agree/Disagree

   A I consider myself well-qualified to participate in politics

   B I think that I am better informed about politics and government than most people

   C I believe my participation in politics will be effective

   D I understand what is going on in government

8 (original) External efficacy (system responsiveness) Agree/Disagree

   A Public officials care a lot about what people like me think – group

   B People like me have a say about what the government does group

   C I trust the government to respond to my needs (accountable)

   D I trust the government to do what is in my best interest

9 Have you attended or participated in a community meeting in the past two years? A public hearing?

10 Have you written a letter or called your alderman?

11 Did your experiences with school closings impact your engagement with other activities?

12 Did your experience with school closings teach you lessons about government you did not know?

13 If so, what lessons?

14 Have you applied them in other situations?

15 If so, what situations?

16 Did your experience with school closings teach you skills you did not have (or help you discover skills you did not know you had)?

17 If so, what skills?

18 Have you applied them in other activities?

19 Have your recent experiences with school closings affected your desire to participate in your community on issues related to education?

20 If so, how and why?

21 Have your recent experiences with school closings affected your perceptions of government leaders?

22 If so, how and why?

Additional Considerations

The Use of Case Studies and Qualitative Methods

As stated by Walsh (2012), "there is a need in our scholarship for listening to the people we study (519)," qualitative interviews, especially, are most useful for understanding citizens' articulation of their own experiences. Additionally, interviews enabled a better understanding of the specific engagement tactics of elites and organizations. Cumulatively, the methods utilized for the analysis highlight how groups affected by closure are identified and given resources to mobilize, and how the process and experience contributes to their feelings about the value of their participation and their evaluations of the lessons learned thereafter.[14]

Middle-Class Blacks

Given that the previous analysis is focused largely on the experiences of low-income Black parents targeted for closure and community organizers, the conclusions certainly raise questions about the attitude and participation of those that do not fit into these categories. I find that in the case of Philadelphia, Black middle-class parents are less affected and in turn participate the least. For example, one Black middle-class parent that did participate agreed that her peers were not as involved, as she explains, "Mt. Airy was like nirvana ... the [closings] weren't in our area so people were not involved." The parent's description of the middle-class neighborhood of Mt. Airy area as "nirvana" complements the experiences of several middle-class parents and community members interviewed.

Yet, even when the Black middle class are involved they view their participation differently than that of the directly impacted. In particular, they focus on their frustration with the participation patterns of those directly affected. As one Black middle-class parent in Philadelphia stated,

> this is how I felt when I went to that meeting: I am fighting for people who don't want to fight. I was tired ... after that meeting

[14] As a consequence of overlapping schedules, parent interviews in Chicago were conducted partially as follow-on interviews after community meetings. Parent interviews in Philadelphia were conducted in person and on the phone.

people left and it was like they closed our school, it's done. For myself, my grandmother does not know how to read but you know what she fought for to make sure my mother went to school. My mother has an associate [degree], I have a bachelor's and I am getting my master's. I was very upset, so emotional. I was to the point of tears. I am coming here to fight for you and it's in your neighborhood.

The previous statement demonstrates how Black middle–class parents care about closure because of their own education struggles but perceive those who are directly affected as people that "don't want to fight." Unsurprisingly, they do not appear to take from these experiences tangible civic skills and lessons in the way that resource-poor groups do. This may be in part due to the fact that many of the middle-class persons who participated were already activists or involved in the community.[15]

As it relates specifically to Chicago, Black middle–class neighborhoods tend to be close in proximity to low-income Black neighborhoods more generally. In addition, more middle-class Blacks live in low-income neighborhoods than middle-class neighborhoods (Massey, 1990; Pattillo-McCoy, 2013). Thus, the sheer number of schools on the original list (330) in Chicago meant that the probability of a school being closed close to a Black middle–class parent's home was quite high. As one businessman in North Lawndale community stated, "I've been living in the North Lawndale community, K-Town, for fifty years. I've seen the changes. You need to stand up, because if your school is not on the list now, one day it might be on the list." The statement demonstrates how middle-class Blacks believed they could be affected eventually and indeed these perceptions influence their decision to participate.

Accordingly, several middle-class Blacks in Chicago participated in the closure process. To justify their participation, several statements such as the following were made: "I am the product of the environment and I have a master's degree ... my school will not be

---

[15] Nonetheless, whether middle-class Blacks participate or not, it remains clear overall that they still consider themselves affected by the issue, albeit indirectly. Multiple parents made comments explicitly stating, "it affected me indirectly because it is hard to find schools." This perception that they too are affected by the closing of public schools contributes to a desire to keep them open. In the end, there was not a single person I spoke to in Philadelphia who believed the school should be closed, irrespective of whether they participated or not.

closed, I am here to support the schools in this room," and "I am standing with schools that are facing closings [and the] Black and Latino students that these closings will affect. I realize I am fortunate because I can teach classes with only twenty students." Both statements demonstrate the extent to which middle-class Blacks come out in support of those affected, even if they were not directly affected. While it is not clear that the closure process shaped them in the same ways it did those who were directly impacted, it is clear that both groups hold similar overall attitudes toward the policy and policy process.

Differences between Chicago and Philadelphia

In terms of the data, while there were similar trends throughout, Chicago mentions skewed more heavily on the issue of race than Philadelphia, and Philadelphia mentions skewed more heavily on the issue of charter schools. The most striking difference was in the respective strengths of the teachers' unions across these two cities. At the time of the investigation, the Chicago Teachers Union was a relatively stronger union with high levels of social, economic, and political capital. The Philadelphia Federation of Teachers was a largely depoliticized union with relatively weaker organizing power but was actively working to strengthen its political power through coalition building. This difference, I suspect, impacted how campaigns to save schools were organized at the school versus the district-wide level. In Chicago, even communities that faced far fewer threats of closure joined the coalition to save schools on the premise that "not one school should be closed." It is unsurprising then that a recently published paper found that Blacks and Latinos in Chicago hold similarly negative attitudes toward school closures despite large differences in experience with the policy. While Philadelphia sought to create a similar collective action strategy through the organization Philadelphia Coalition in Alliance for Public Schools (PCAPS) – a coalition of youth, parent, and union groups working together to combat closures across the city – the union lacked political muscle. This appeared to result in a much more individualized fight against closures, where schools were more likely to work toward saving their own school rather than all schools. For example, in Chicago each community meeting boasted high levels of attendance, because all those affected were asked to attend the meetings of all other schools threatened. In Philadelphia, on the other hand, some community meetings had very low levels of participation, while others stood out for exceptionally high levels of participation.

In the short term, it appeared that the most organized schools were saved from being closed. In the long term, Philadelphians appeared to gain some clear political successes including the election of Democrats Mayor Jim Kenney and Governor Tom Wolf, who both appeared sympathetic to their demands; school advocates elected on the city council; the dissolution of the school board; and a lower rate of new charter school openings. Chicagoans, in contrast, reelected Rahm Emanuel, despite a significant decline in support for him among those affected by closure, and elected a Republican governor, Bruce Rauner, who appeared to be unsympathetic to their demands. Chicago also retained a mayoral-appointed school board, rather than an elected school board, and suffered an even higher enrollment decline, leading to a proposal by the district in 2017 to close more schools.

Regardless of these varied political outcomes, by 2017 the general responses from those interviewed in Chicago and Philadelphia revealed a similar belief in the idea that the adverse effects of the policy are seen once possible school closure is announced and last long after decisions are made. As a CPS official involved in the closures explained, "the minute you tell a teacher that their school is closing in a year is the minute that school becomes unstable, because teachers immediately begin looking for jobs ... and it becomes a chaotic school environment ... extended across a whole year ... You see a huge uptick in a need for substitute teachers" (interview, school district leader, Chicago Public Schools, 2015). For example, in the case of Steele, the "principal was forced out ... and then the first year [they] lost 50 percent of [their] teachers." The example of Steele demonstrates how *just the action of putting a school on a closure list can induce setbacks, even if the school ultimately achieves the desired outcome of staying open*. Once this occurs, the same persons that fought the hardest often become too "tired and overwhelmed" to fight again, contributing to the CPD of those communities. In sum, communities learn that, even if they successfully save their school from closure, the damage has already been done.

BIBLIOGRAPHY

Achen, C. H., & Bartels, L. M. (2016). *Democracy for realists: Why elections do not produce responsive government.* Princeton, NJ: Princeton University Press.

Ahmed-Ullah, N. S. (2012). School closings discriminatory, coalition tells US Education Department. *Chicago Tribune*, June 21. www.chicagotribune.com/news/ct-xpm-2012-06-21-ct-met-cps-school-closing-complaint-20120621-story.html.

Ahmed-Ullah, N. S., Chase, J., & Secter, B. (2013). CPS approves largest school closure in Chicago's history. *Chicago Tribune*, May 23. www.chicagotribune.com/news/ct-xpm-2013-05-23-chi-chicago-school-closings-20130522-story.html.

Alex-Assensoh, Y. M. (1997). Race, concentrated poverty, social isolation, and political behavior. *Urban Affairs Review, 33*(2), 209–227.

Alex-Assensoh, Y. M. (2002). Social capital, civic engagement, and the importance of context. In S. L. McLean et al. (eds.), *Social capital: Critical perspectives on community and "bowling alone"* (p. 203). New York: New York University Press.

Allen, D. (2009). *Talking to strangers: Anxieties of citizenship since Brown v. Board of Education.* Chicago: University of Chicago Press.

Allen, A., & Plank, D. N. (2005). School board election structure and democratic representation. *Educational Policy, 19*(3), 510–527.

Allison, P. D. (1999). Comparing logit and probit coefficients across groups. *Sociological Methods and Research, 28*(2), 186–208.

Alsbury, T. L., & Shaw, N. L. (2005). Policy implications for social justice in school district consolidation. *Leadership and Policy in Schools, 4*(2), 105–126.

American Community Survey. (2015). 2009–2013 ACS 5-year estimates. www.census.gov/programs-surveys/acs/technical-documentation/table-and-geography-changes/2013/5-year.html.

Anderson, M. R. (2009). Beyond membership: A sense of community and political behavior. *Political Behavior*, *31*(4), 603.

Arceneaux, K., & Stein, R. M. (2006). Who is held responsible when disaster strikes? The attribution of responsibility for a natural disaster in an urban election. *Journal of Urban Affairs*, *28*(1), 43–53.

Arnstein, S. R. (1969). A ladder of citizen participation. *Journal of the American Institute of Planners Association*, *35*(4), 219. https://doi.org/10.1080/01944366908977225.

Ayers, W., & Klonsky, M. (2006). Chicago's Renaissance 2010: The small schools movement meets the ownership society. *Phi Delta Kappan*, *87*(6), 453–457.

Barker, L. J. (1988). *Our time has come: A delegate's diary of Jesse Jackson's 1984 presidential campaign*. Urbana: University of Illinois Press.

Barnes, C. (2020). *State of empowerment: Low-income families and the new welfare state* (p. 179). Ann Arbor: University of Michigan Press.

Bastress, R. M. (2003). The impact of litigation on rural students: From free textbooks to school consolidation. *Nebraska Law Review*, *82*, 9.

Berger, M. A. (1983). Why communities protest school closings. *Education and Urban Society*, *15*(2), 149–163.

Berry, C. R., & Howell, W. G. (2007). Accountability and local elections: Rethinking retrospective voting. *Journal of Politics*, *69*(3), 844–858.

Besley, T., Pande, R., & Rao, V. (2005). Participatory democracy in action: Survey evidence from South India. *Journal of the European Economic Association*, *3*(2–3), 648–657. https://doi.org/10.1162/jeea.2005.3.2-3.648.

Bierbaum, A. H. (2018). School closures and the contested unmaking of Philadelphia's neighborhoods. *Journal of Planning Education and Research*. https://doi.org/10.1177/0739456X18785018.

Bischoff, K. (2008). School district fragmentation and racial residential segregation: How do boundaries matter? *Urban Affairs Review*, *44*(2), 182–217.

Bobo, L. (1983). Whites' opposition to busing: Symbolic racism or realistic group conflict? *Journal of Personality and Social Psychology*, *45*(6), 1196–1210.

Bobo, L. (1998). Race, interests, and beliefs about affirmative action: Unanswered questions and new directions. *American Behavioral Scientist*, *41*(7), 985–1003.

Bobo, L., & Gilliam, F. D. (1990). Race, sociopolitical participation, and Black empowerment. *American Political Science Review*, *84*(2), 377–393.

Bourgeois, L. 2013. *Solidarité*. Paris: Hachette Livre BNF.

Brady, H. E., Verba, S., & Schlozman, K. L. (1995). Beyond SES: A resource model of political participation. *American Political Science Review*, *89*(2), 271–294.

Bruch, S. K., & Soss, J. (2018). Schooling as a formative political experience: Authority relations and the education of citizens. *Perspectives on Politics*, *16*(1), 36–57. https://doi.org/10.1017/S1537592717002195.

Bulkley, K. E. (2007). Bringing the private into the public: Changing the rules of the game and new regime politics in Philadelphia public education. *Educational Policy*, 21(1), 155–184.

Bulkley, K. E., Henig, J. R., & Levin, H. M. (2010). *Between public and private: Politics, governance, and the new portfolio models for urban school reform.* Cambridge, MA: Harvard Education Press.

Burch, T. (2013). *Trading democracy for justice: Criminal convictions and the decline of neighborhood political participation.* Chicago: University of Chicago Press.

Burdick-Will, J., Keels, M., & Schuble, T. (2013). Closing and opening schools: The association between neighborhood characteristics and the location of new educational opportunities in a large urban district. *Journal of Urban Affairs*, 35(1), 59–80.

Bushaw, W. J., & Lopez, S. J. (2010). The 42nd annual Phi Delta Kappa/Gallup Poll of the public's attitudes toward the public schools. *Phi Delta Kappan*, 91 (1), 8–23.

Bushaw, W. J., & Lopez, S. J. (2013). The 45th annual Phi Delta Kappa/Gallup Poll of the public's attitudes toward the public schools. *Phi Delta Kappan*, 95 (1), 9–25.

Cain, B. E., Citrin, J., & Wong, C. (2000). *Ethnic context, race relations, and California politics.* San Francisco: Public Policy Institute of California.

Campbell, A. L. (2003a). *How policies make citizens: Senior political activism and the American welfare state.* Princeton, NJ: Princeton University Press.

Campbell, A. L. (2003b). Participatory reactions to policy threats: Senior citizens and the defense of social security and Medicare. *Political Behavior*, 25(1), 29–49. https://doi.org/10.1023/A:1022900327448.

Campbell, A., Gurin, G., & Miller, W. E. (1954). *The voter decides.* Evanston, IL: Row, Peterson and Co.

Caref, C., Hainds, S., Hilgendorf, K., Jankov, P., & Russell, K. (2012). *The Black and White of education in Chicago's public schools. Class, Charters & Chaos: A Hard Look at Privatization Schemes Masquerading as Education Policy.* Chicago: Chicago Teachers Union. www.ctunet.com/root/text/CTU-black-and-white-of-chicago-education.pdf.

Carmichael, S. (1967). *Black power and the Third World.* Address to the Organization of Latino American Solidarity. August. www.freedomarchives .org/Documents/Finder/Black%20Liberation%20Disk/Black%20Power!/ SugahData/Books/Carmichael.S.pdf.

Carmichael, S., Ture, K., & Hamilton, C. V. (1992). *Black power: The politics of liberation in America.* New York: Vintage.

Caskey, J., & Kuperberg, M. (2014). The Philadelphia School District's ongoing financial crisis. *Education Next*, 14(4).

Chicago Public Schools. (2012). CPS announces five-year moratorium on facility closures starting in fall 2013. Press release, November 26. http://cps.edu/News/Press_releases/Pages/11_26_2012_PR1.aspx.

Chicago Public Schools. (2013). School Data – Demographics. http://cps.edu/SchoolData/Pages/SchoolData.aspx.

Chong, D., & Rogers, R. (2005). Racial solidarity and political participation. *Political Behavior*, 27 (4), 347–374.

Clark, M. (2013). 9-year-old activist saves Chicago school, dreams big. NBC News, May 28.

Cobb, C. (1997). Revolution: From Stokely Carmichael to Kwame Ture. *The Black Scholar*, 27(3/4), 32–38.

Cohen, C. J. (1999). *The boundaries of blackness: AIDS and the breakdown of Black politics*. Chicago: University of Chicago Press.

Cohen, C. J., & Dawson, M. C. (1993). Neighborhood poverty and African American politics. *American Political Science Review*, 87(2), 286–302.

Cohen, J., Golden, M., Quinn, R., & Simon, E. (2018). Democracy thwarted or democracy at work? Local public engagement and the new education policy Landscape. *American Journal of Education*, 124(4), 411–443.

Cohen, L., Marion, L., & Momson, K. (2018). *Research methods in education*. 8th ed. London: Routledge.

Cohen, R. M. (2016). School closures: A blunt instrument. *The American Prospect*, April 11. https://prospect.org/power/school-closures-blunt-instrument.

Collins, J. E. (2021). Does the meeting style matter? The effects of exposure to participatory and deliberative school board meetings. American Political Science Review, 115(3), 790–804.

Colton, D., & Frelich, A. (1979). Enrollment decline and school closings in a large city. *Education and Urban Society*, 11(3), 396–417.

Conner, J., & Rosen, S. (2013). How students are leading us: Youth organizing and the fight for public education in Philadelphia. *Penn GSE Perspectives on Urban Education*, 10(1), n1.

Craig, S. C., & Maggiotto, M. A. (1982). Measuring political efficacy. *Political Methodology*, 8(3), 85–109.

Cuban, L. (1979). Shrinking enrollment and consolidation: Political and organizational impacts in Arlington, Virginia 1973–1978. *Education and Urban Society*, 11(3), 367–395.

Cucchiara, M. (2013). *Marketing schools, marketing cities: Who wins and who loses when schools become urban amenities*. Chicago: University of Chicago Press.

Cucchiara, M., Gold, E., & Simon, E. (2011). Contracts, choice, and customer service: Marketization and public engagement in education. *Teachers College Record*, 113(11), 2460–2502.

Darity Jr., W. A., & Mullen, A. K. (2020). *From here to equality: Reparations for Black Americans in the twenty-first century*. Chapel Hill: University of North Carolina Press.

Davis, A. Y. (2016). *Freedom is a constant struggle: Ferguson, Palestine, and the foundations of a movement*. Chicago: Haymarket Books.

Dawson, M. C. (1994). *Behind the mule: Race and class in African-American politics*. Princeton, NJ: Princeton University Press.

Dawson, M. C. (2011). *Not in our lifetimes: The future of Black politics*. Chicago: University of Chicago Press.

Dawson, M. C. (2018). Racial capitalism and democratic crisis. *Items: Insights from Social Sciences*, December 4. https://items.ssrc.org/race-capitalism/racial-capitalism-and-democratic-crisis.

Dawson, M. C., & Wilson III, E. J. (1991). Paradigms and paradoxes: Political science and African-American politics. In W. Crotty (ed.), *Political science: Looking to the future*, vol. 1 (pp. 189–237). Evanston, IL: Northwestern University Press.

Dean, J. (1981). *Dealing with decline: The politics of public school closings*. New York: ERIC Clearinghouse on Urban Education, Institute for Urban and Minority Education, Teachers College, Columbia University.

Deeds, V., Pattillo, M. (2015). Organizational "failure" and institutional pluralism: A case study of an urban school closure. *Urban Education*, 50(4), 474–504.

DeJarnatt, S. L. (2013). Community losses: The costs of education reform. *University of Toledo Law Review*, 45, 579.

De la Garza, R. O. (2004). Latino politics. *Annual Review of Political Science*, 7 (1), 91–123.

De la Torre, M., & Gwynne, J. (2009). *When schools close: Effects on displaced students in Chicago Public Schools*. Chicago: Consortium on Chicago School Research.

Desimone, L. M. (1993). Racial discourse in a community: Language and the social construction of race. *Journal of Negro Education*, 62(4), 414–418.

Dolan, K. (2011). Do women and men know different things? Measuring gender differences in political knowledge. *Journal of Politics*, 73(1), 97–107.

Dryfoos, J. G. (2000). Evaluation of community schools: Findings to date. http://76.227.216.38/assets/1/AssetManager/Evaluation%20of%20Community%20Schools_joy_dryfoos.pdf.

Duncan, A. (2006). Chicago's Renaissance 2010: Building on school reform in the age of accountability. *Phi Delta Kappan*, 87(6), 457–458.

Duncan, A. (2009, July). Partners in reform: Remarks of Arne Duncan to the National Education Association. US Department of Education. www2.ed.gov/news/pressreleases/2009/07/07022009.html.

Edwards, B., & McCarthy, J. D. (2004). Resources and social movement mobilization. In D. A. Snow, S. A. Soule, & H. Kriesi (eds.), *The Blackwell companion to social movements* (pp. 116–152). New York: Wiley Publishing.

Eltagouri, M., & Perez, J., Jr. (2016). After hunger strike, Dyett reopens as arts-focused neighborhood high school. *Chicago Tribune*, September 6. www .chicagotribune.com/news/ct-dyett-high-school-reopening-met-20160906-story.html.

Emanuel, A. (2019). Merged Chicago school searches for elusive balance in its fractured community. *Chalkbeat Chicago*, March 12.

Emerson, R. M., Fretz, R. I., & Shaw, L. L. (1995). *Writing ethnographic notes.* Chicago: University of Chicago Press.

England, W., & Hamann, E. T. (2013). Segregation, inequality, demographic change, and school consolidation. *Great Plains Research*, 23, 171–183.

Ewing, E. L. (2018). *Ghosts in the schoolyard: Racism and school closings on Chicago's South Side.* Chicago: University of Chicago Press.

Faust, J. F. (1976). The social and political factors affecting the closing of schools in a period of declining enrollments in a large urban school system. Dissertation. University of Cincinnati.

Feldman, M. S. (1995). *Strategies for interpreting qualitative data.* Thousand Oaks, CA: Sage.

Finkel, S. E. (1985). Reciprocal effects of participation and political efficacy: A panel analysis. *American Journal of Political Science*, 29(4), 891–913.

Forgette, R., King, M., & Dettrey, B. (2008). Race, Hurricane Katrina, and government satisfaction: Examining the role of race in assessing blame. *Publius: The Journal of Federalism*, 38(4), 671–691.

Frasure-Yokley, L., Masuoka, N., & Barreto, M. A. (2019). Introduction to dialogues: Linked fate and the politics of groups and identities. *Politics, Groups, and Identities*, 7(3), 610–614. https://doi.org/10.1080/21565503 .2019.1638802.

Fung, A., & Wright, E. O. (2003). *Deepening democracy: Institutional innovations in empowered participatory governance.* London: Verso.

Gay, C. (2001). The effect of Black congressional representation on political participation. *American Political Science Review*, 95(3), 589–602.

Gay, C. (2002). Spirals of trust? The effect of descriptive representation on the relationship between citizens and their government. *American Journal of Political Science*, 46(4), 717–732.

Gay, C. (2004). Putting race in context: Identifying the environmental determinants of Black racial attitudes. *American Political Science Review*, 98 (4), 547–562.

Gay, C., & Tate, K. (1998). Doubly bound: The impact of gender and race on the politics of Black women. *Political Psychology*, 19(1), 169–184.

Gershon, S. A., Montoya, C., Bejarano, C., & Brown, N. (2019). Intersectional linked fate and political representation. *Politics, Groups, and Identities*, 7(3), 642–653.

Gilens, M. (1995). Racial attitudes and opposition to welfare. *Journal of Politics*, 57(4), 323–349.

Gillespie, M. (1999). Americans want integrated schools, but opposed school busing. *Gallup*, September 27. https://news.gallup.com/poll/3577/americans-want-integrated-schools-oppose-school-busing.aspx.

Good, R. M. (2017). Invoking landscapes of spatialized inequality: Race, class, and place in Philadelphia's school closure debate. *Journal of Urban Affairs*, 39 (3), 358–380.

Gomez, B. T., & Wilson, J. M. (2008). Political sophistication and attributions of blame in the wake of Hurricane Katrina. *Publius: Journal of Federalism*, 38(4), 633–650.

Gordon, M. F., De la Torre, M., Cowhy, J. R., Moore, P. T., Sartain, L., & Knight, D. (2018). *School closings in Chicago: Staff and student experiences and academic Outcomes. Research Report.* University of Chicago Consortium on School Research.

Gordy, S. (2009). *Finding the lost year.* Fayetteville: University of Arkansas.

Greer, C. M. (2013). *Black ethnics: Race, immigration, and the pursuit of the American dream.* New York: Oxford University Press.

Gurin, P., & Epps, E. (1975). *Black consciousness, identity, and achievement: A study of students in historically Black colleges.* New York: John Wiley & Sons.

Gurin, P., & Markus, H. (1989). Cognitive consequences of gender identity. In S. Skevington & D. Baker (eds.), *The social identity of women* (pp. 152–172). London: Sage.

Hajnal, Z. L. (2009). Who loses in American democracy? A count of votes demonstrates the limited representation of African Americans. *American Political Science Review*, 103(1), 37–57.

Hamilton, R. J. (2020). The Hahnemann University Hospital closure and what matters: A department chair's perspective. *Academic Medicine*, 95(4), 494–498.

Han, C., Raymond, M. E., Woodworth, J. L., Negassi, Y., Richardson, W. P., & Snow, W. (2017). *Lights off: Practice and impact of closing low-performing schools.* Stanford, CA: Center for Research on Education Outcomes.

Han, H. (2009). *Moved to action: Motivation, participation, and inequality in American politics.* Stanford, CA: Stanford University Press.

Han, H. (2014). *How organizations develop activists: Civic associations and leadership in the 21st century.* New York: Oxford University Press.

Harris, F. C., Sinclair-Chapman, V., & McKenzie, B. D. (2005). Macrodynamics of Black political participation in the post-civil rights era. *Journal of Politics*, 67(4), 1143–1163.

Harris-Lacewell, M. V. (2006). *Barbershops, bibles, and BET: Everyday talk and Black political thought.* Princeton, NJ: Princeton University Press.

Henig, J. R. (1995). *Rethinking school choice: Limits of the market metaphor.* Princeton, NJ: Princeton University Press.

Henig, J. R., Hula, R. C., Orr, M., & Pedescleaux, D. S. (2001). *The color of school reform: Race, politics, and the challenge of urban education.* Princeton, NJ: Princeton University Press.

Hess Jr., G. A., & Easton, J. Q. (1991). *Who's making what decisions: Monitoring authority shifts in Chicago school reform.* Chicago: American Educational Research Association Annual Meeting.

Hicks, W. D. (2013). Initiatives within representative government: Political competition and initiative use in the American states. *State Politics & Policy Quarterly, 13*(4), 471–494. https://doi.org/10.1177/1532440013502797.

Hochschild, J. L. (1993). Middle-class Blacks and the ambiguities of success. In P. M. Sniderman, P. E. Tetlock, & E. G. Carmines (eds.), *Politics and the American dilemma* (pp. 48–72). Stanford, CA: Stanford University Press.

Hochschild, J. L. (1995). *Facing up to the American dream.* Princeton, NJ: Princeton University Press.

Hochschild, J. L. (2006). Ambivalence about equality in the United States or, did Tocqueville get it wrong and why does that matter? *Social Justice Research, 19* (1), 43–62.

Hochschild, J. L., & Scott, B. (1998). Trends: Governance and reform of public education in the United States. *Public Opinion Quarterly, 62*(1), 79–120.

Hochschild, J. L., & Scovronick, N. (2003). *The American dream and the public schools.* New York: Oxford University Press.

Hooker, J. (2016). Black Lives Matter and the paradoxes of US Black politics: From democratic sacrifice to democratic repair. *Political Theory, 44*(4), 448–469.

Howell, W. G., & Peterson, P. E. (2006). *The education gap: Vouchers and urban schools* (rev. ed.). Washington, DC: Brookings Institution Press.

Howell, W. G., & West, M. R. (2009). Educating the public. *Education Next, 9* (3), 40–47.

Ingram, H., & Schneider, A. L. (1995). Social construction (continued): Response. *American Political Science Review, 89*(2), 441–446.

Jack, J., & Sludden, J. (2013). School closings in Philadelphia. *Penn GSE Perspectives on Urban Education, 10*(1), n1.

Jackman, M. R., & Jackman, R. W. (1973). An interpretation of the relation between objective and subjective social status. *American Sociological Review, 38*(5), 569–582.

Jacobsen, R., & Saultz, A. (2012). The polls—trends: Who should control education? *Public Opinion Quarterly, 76*(2), 379–390.

Karpowitz, C. F., Mendelberg, T., & Shaker, L. (2012). Gender inequality in deliberative participation. *American Political Science Review, 106*(3), 533–547.

Kathlene, L. (1994). Power and influence in state legislative policymaking: The interaction of gender and position in committee hearing debates. *American Political Science Review*, 88(3), 560–576.

Kaufmann, K. M. (2004). *The urban voter: Group conflict and mayoral voting behavior in American cities*. Ann Arbor: University of Michigan Press.

Kinder, D. R., & Sears, D. O. (1981). Prejudice and politics: Symbolic racism versus racial threats to the good life. *Journal of Personality and Social Psychology*, 40(3), 414–431.

King, G. (1986). How not to lie with statistics: Avoiding common mistakes in quantitative political science. *American Journal of Political Science*, 30(3), 666–687.

King, M. L. Jr. (1986). *I have a dream: Writings and speeches that changed the world*. San Francisco: Harper (Teaching America History).

King, M. L. Jr. (2010). *Where do we go from here? Chaos or community* (vol. 2). Boston: Beacon Press.

Kluegel, J. R., & Smith, E. R. (1983). Affirmative action attitudes: Effects of self-interest, racial affect, and stratification beliefs on Whites' views. *Social Forces*, 61(3), 797–824.

Kohn, M. (2020). Public goods and social justice. *Perspectives on Politics*, 18(4), 1104–1117.

Kuklinski, J. H., Cobb, M. D., & Gilens, M. (1997). Racial attitudes and the "New South." *Journal of Politics*, 59(2), 323–349.

Laird, C. (2019). Black like me: How political communication changes racial group identification and its implications. *Politics, Groups, and Identities*, 7(2), 324–346.

Lane, R. E. (1959). *Political life: Why people get involved in politics*. New York: Free Press

Ledbetter, C. R. (2006). The fight for school consolidation in Arkansas, 1946–1948. *Arkansas Historical Quarterly*, 65(1), 45–57.

Lee, J., & Lubienski, C. (2016). The impact of school closures on equity of access in Chicago. *Education and Urban Society*, 49(1), 53–80.

Leighley, J. (1996). Group membership and the mobilization of political participation. *Journal of Politics*, 58(2), 447–463.

Leong, N. (2013). Racial capitalism. *Harvard Law Review*, 126(8), 2151–2226.

Lerman, A. E., & McCabe, K. T. (2017). Personal experience and public opinion: A theory and test of conditional policy feedback. *The Journal of Politics*, 79(2), 624–641.

Lerman, A. E., & Weaver, V. M. (2014). *Arresting citizenship: The democratic consequences of American crime control*. Chicago: University of Chicago Press.

Levinson, M. (2012). *No citizen left behind* (vol. 13). Cambridge, MA: Harvard University Press.

Lieberson, S., & Waters, M. C. (1988). *From many strands: Ethnic and racial groups in contemporary America.* New York: Russell Sage Foundation.

Limm, D. (2013). City Council passes resolution to support moratorium on school closings. The Philadelphia Public School Notebook, January 24. http://thenotebook.org/blog/135544/city-council-passes-resolution-suppor.

Lipman, P. (2009). Making sense of Renaissance 2010 school policy in Chicago: Race, class, and the cultural politics of neoliberal urban restructuring. Great Cities Institute Publication. NO: GCP-09-02. https://greatcities.uic.edu/2009/01/01/making-sense-of-renaissance-2010-school-policy-in-chicago-race-class-and-the-cultural-politics-of-neoliberal-urban-restructuring-gcp-09-02.

Lipman, P. (2011). *The new political economy of urban education: Neoliberalism, race, and the right to the city.* New York: Routledge.

Lipman, P. (2015). Large education policy under Obama. *Journal of Urban Affairs, 37*(1), 57–61.

Logan, J. R., & Burdick-Will, J. (2016). School segregation, charter schools, and access to quality education. *Journal of Urban Affairs, 38*(3), 323–343. https://doi.org/10.1111/juaf.12246.

Loveless, T. (2007). The peculiar politics of No Child Left Behind. In A. Gamoran (ed.), *Standards-based reform and the poverty gap: Lessons for No Child Left Behind* (pp. 253–285). Washington, DC: Brookings Institution Press.

Lublin, D., & Tate, K. (1995). Racial group competition in urban elections. In P. Peterson (ed.), *Classifying by race* (pp. 245–261). Princeton, NJ: Princeton University Press.

Macedo, S., & Karpowitz, C. F. (2006). The local roots of American inequality. *PS: Political Science & Politics, 39*(1), 59–64.

Malhotra, N., & Kuo, A. G. (2009). Emotions as moderators of information cue use: Citizen attitudes toward Hurricane Katrina. *American Politics Research, 37*(2), 301–326.

Manna, P. (2006). *School's in: Federalism and the national education agenda.* Washington, DC: Georgetown University Press.

Marable, M. (2007). *Race, reform and rebellion: The second Reconstruction and beyond in Black America, 1945–2006.* New York: Macmillan International Higher Education.

Marsh, W. Z. C., & Ramírez, R. (2019). Unlinking fate? Discrimination, group-consciousness, and political participation among Latinos and whites. *Politics, Groups, and Identities, 7*(3), 625–641. https://doi.org/10.1080/21565503.2019.1638799.

Massey, D. S. (1990). American Apartheid: Segregation and the making of the underclass. *American Journal of Sociology, 96*(2), 329–357.

Massey, D. S., & Denton, N. A. (1998). *American apartheid: Segregation and the making of the underclass.* Cambridge, MA: Harvard University Press.

Masuoka, N., & Junn, J. (2013). *The politics of belonging: Race, public opinion, and immigration*. Chicago: University of Chicago Press.

McClain, P. D., Carew, J. D. J., Walton, E., & Watts, C. S. (2009). Group membership, group identity, and group consciousness: Measures of racial identity in American politics. *Annual Review of Political Science*, 12(1), 471–485.

McDonald, B. (2015). A hunger strike in Chicago. *New York Times*, September 8. www.nytimes.com/video/us/100000003895513/a-hunger-strike-in-chicago.html?smid=tw-share.

McGuinn, P. J. (2006). *No Child Left Behind and the transformation of federal education policy, 1965–2005*. Lawrence: University Press of Kansas.

McPherrin, M. J. (1979). A case study of declining enrollment in a large suburban school district. Dissertation. Northern Illinois University.

Mettler, S. (2005). *Soldiers to citizens: The GI Bill and the making of the greatest generation*. New York: Oxford University Press.

Mettler, S., & Soss, J. (2004). The consequences of public policy for democratic citizenship: Bridging policy studies and mass politics. *Perspectives on Politics*, 2(1), 55–73.

Michener, J. (2017). People, places, power: Medicaid concentration and local political participation. *Journal of Health Politics, Policy and Law*, 42(5), 865–900.

Michener, J. (2018a). *Fragmented democracy: Medicaid, federalism, and unequal politics*. New York: Cambridge University Press.

Michener, J. (2018b). The politics and policy of racism in American health care. *Vox*, May 24. www.vox.com/polyarchy/2018/5/24/17389742/american-health-care-racism.

Michener, J. D. (2019). Policy feedback in a racialized polity. *Policy Studies Journal*, 47(2), 423–450.

Miles, M. B., & Huberman, A. M. (1994). *Qualitative data analysis: An expanded sourcebook*. Beverly Hill, CA: Sage Publications.

Moe, T. M. (2001). *Schools, vouchers, and the American public*. Washington, DC: Brookings Institution.

Morel, D. (2018). *Takeover: Race, education, and American democracy*. New York: Oxford University Press.

Morel, D., & Nuamah, S. A. (2020). Who governs? How shifts in political power shape perceptions of local government services. *Urban Affairs Review*, 56(5), 1503–1528.

National Council for Education Statistics. (2013). Common Core of Data: Public Elementary/Secondary School Universe Survey. US Department of Education. http://nces.ed.gov/ccd/pubschuniv.asp.

National Opinion Research Center (NORC) at the University of Chicago. (2013). The Joyce Foundation education survey. www.norc.org/PDFs/Joyce_Tribune_

NORC%20education%20survey_with_percent_tables_2-DTP%20Formatted
.pdf.

Neal, Z. P., & Watling Neal, J. (2012). The public school as a public good: Direct and indirect pathways to community satisfaction. *Journal of Urban Affairs*, 34 (5), 469–486.

Niemi, R. G., Craig, S. C., & Mattei, F. (1991). Measuring internal political efficacy in the 1988 National Election Study. *American Political Science Review*, 85(04), 1407–1413.

Nuamah, S. A. (2019a). *How girls achieve*. Cambridge, MA: Harvard University Press.

Nuamah, S. A. (2019b). A spoke in a wheel. In E. B. Duncan-Shippy (ed.), *Shuttered schools: Race, community, and school closures in American cities* (pp. 259–286). Charlotte, NC: Information Age Publishing.

Nuamah, S. A. (2020). The paradox of educational attitudes: Racial differences in public opinion on school closure. *Journal of Urban Affairs*, 42(4), 554–570.

Nuamah, S. A. (2021a). The cost of participating while poor and Black: Toward a theory of collective participatory debt. *Perspectives on Politics*, 19(4), 1115–1130.

Nuamah, S. A. (2021b). "Every year they ignore us": Public school closures and public trust. *Politics, Groups, and Identities*, 9(2), 239–257.

Nuamah, S. A., & Ogorzalek, T. (2021). Close to home: Place-based mobilization in racialized contexts. *American Political Science Review*, 115(3), 757–774.

Nuamah, S. A., Good, R., Bierbaum, A., & Simon, E. (2020). School closures always hurt. They hurt even more now. *Education Week*. www.edweek.org/ leadership/opinion-school-closures-always-hurt-they-hurt-even-more-now/ 2020/06.

Oliver, J., & Ha, S. (2007). Vote choice in suburban elections. *American Political Science Review*, 101(3), 393–408.

Olson, M., Jr. (1965). *The logic of collective action: Public goods and the theory of groups*. Cambridge, MA: Harvard University Press.

Orr, M., & Rogers, J. (eds.) (2011). *Public engagement for public education: Joining forces to revitalize democracy and equalize schools*. Stanford, CA: Stanford University Press.

Pateman, C. (1970). *Participation and democratic theory*. New York: Cambridge University Press.

Peterson, P. E., & Chingos, M. M. (2009). Impact of for-profit and non-profit management on student achievement: The Philadelphia intervention, 2002–2008. Programme on Education Policy and Governance Working Papers Series PEPG, 09-02.

Phoenix, D. L. (2019). *The anger gap: How race shapes emotion in politics*. New York: Cambridge University Press.

Pierson, P. (1993). When effect becomes cause: Policy feedback and political change. *World Politics*, 45(04), 595–628.

Pinderhughes, D. M. (1987). *Race and ethnicity in Chicago politics: A reexamination of pluralist theory*. Urbana: University of Illinois Press.

Polletta, F. (2012). *Freedom is an endless meeting: Democracy in American social movements*. Chicago: University of Chicago Press.

Pride, R. A. (2000). Public opinion and the end of busing: (Mis)perceptions of policy failure. *Sociological Quarterly*, 41(2), 207–225.

Reckhow, S., & Snyder, J. W. (2014). The expanding role of philanthropy in education politics. *Educational Researcher*, 43(4), 186–195.

Rich, W. C. (1996). The moral choices of garbage collectors: Administrative ethics from below. *American Review of Public Administration*, 26(2), 201–212.

Robinson, C. (1983, 2000) *Black Marxism: The making of the Black radical tradition*. Chapel Hill: University of North Carolina Press.

Rogers, M. L. (2014). Introduction: Disposable lives. *Theory & Event*, 17(3).

Rogers, R. R. (2006). *Afro-Caribbean immigrants and the politics of incorporation: Ethnicity, exception, or exit*. New York: Cambridge University Press.

Rose, D. (2018). *Citizens by degree: Higher education policy and the changing gender dynamics of American citizenship*. New York: Oxford University Press.

Russo, A. (ed.) (2004). *School reform in Chicago: Lessons in policy and practice*. Cambridge, MA: Harvard Education Press.

Sampson, R. (2012). *Great American city: Chicago and the enduring neighborhood effect*. Chicago: University of Chicago Press.

Schneider, A., & Ingram, H. (1993). Social construction of target populations: Implications for politics and policy. *American Political Science Review*, 87(2), 334–347.

Schneider, A., & Ingram, H. (2005). *Deserving and entitled: Social constructions and public policy*. Albany: State University of New York Press.

School Reform Commission Report. (2013). School District of Philadelphia. http://webgui.phila.k12.pa.us/offices/s/src/meeting-minutes/2013-meeting-minutes.

Schuman, H. (1997). *Racial attitudes in America: Trends and interpretations*. Cambridge, MA: Harvard University Press.

Sidney, M. S. (2002). The role of ideas in education politics: Using discourse analysis to understand barriers to reform in multiethnic cities. Urban Affairs Review, 38(2), 253–279.

Skocpol, T., & Fiorina, M. P. (1999). Making sense of the civic engagement debate. In T. Skocpol & M. P. Fiorina (eds.), *Civic engagement and American democracy*. Washington, DC: Brookings Institution.

Skogan, W. G., & Hartnett, S. M. (1997). *Community policing, Chicago style*. New York: Oxford University Press.

Smith, S. R., & Ingram, H. M. (1993). *Public policy for democracy*. Washington, DC: Brookings Institution Press.

Spence, L. K. (2015). *Knocking the hustle: Against the neoliberal turn in Black politics*. New York: Punctum Books.

Soss, J. (1999). Lessons of welfare: Policy design, political learning, and political action. *American Political Science Review*, 93(2), 363–380.

Soss, J., & Schram, S. F. (2007). A public transformed? Welfare reform as policy feedback. *American Political Science Review*, 101(1), 111–127.

Soss, J., & Weaver, V. (2017). Police are our government: Politics, political science, and the policing of race–class subjugated communities. *Annual Review of Political Science*, 20, 565–591.

Swain, C. M. (1995). *Black faces, Black interests: The representation of African Americans in Congress*. Cambridge, MA: Harvard University Press.

Tate, K. (1994). *From protest to politics: The new Black voters in American elections*. Cambridge, MA: Harvard University Press.

Tate, K. (2004). *Black faces in the mirror: African Americans and their representatives in the US Congress*. Princeton, NJ: Princeton University Press.

Tieken, M. C., & Auldridge-Reveles, T. R. (2019). Rethinking the school closure research: School closure as spatial injustice. *Review of Educational Research*, 89(6), 917–953.

Tilsley, A. (2017). Subtracting schools from communities. Urban Institute, March 23. www.urban.org/features/subtracting-schools-communities.

Todd-Breland, E. (2018). *A political education: Black politics and education reform in Chicago since the 1960s*. Chapel Hill: University of North Carolina Press.

Trounstine, J. (2016). Segregation and inequality in public goods. *American Journal of Political Science*, 60(3), 709–725.

Trounstine, J. (2018). *Segregation by design: Local politics and inequality in American cities*. New York: Cambridge University Press.

US Census Bureau. (2019). American Community Survey (ACS) 2009–2013 ACS 5-year estimates. www.census.gov/programs-surveys/acs/technical-documentation/table-and-geography-changes/2013/5-year.html.

US Department of Education, Office of Planning, Evaluation and Policy Development. (2010). ESEA Blueprint for Reform. Washington, DC: Education Publications Center.

US Department of Education, National Center for Education Statistics. (2018). *Digest of education statistics, 2016* (NCES 2017-094), Table 216.95.

US National Commission on Excellence in Education. (1983). *A nation at risk: The imperative for educational reform: A report to the nation and the Secretary of Education, US Department of Education*. Washington, DC: US National Commission on Excellence in Education.

Useem, E. (2009). Big city superintendent as powerful CEO: Paul Vallas in Philadelphia. *Peabody Journal of Education, 84*(3), 300–317.

Valencia, R. R. (1980). The school closure issue and the Chicano community. *Urban Review, 12*(1), 5–21.

Valencia, R. R. (1984a). The school closure issue and the Chicano community: A follow-up study of the Los Angeles case. *Urban Review, 16*(3), 145–163.

Valencia, R. R. (1984b). School closures and policy issues. Policy Paper No. 84-C3.

Verba, S., Schlozman, K., & Brady, H. (1995). Beyond SES: A resource model of political participation. American Political Science Review, *89*(2), 271–294.

Vergari, S. (2007). The politics of charter schools. *Educational Policy, 21*(1), 15–39. https://doi.org/10.1177/0895904806296508.

Walsh, K. C. (2012). Putting inequality in its place: Rural consciousness and the power of perspective. *American Political Science Review, 106*(03), 517–532.

Watkins-Hayes, C. (2009). *The new welfare bureaucrats.* Chicago: University of Chicago Press.

White, I. K., & Laird, C. N. (2020). *Steadfast democrats.* Princeton, NJ: Princeton University Press.

Yaccina, S. (2013). Protests fail to deter Chicago from shutting 49 schools. *New York Time,* May 22. www.nytimes.com/2013/05/23/education/despite-protests-chicago-closing-schools.html.

Zepeda-Millán, C. (2016). Weapons of the (not so) weak: Immigrant mass mobilization in the US South. *Critical Sociology, 42*(2), 269–287.

INDEX

For EU product safety concerns, contact us at Calle de José Abascal, 56–1°, 28003 Madrid, Spain or eugpsr@cambridge.org.

www.ingramcontent.com/pod-product-compliance
Ingram Content Group UK Ltd.
Pitfield, Milton Keynes, MK11 3LW, UK
UKHW020352140625
459647UK00020B/2430